MULTIPLE VOICES,
MULTIPLE TEXTS

MULTIPLE VOICES, MULTIPLE TEXTS

Reading in the Secondary Content Areas

Reade Dornan

Michigan State University

Lois Matz Rosen

The University of Michigan–Flint

Marilyn Wilson

Michigan State University

BOYNTON/COOK PUBLISHERS
HEINEMANN
Portsmouth, NH

Boynton/Cook Publishers
A subsidiary of Reed Elsevier Inc.
361 Hanover Street
Portsmouth, NH 03801-3912
Offices and agents throughout the world

The author and publisher wish to thank those who have generously given permission to reprint borrowed material:

Fig. 2–1 from *The Psychology and Pedagogy of Reading* by Edmund Burke Huey. Copyright © 1908. Reprinted by permission of The MIT Press.

Fig. 2–2 from *English 3200: A Programed Course in Grammar and Usage*, Second Edition by Joseph C. Blumenthal. Copyright © 1972 by Harcourt Brace & Company. Reprinted by permission of the publisher.

Fig. 3–1 from *Reading Strategies: Focus on Comprehension*, Second Edition by Yetta Goodman, Dorothy Watson, and Carolyn Burke. Copyright © 1996. Reprinted by permission of Richard C. Owen Publishers, Inc.

Fig. 3–4 from *Reading Miscue Inventory: Procedure for Diagnosis and Evaluation* by Yetta Goodman and Carolyn Burke. Copyright © 1972 by Allyn & Bacon.

"A Recipe for Cloze Testing" and "Answers for a Recipe for Cloze Testing" adapted from *Content Area Reading: An Integrated Approach*, Third Edition by Readance et al. Copyright © 1989 by Kendall/Hunt Publishing Company. Used with permission.

"Some Possible Elements for Reading and Writing Portfolios" adapted from *Portfolio Assessment in the Reading-Writing Classroom* by Robert J. Tierney, Mark A. Carter, and Laura E. Desai. Copyright © 1991. Reprinted by permission of Christopher Gordon Publishers, Inc.

Excerpts from Collins, Cathy. (1988). Content mastery strategies aid class discussion. *The Reading Teacher*, 40, 816–818. Reprinted with permission of Cathy Collins Block and the International Reading Association. All rights reserved.

"NCTE Guidelines for Using Journals in School Settings." Copyright 1987 by the National Council of Teachers of English. Reprinted with permission.

Fig. 9–5 from *Teaching Writing in the Content Areas: Middle School/Junior High*, by Stephen N. Tchudi and Margie C. Huerta. Copyright 1983. Washington, D.C.: National Education Association. Reprinted by permission of the NEA Professional Library.

Fig. 9–9 reprinted by permission of Dan Kirby and Tom Liner with Ruth Vinz: *Inside Out: Developmental Strategies for Teaching Writing* (Boynton/Cook, A subsidiary of Reed Elsevier Inc., Portsmouth, NH, 1988).

Cataloguing-in-Publication Data is on file with the Library of Congress.
ISBN 0-86709-417-6

Editors: Peter Stillman and William Varner
Production: Renée Nicholls
Cover design: Jenny Jensen Greenleaf
Manufacturing: Louise Richardson

Printed in the United States of America on acid-free paper
01 00 99 98 97   DA   6 5 4 3 2 1

To those who inspired our love of reading:
Lila Chisman Day, who made reading illicit and inviting;

Claire Whitman Matz, who read me to sleep every night of my childhood; and Benjamin Matz, who took me to the library on Friday nights to load up on books for the week ahead.

To those who enriched our understanding of literacy: Stu, who provided the support; and Tim and Ann, whose developing literacies provided the surprise and confirmations—and most of all, the joy.

CONTENTS

FOREWORD

Debates about how to teach reading in schools have been heated throughout the twentieth century. The major argument boils down to a choice between the following:

1. whether children should be taught explicitly to read through prerequisite skills before they will be able to read to learn; or
2. whether children learn to read and use the language cueing systems as a result of reading to learn.

The argument is based on the proponents' views of learning and teaching written language. Those who have a word-recognition view of reading believe that it is necessary to isolate specific features of reading (letters, sounds, words, bound morphemes) and teach them explicitly to young children before allowing them to read for real purposes. Those who have a meaning-centered view of reading development believe that readers learn about written language (phonics relationships and the importance of grammar and meaning) in an integrated way by being immersed in rich reading experiences that help them focus on the construction of a meaningful text at the same time as they learn about the conventions of written language.

In many places in the world this argument is only an issue in the early grades. Some countries do not focus on reading as a subject beyond this level. In the United States and elsewhere, where educators believe that all children should be educated through high school and become highly literate, the teaching and learning of reading throughout the elementary and secondary years and extending into colleges and universities is the focus of extensive research and curriculum development. We have developed special classes for those students who are not considered successful readers, especially in middle and high schools. And we have also discovered that it is necessary for teachers in all subject areas to understand the reading process and how students learn to read in order to know how to extend students' reading capabilities to specific fields or content areas. Extending the teaching of reading to older students brings us back to the argument we started with. If we believe that readers learn to read at the same time that they are reading to learn, then teaching reading is not just the domain of teachers who work with beginning readers or those struggling to learn to read. Rather the teaching of reading is the domain of every teacher who uses reading to help students learn about the content and knowledge of their subject areas.

At the heart of *Multiple Voices, Multiple Texts: Reading in the Secondary Content Areas* is the belief that as readers use written language to understand the world in which they live, they learn more about how to read at the same time. In other words, learning to read is a lifelong process. Each of us knows very well that, no matter how competent we are as readers, we have to pay lawyers to read contracts for us so that we do not get ourselves in legal trouble. If we want to understand contracts, we need knowledgeable support. Every time we read a new genre or explore beliefs and knowledge with which we are not familiar, we learn to adapt strategies to help us understand how to read in these new areas. When we read in the specialized fields of others, such as computer manuals or medical reports, we know we need help to understand the new meanings and the specialized grammatical forms and vocabulary that we encounter. Proficient readers have many strategies to help them make their way into new written forms and meanings. They are confident in their own abilities and patient with their struggles through the text. Most teachers are such confident readers and take such struggles into new texts for granted.

However, for students who do not take reading for granted, who do not have a strong background in a particular field of study, or who find reading is difficult or traumatic, it is important to have the support of a professional who understands the reading process, knows how people learn to read, and supports the development of reading throughout the school experience. The role of teaching, therefore, takes on great importance. As described in *Multiple Voices, Multiple Texts,* knowledgeable subject area teachers are best able to organize curriculum and instruction that provides the rich background of content knowledge, language, and experience that allows students to construct meaning in response to a range of written materials. In some way the greatest task that teachers face is to help students understand that reading to learn is easy and enjoyable and that everyone is capable of doing it. We support the premise of the authors that the best way to learn to read is to be engaged in reading—to use reading to learn about the aspects of the world that are important to the reader.

However, many people are taught to read with materials that are boring, uninteresting, and not relevant to their lives. They are taught to read with the focus on sounding out every word slowly and carefully, knowing the meaning of single isolated words, and searching the text for simple, correct answers. Readers who are not engaged in reading, readers for whom reading is not an integral part of their daily lives, interpret the messages that come from narrow views of teaching reading and instructional materials in such ways that often result in unproductive reading strategies. Even worse, there are those who learn to read in such settings and decide that reading in school has little meaning for them. Such readers read as little as possible.

Reade Dornan, Lois Matz Rosen, and Marilyn Wilson are experienced at exploring and resolving such issues with teachers. They are knowledgeable about the reading and writing processes, how humans become literate and how teachers can support literacy learning. In this book we continue to learn from these women as we have learned from them over the years. We participated in many lively discussions when we traveled from Detroit to East Lansing to work with the English department at Michigan State University to discuss ways to develop a university reading program for secondary English teachers. Through their many years of teaching and research they continue to develop ways for secondary teachers to understand the reading process and the learning and teaching of reading. A large portion of their book is focused on innovative practices and understandings to help teachers support the ever growing literacy needs of our democratic society. The authors make clear that traditional approaches to literacy learning and teaching in schools are no longer acceptable.

The knowledge, ideas, beliefs, and concerns explored here are as helpful for upper elementary and middle school teaching as they are for secondary schools and junior colleges. This book is especially important for content area teachers to consider their role in their students' lifelong process of developing expertise in a variety of fields through the power of reading and writing. The authors share their expertise in a number of ways. They use the ideas and voices of outstanding teachers with whom they have worked. They provide examples of students' work to show the multifaceted, complex, and pluralistic aspects of literacy. They encourage their readers to expand their understanding of the reading process by presenting multiple views of reading and the history of reading and reading instruction.

In this book, teachers are invited to think about the issues that affect the teaching of reading. The authors discuss the selection of materials, show concern for the wide spectrum of students that make up classrooms, and present ways to assess students' reading at the same time they caution teachers about the misuse of testing. The book is concerned with innovative teaching strategies to support readers as they search for knowledge in their written texts. These strategies have been developed and used by the authors for many years. The authors not only present lessons as exemplars, they encourage teachers to adapt the teaching strategies to their own styles and the needs of their students.

Teaching reading beyond the early grades is complex in many ways. It is best taught not as a separate subject but as an integral part of the teaching of ideas, knowledge, and beliefs. This means the teacher needs to be knowledgeable about the process, how it works and how to adapt it to meet the specific needs of different kinds of literature and different kinds of literacy in a variety of contexts and with the rich diversity of students in our schools today.

Yetta M. Goodman and Kenneth S. Goodman

CHAPTER ONE

Introduction

A Classroom Vignette

The wooden door to 103 with the old-fashioned opaque glass is held open by a rubber doorstop to prevent the crossventilation from blowing it shut. It's 8:03 a.m. on a September morning in this urban school, just before the eighth graders will start trekking in for their English/social studies class. Toby Curry has been here since 7:15, getting organized for the day ahead. Toby's desk is located in the corner of the room, almost obscured by the students' desks and tables that fill the room's center, and by the amount of material on the walls: students' creative writing prominently displayed on the bulletin board in the "Are You a Poet and Didn't Know It" corner; student-written booklets developed from their I-search papers tacked to the bulletin board; artwork, time lines, and illustrations of the stories and books the students are reading. Stacks of student folders are piled on the filing cabinet and the adjacent table, and shelves lining the walls are filled with children's picture books, young adult novels, biographies and autobiographies, nonfiction books, informational books, and some old encyclopedias. A spinning book rack in the corner holds the books that don't fit on the shelves. Two computers sit on a table against the far wall under the windows, along with cardboard mailboxes for each person in the room, including the teacher. The room abounds with reading and writing and student energy.

On a tour of the classroom for the visitors, Marcus shows off his illustrated and bound I-search paper on Italy; Ebony talks enthusiastically about the genre groups in romance, science fiction, and sports, in which the students discuss their reading; Denise talks about the writing they all do in response to their reading, including work in their reading journals. Surveying this activity, the intern teacher concludes, "I've never seen a class where there's so much reading going on." Not all the classrooms in this school are this actively literate and energized, but the majority are similar to Toby's.

We could be describing ambitious students in a well-funded suburban school, economically privileged and fully equipped with the latest computer hardware and athletic facilities. The truth is that this is not a private or suburban school. It is the Dewey School, located in the Cass Corridor in inner-city Detroit, a public school of 550 students from prekindergarten through eighth grade, with a mix of learning-disabled students mainstreamed in all the class-rooms and with limited resources. This whole language school draws 50 percent of its students from around the city and the remainder from the immediate neighborhood. Ninety-five percent of the students are African American. Five to ten percent are homeless. About 10 percent have been classified as learning-disabled. Each classroom has thirty to thirty-five students, the rooms are small and crowded, and across the street are buildings with boarded-up windows, adult bookstores, and liquor stores.

A bleak setting indeed. But offsetting the bleakness of the physical environment are the faces of motivated students engaged in learning, willing and eager to develop as readers and writers—proud of their poetry, fiction, and historical research. They have become reflective thinkers, critical readers and writers. There is a richness of spirit about kids and learning that has transformed what ordinarily would have been a traditional classroom and school into one in which literacy is developing and flourishing, and excitement about learning is visible on the faces of the students and in their voices as they talk about their writing prominently displayed in the room.

Their teacher, Toby Kahn Curry, who has orchestrated this assortment of voices, is a down-to-earth teacher, aware of student needs, reflective about their work together, and a strong believer in giving students responsibility for their learning. Well-read and intelligent, Toby articulates the beliefs that underlie this classroom—why they write in journals, why they respond in writing to litera-ture, what the connections are between reading and writing.

In another school, in an eleventh-grade chemistry classroom, Chris Jackson walks among the students as they work in teams trying to identify the elements of their mystery solutions. Trade books and issues of *Scientific American, Omni,* and *The Smithsonian* line the bookshelves. For students interested in medical fields, Chris has brought in a collection of materials: an old *Physician's Desk Reference,* a Merck manual, and a vertical file of articles pulled from the popular media. This classroom is also filled with student work, along with the traditional periodic table of elements. One area contains student-written reports on real-world applications of chemistry to biology and industry. On one wall hang posters from last year's science fair, illustrating the collaborative research projects Chris's students presented to other science classes in the school. Pieces of drying fruit hang from the ceiling at one end of the room. The students do not yet understand why the fruit is hanging there, but eventually Chris will ask them, in a journal entry, to formulate a theory speculating on the oxidation process of each piece of fruit—an assignment that stimulates their curiosity and makes science relevant to their everyday lives.

Chris Jackson moves from one group to another, prodding students' think-ing about the connections between their experiments and the principles dis-cussed in the textbook. Later each group will write a collaborative learning log entry that reflects on how they solved the problem and how they will use the process to determine other solutions.

Like Toby's, Chris's classroom is in a public school with a diverse student body, and, like Toby, Chris is dedicated to encouraging students to think critically about their work in this class, to engage personally in the process of learning, and to reflect on the place of chemistry in their lives.

The methods practiced by Chris and Toby reflect a movement among late-twentieth-century teachers to integrate reading and writing in meaningful assignments. Taking their cues from primary school methodology in whole language learning, secondary teachers across the curriculum are finding that when students articulate their ideas for themselves and for others to read and absorb, they invest more of themselves in their work and they deepen their understanding by writing and listening. The learning is by necessity social. If collaboration and meaning-making through reading and writing are two pillars of the whole language classroom, then authentic texts form the third. To convince students that their learning is worthwhile, the texts must be relevant, functional, and useful, and the curriculum should be responsive to student needs and interests.

These classrooms exemplify the transactional model of teaching, with teachers as facilitators, rather than lecturers, who create the environment and structures that permit students to become independent learners. In the transactional classroom, learning is an active process in which students, often working collaboratively, become risk-takers as they explore areas of study through reading and writing. Learning is approached holistically and skills learned in context. The contrasting paradigm is the transmission model of teaching in which the teacher dispenses knowledge, signaling students that they will be told in time what to do, that they need not initiate inquiry but should passively accept the information given by the teacher or the text. It is a view of learning that privileges sequential learning of skills, moving from parts to wholes. This book is based on the transactional model of learning and presents a classroom model that integrates reading, writing, listening, and speaking within a whole language framework.

What We Are About

The title of this text, *Multiple Voices, Multiple Texts,* reflects our view of literacy as multifaceted, complex, and pluralistic rather than one-dimensional. First it suggests the need to help a wide range of learners from varying kinds of communities to find voice through literacy. Because the demographics of the American schools continue to change and minority populations will become majority populations in the twenty-first century, educational institutions must begin to recognize that simplistic assumptions about literacy that reflect mainstream, middle-class values and practices should be reconsidered. If educators hope to increase the level of literacy of *all* learners, a monolithic view of literacy is neither sufficient nor desirable.

The title also implies the use of classroom materials that are multiple in number, varied in kind, and differentiated on the basis of student need and interest. Some of these texts are generated by teacher and student for others to read, and some are gathered for classroom consumption from the popular media, from textbook publishers, and from the trade book market. The basal reader or the course textbook is insufficient for the task of opening students to the power of literacy. Classrooms in all disciplines need to explore materials that go beyond the blandness of anthologies and the density of content area texts to real-world reading for young adults. Another view implicit in the title is that literacy should empower learners if they are encouraged to use it as a means of reflection and critique. National assessments that pit one school against the next and test scores that function as gatekeepers regardless of validity silence alternative and oppositional voices. This book argues that literacy must be redefined to underscore the relationship between literacy and action, between *knowing* how to read and write and *using* these skills to change the world or at least a corner of it.

A Summary of the Chapters

In this text, we explore issues of theory as well as of practice for reading in all the disciplines, not just English. We have no prescription for reading instruction in each of the content areas because we believe that successful methods and approaches to reading in the disciplines grow out of an articulated theory of reading as a sociolinguistic process and an understanding of how that process operates in the various disciplines. We believe that once teachers understand the *why* of reading they can begin to understand the *how*. Nevertheless, we suggest practices in which the theory might be applied in classrooms across the curriculum.

We begin this text with a chapter on the history of the debates about reading in the twentieth century. Theories of reading and issues of learning are explored next in Part One, "Understanding Reading." Chapter Three, "The Reading Process: Who's in Charge?" focuses on the complexities of reading as a socio-psycholinguistic process and leads to a discussion in Chapter Four of those complexities of language and literacy acquisition as they affect how children learn to read and write. Chapter Four also moves into a discussion of the impact of differing linguistic patterns and cultural experiences on literacy development.

Part Two, "Preparing to Teach," acknowledges that teachers need to assess both classroom materials and the students who will use them, in order to create effective instructional programs that incorporate whole language principles and are responsive to the broad range of students in contemporary classrooms. Chapter Five deals with the evaluation and selection of classroom texts for the best match between the text and the student. For pragmatic reasons, we have broadened the concept of text to include a wide variety of both print and non-print materials. Chapter Six, on student assessment, helps teachers to understand and minimize the negative effect of standardized tests on students, schools, and community and to explore a spectrum of informal assessment practices that foster whole language approaches in the classroom, including authentic assessment and portfolio assessment.

Part Three, "Theory into Practice," begins by arguing that a multicultural population brings not only diverse backgrounds to the classroom but also multiple intelligences. Chapter Seven lays out the possibilities of open inquiry through vocabulary, critical thinking, question-asking, aesthetic response, and metacognition. Chapter Eight begins with a definition of comprehension and demonstrates how the principles of comprehension can aid in the design of everyday lesson plans and unit plans, using pre-, during, and post-reading strategies. Both chapters contain many practical reading strategies for translating theory into practice. Chapter Nine deals with writing as a thinking tool for understanding course content. It provides a rationale for writing to learn and offers numerous concrete suggestions for using writing in the content area classroom. As teacher-educators working with both preservice and experienced teachers, we have come to understand the need for sound theory as the basis for sound classroom practice. This book is an attempt to address the issues that we have been struggling with over the years of our teaching: the major theoretical issues, the reading process, the politics of literacy, and the application of theory to classroom practice. We invite you to join us in the exploration of these issues.

CHAPTER TWO

The History of Reading Movements in the Twentieth Century

Introduction

Toward the end of the nineteenth century in America, several events began to change the nature of education. These, in turn, affected the way reading and writing were taught. One change was in the way adults began to think about children: less as little creatures who needed to be civilized and reformed and more as individuals with the capacity for reason and the human potential for intellectual growth. The traditional view had been that the only effective education methodology was a step-by-step procedure that instructed in manageable increments. Once children mastered one part of the lesson, they should then be led to the next. In effect, this pedagogical approach relied on drill and discipline to teach reading and writing. Countering this time-honored view, reformers like John Dewey (1859–1952) believed that education should value each child as an individual to be nurtured, as a whole person taking steps toward a higher-quality life. Dewey and others called for educating children to think and speak for themselves. This change in attitude triggered a variety of experiments in progressive education that have marked educational reform throughout the twentieth century.

While schools were testing new approaches to classroom practice, education visionaries were also borrowing ideas from the scientists of their day who offered an explosion of knowledge about the human mind and body. Darwin with his paradigmatic shift in biology in 1871 and Freud and Jung with their insights into the human psyche, William James (1842–1910) and G. Stanley Hall (1846–1924) with their interest in cognitive processes and physiology were among dozens of scientists who added fuel to the social sciences. So when Edward L. Thorndike with his studies in behaviorism and E. B. Huey with his studies on reading cognition followed just after the turn of the century, educators were ready to listen. What is important for our purposes here is that the theories of Thorndike and Huey spoke to two different camps in education. Disciplinarians embraced Thorndike's behaviorist model, which explained how the stimulus response might work in education and how to test for student performance on each part of any learning procedure. The alternative group of educators, believing that children learn best when relying on their natural instincts for language, subscribed to Huey's conclusion that in the process of reading, readers do not naturally approach the text letter by letter, but in wholes based on its meaning.

These competing scientific views were eventually codified into the two distinct views of reading that are current today. On the one hand are the supporters of phonics, who believe that reading is a matter of getting the meaning from the text by learning to identify letters. They also believe that reading is a linear process with an orderly sequence, that reading is a mastery of skills and an exact process. On the other hand are the psycholinguists and whole language advocates, who believe that meaning resides in a negotiation between reader and text. They further believe that reading depends on an interaction between thought and language, that reading begins when the reader brings meaning to text, and that the reader's own emphasis aids in constructing meaning. This chapter explores the history of ideas that fed both approaches to reading.

Experimental Schooling and John Dewey

John Dewey's educational philosophy represented a radical departure from William McGuffey and many other nineteenth-century educators. Although McGuffey's readers were very popular in his time, Dewey objected to educational methods that forced children to learn exactly alike, which is what the readers did. Using a controlled vocabulary and passages written for classroom consumption, McGuffey's graduated readers were used for recitation, drill, and mastery. Dewey resisted the idea that the young needed to memorize a vast accumulation of disconnected facts, rules, and definitions, and he protested meaningless skills. He was adamant that the young should learn to evaluate their own experiences and draw their own reasoned conclusions. On the surface, Dewey's pedagogy resembles classic scientific inquiry with its test of assumptions against the evidence, its examination of the data for evidence, its warrants and good reasons. However, he added the notion of collaboration, through which children can learn how to participate in a democratic society. Dewey envisioned education as the key to a vital democracy. Democracy was not just an occasional duty, but a "personal way of life"; in a democracy, problems have to be worked out by "reflective thinking," that is, by achieving community solutions through logical processes. Dewey's concept of the inquiry-based lesson, which begins with problems to solve, has had a profound influence on our contemporary definition of critical thinking and our purposes for schooling children to the age of majority.

Dewey's singular contribution, however, lies in his model for learning, which builds on the child's own experience. While most educators of his time stressed authoritarian learning methods—that is, memorizing facts and transmitting fixed bodies of knowledge—Dewey advocated a model of education that begins with the child's knowledge and world of experience. The most instructive experience is one that flows out of normal daily interaction that the child enjoys, much like the natural ebb and flow of activities that teach a child in the home. Dewey writes, "Every experience is a moving force. Its value can be judged only on the ground of what it moves toward and into" (1938, 38). It's not a fixed entity but a process, an ongoing flow of events that makes education a lifelong endeavor.

As an example, Dewey describes the process of learning how to cook an egg. In this lesson, the teacher rules out teaching by rote, asking the child instead how a cook might decide what to do without looking at a cookbook. The teacher wants the students to understand the reasons for what they are doing. The children build on this experience to explore the nutritional value of eggs, the amount of fat in the white and the yolk, and their properties at various temperatures. The lesson is carefully orchestrated by the teacher, but the initial impulse begins with the child's wanting to learn to cook, then raising questions and drawing conclusions about the results. Using this disciplined method of inductive inquiry and problem solving, Dewey found science in the carpenter's shop and chemistry in the barn.

Dewey also called attention to the potential of interactive learning, of learning through social discourse. To encourage social interaction, he endorsed physical movement in the classroom, freeing children from their desks and shaping a more collaborative form of education. And his method of embedding language skills in the total educational experience presaged much of what is happening in whole language classrooms today. To that end, Dewey took learning beyond the text and the school building into the neighborhood and community.

Edward L. Thorndike

Edward L. Thorndike was a pre-Skinnerian behaviorist who believed that learning could be understood by the way the neural system responded to a given situation. Drawing on biology and scientific discussions about determinism and inherited traits, Thorndike developed an entire study around the connections between situations and human responses to them. From other scientists studying human behavior, he had already concluded that certain sequences in training produce the most efficient results and that rewards positively reinforce certain behaviors while punishments diminish the frequency of others. After developing his stimulus-response theories, Thorndike regarded the process of learning as simply a matter of strengthening some bonds and weakening others. He wrote in his *Principles of Teaching* (1906) that teachers should "often study how to utilize inborn tendencies, how to form habits, and how to develop interests, and the like with reference to what changes in intellect and character are to be made" (quoted in Shannon 1989, 19). But, he reasoned, educators need first to analyze and classify the traits of mind and character, the skills, needs, and abilities that each child brings to the school. Given a complete profile of a child's intellectual and physical makeup, teachers can go to work shaping and conditioning her habits.

Thorndike's theories have had tremendous implications for reading in the twentieth century. They gave credence to many new courses for improving health, citizenship, and right character. If all learning is a matter of habit formation, educators surmised, then civic and moral behavior could be achieved through rigorous training and discipline. Penmanship training, which dominated classrooms for decades, also owes its rationale to Thorndike's ideas. Furthermore, his theories have justified a whole new industry in testing, particularly intelligence tests and the measurements of rates of learning. (No) thanks to Thorndike, testing has become a standard practice in all aspects of education, especially because certain learning outcomes—such as the acquisition of specific facts and skills—can be easily assessed. Educators' faith in testing led to a spate of reading tests in the 1940s and '50s that dissected the act of reading into small, testable fragments like phonics.

These reading tests, some still in use today in some schools, offer information of relatively little value to the teacher, since they attempt to determine whether the child has mastered vowel combinations, attained a certain reading speed, or remembered the antonym of a given word. But for architects of curriculum, they can justify course offerings, including remedial reading classes, as well as course design.

In Thorndike's day, intelligence tests were considered a valuable tool for categorizing and tracking a growing population of school-age children. Educators, faced with complex school placements for a surge of immigrants from Europe and the migration of many Americans from the farms to the cities, used the testing instruments available to label and sort. The tests were also used to help with vocational selection. Once a child's inherited traits and native ability had been established, he or she could be channeled—for better or worse—toward a certain educational path. Based on the results of these tests, schools began to offer a wider assortment of subjects to prepare boys and girls for the relatively new professions of secretary and bookkeeper and for the skilled trades at all levels. Unfortunately, instruments that have sometimes been used to benefit children have more often become a social and economic weapon to diminish their untestable achievements. Not only that, they have been taken up by warring factions, both inside and outside the academic community, to discredit their political opponents.

E. B. Huey

E. B. Huey's work developed in a totally different direction from that of Thorndike and his followers. Huey's seminal book *The Psychology and Pedagogy of Reading* (1908), which appeared just two years after Thorndike's *Principles of*

Teaching, focused attention on internal workings of the mind, rather than external forms of behavior. Convinced that word meanings do not exist in isolation or in lists, Huey began examining the physiological studies conducted in Germany, Paris, and the United States to prove that eye movements varied with the reader's familiarity with the material. The more the reader knows, Huey concluded, the less time the eye takes for visual perception. The less the reader knows, the longer the eye fixes on the print. In short, not every reader goes through the same mechanical motions, and eye fixations vary in number and duration according to the subject matter. Huey also cited the work of J. M. Cattell, who discovered that readers do not scan letter by letter or even syllable by syllable, but as they read, they chunk several letters and words to take in whole phrases with one eye fixation. Furthermore, he found that it took twice as long to read *unrelated* letters or words aloud as to read the same number of words combined into meaningful units. Cattell corroborated the work of others who asserted that what we cannot see is "mentally supplied" by our mind's eye "somewhat as we recognize a friend from a glimpse of his hat and cane or by his bowed form" (Huey 1908, 63). Huey added to Cattell's work by demonstrating that isolated letters or words take more time to read than words in familiar phrases. Eight-letter words, for example, do not take eight times longer to read than single letters. Indeed, a list of twenty-five eight-letter words (Figure 2–1) only takes 2.3 seconds longer to read (19.6 seconds) than the same number of four-letter words (17.3 seconds).

In his own experiments Huey also discovered that the first half of a word is more important for understanding than the second half, and that we can read most words that are missing the bottom half of their letters or their vowels, as long as the words appear in meaningful passages. "*Meaning leads* and the idea of the whole dominates the parts," wrote Huey. "The sentence is *not* naturally composed of words which originally existed independently, just as we shall find that the word is not a mere collection of syllables and letters" [italics in original] (125). Most of these turn-of-the-century experimenters were coming to the same conclusion: to read efficiently, the eye does not process each individual letter. The point of many of their findings is that we do not depend on the print for reading and we certainly do not depend on sounding out each letter, because readers first bring meaning to the page and they use the print merely to confirm what they expect to see. Huey concluded that prior knowledge is more important than the perception of any single letter in print.

Huey's conclusions confirmed what educators in the natural language movement had been saying for years. His experiments confirmed again and again that phonics training, a cornerstone of traditional language arts pedagogy, when used alone was not an effective method for teaching reading. His work, however, was largely ignored by the American educational community, which had by that time invested 150 years in instructional materials and lesson plans using the phonics approach.

By the turn of the century, when Huey published the results of his experiments, the teaching of phonics was so entrenched that it had become tedious and mechanical. For example, there is Rebecca Pollard's step-by-step procedure

y	pool	analysis	anthropology
w	rugs	habitual	independence
u	mark	occupied	histological
s	send	inherent	astronomical
q	list	probable	tautological
o	more	summoned	paleontology
m	pick	devotion	consummation
k	stab	remarked	concomitance
i	neck	overcome	epistemology
g	your	resolute	irritability
e	dice	elements	somnambulism
c	font	conclude	minimization
a	earl	numbered	malleability
z	whit	struggle	emblematical
x	ants	division	permeability
v	role	research	etymological
t	sink	original	quantitative
r	rust	involved	ascertaining
p	ware	obstacle	definiteness
n	fuss	relative	sociological
l	tick	physical	legitimately
j	rasp	pastness	scientifical
h	mold	lacteals	institutions
f	hive	sameness	governmental
d	four	distract	emphatically

50 letters in an average of 15.7 seconds.
50 four-letter words in an average of 17.3 seconds.
50 eight-letter words in an average of 19.6 seconds.
50 twelve-letter words in an average of 28.5 seconds.
50 sixteen-letter words in an average of 54.1 seconds.

FIGURE 2–1. E. B. Huey Experiment

for a phonics lesson, as described in her book *Synthetic Method* (1899). It demonstrates how complicated and codified reading lessons had become since early colonial times:

First: Oral instructional excerpts from Johnny's Story, using stencils and songs when teaching sounds; talk about the new sound; developing words by families; reasons for marking, etc.

Second: Blackboard drill, which should include the marking on the board by pupils, in turn, of all the letters, words, and sentences given in the lesson.

Third: Independent marking of the lesson by pupils at their seats.

Fourth: Writing, from the teacher's dictation, the letters, family names, words, and keys of the lesson.

Fifth: Recitation; pupils pronouncing the words and reading the sentences of the lesson. (Smith, 132)

Pollard's carefully detailed instructions were not unusual. Nearly every reader of her day had its own instructions to teachers for drilling students not only in phonics, but also in points of grammar, vocabulary acquisition, and spelling. After noting this method's de-emphasis on meaning and after realizing that students were forced to read against their natural inclinations, many reading specialists began to look around for holistic approaches. Advocates for the skills approach nevertheless persist to this day, many of them using "new and improved" instructions for making phonics work. The difference between Pollard's methods and those used nearly a hundred years later in phonics classes lies largely in the addition of the expensive computer software, teacher's manuals, workbooks, and overhead transparencies that now accompany the text.

Methods That Supported Both Views of Reading

Following this period of intense scientific investigation came a variety of reading programs that have attempted in one way or another to apply scientific findings. By the 1920s, many changes had already taken place in language arts classes. Silent reading was adopted on a wholesale basis to replace recitation and reading aloud. Techniques for teaching children to read without subvocalizing (moving their lips or tongues) brought new discussions to teacher education classes in the 1920s. The scientific movement was also responsible for flash cards, diagnostic tests and remediation, and "seat work," which included workbook exercises for each skill. With the introduction of devices to measure performance, attention was suddenly given to speed work, increasing the number of words that readers took in during an eye fixation and attempts were made to ensure that each student's eye movements shifted from left to right. Some clinicians even suggested body movements and exercises to improve oral reading, silent reading, word recognition, and rate through left/right eye coordination. In the 1950s and '60s many of these efforts culminated in the use of tachistoscopes and other devices to build up reading speed.

The computer is, of course, a recent attempt to teach reading using machines that can drill students. An earlier example is Stanley L. Pressey's 1924 "teaching machine," which was programmed to reward right answers and send students with wrong answers for additional instruction. Nila Banton Smith describes it in her classic history of reading: "In using the teaching machine the student sits at the machine and makes his responses to a preprogrammed set of questions or exercises that are presented to him. After making each response the answer is flashed to him automatically, or he may pull a knob, turn a crank, push a lever or button, slide a panel or use some other arrangement for the purpose of revealing the answer" (Smith 1986, 398). Since that time, programmed learning has appeared in many guises, including large workbooks and expensive computer software that take students through seemingly endless steps based on student responses (398–401). An example of programmed learning taken from a workbook that was popular in its time is found in Figure 2–2.

As the century has progressed, positions have hardened around pedagogical methods in language arts. Supporters of the basic-skills approach have found allies in the textbook industry, primarily among publishers of basal readers. These texts, whose antecedents include the McGuffey readers, come in a wide variety of styles, but they promote the following features: control for vocabulary that becomes increasingly difficult with longer words in each volume; mass appeal stories, which are monitored for controversial content; and sentence complexity. Because they are sold in all regions of the United States, these books reflect only mainstream, middle-class values about race, class, and gender. For example, before the civil rights movement of the 1950s and '60s, only textbooks from small presses included pictures of minorities. To this day, anthologies for the secondary level include only "safe" canonical literature, tried and true stories and essays that the public has found acceptable and advisable for student consumption. Middle school anthologies are largely filled with innocuous stories and essays about nature and school experiences written by unknown or relatively unknown authors. They generally avoid subject matter that deals with social issues, sex, death, religion, and violence. This policy has often meant the

---

whose
1. **A local firm got the order.** ~~Its~~ *bid was the lowest.*
   a.   **A local firm** *whose bid was the lowest* **got the order.**
   b.   **A local firm got the order** *whose bid was the lowest.*
In which sentence is the clause properly placed? _____

2. Change the italicized sentence to an infinitive phrase:
   We boiled our drinking water. *This killed all the bacteria.*

   _____

   _____

3. a.   **When I sit down to study, someone usually disturbs me.**
     b.   **No sooner do I sit down to study than someone usually disturbs me.**
    The verb **sit** in sentence *a* becomes _____ in sentence *b*.

FIGURE 2–2. Programmed Grammar

exclusion of mythology and fairy tales and other authentic literature that has satisfied children's psychological needs and imagination for more than a hundred years. On the high school level, basal readers have taken the form of graded reading kits based on the concept of "mastery" learning. To demonstrate proficiency, students must answer canned questions at one level before graduating to the next level. The text's reading level is usually determined by one of the readability formulas described in Chapter Five, which measure a combination of length of word and sentence with no appreciable consideration of the student's interest or prior knowledge of the subject matter.

Historical Overview

Both camps in reading theory—the controlled vocabulary approach and the whole text approach—have experienced dead-ends in their response to the scientific research that has fed teacher education during the twentieth century. Trying to improve on phonics was a movement spearheaded by Sir James Pitman. In an attempt to make reading easier, the Pitman Augmented Roman Alphabet added extra letters to the alphabet to include phonological symbols with closer sight-sound correspondence. Developments in the 1960s led to the "Initial Teaching Alphabet" and the I/T/A method of teaching reading.

The idea was to teach reading using the sound symbols in the first year or two and then to gradually introduce the traditional alphabet. The content of the books was appealing with many fanciful as well as realistic narratives, and one volume was wholly given over to dinosaurs. Beginning activities included handwriting, creative writing, spelling, and thinking. I/T/A was eventually dropped, however, because the phonics-like method was cumbersome and few parents or teachers were persuaded that it was effective.

Early use of natural language also had its failures when it endorsed "whole word" instruction, even though the words were not being learned in their contexts. One program introduced in the 1920s, the "look-say" method (sometimes called the "look-and-say" or "Sight Word" approach), used pictures and flash cards instead of phonics instruction to encourage young readers to connect the spoken word with the printed word. It was incorporated as one of several approaches in the Dick and Jane books. The point was to foster instant whole word recognition rather than fixate on sounding out the letters. The problem with the look-say method was that the words were just as isolated and meaningless linguistically as words learned with phonics rules. The look-say approach was the trend in many schools between 1920 and 1935. After that period, it was combined with other methods.

Another, similar, whole word approach was the so-called "linguistic" method, which used rhyming words in sentence form, largely to reinforce the sight-sound correspondence between print and spoken word. The sentences tended to work hard the vowel sounds: Nan can fan Dan, Tom wants Ron's lock, and Odd ox swats Tom's socks. Developed by Leonard Bloomfield in the

1940s, it remained popular in some schools into the '60s, even though the sentences were nonsensical and did not teach children to make meaning out of the text. Although these experimental approaches are often attributed to those advocating natural language, in fact they fell far short of any effort to bring meaning to reading.

Responses to Fears About Literacy Levels

A dissatisfied public is not new to education circles. Each time we experience significant political or economic changes, America suddenly requires a more sophisticated workforce and the schools are forced to raise the literacy requirements. Each time the schools go through such a crisis, phonics and other skills approaches become popular as quick solutions.

Reformers were particularly vocal in the nineteenth century when manufacturing and the business sector needed more literate workers. Not coincidentally, Harvard President Charles Eliot deplored the level of composition among its college freshmen in 1871—two years after the president of Cornell complained about the ignorance of its students. In 1907, when half the students enrolled at Harvard, Princeton, Yale, and Columbia supposedly did not meet their entrance requirements, remedial courses were instituted to address this crisis in education. They were put in place at a time when the workplace demanded a more standardized business correspondence, and company presidents needed to be better read. This was also the time of the great migration from Europe, when immigrants who wanted to become secretaries or traveling salesmen needed to be able to write and speak in standard English. Remedial reading courses were widely installed in all major colleges by the late 1930s. These classes again increased in number as a large influx of underprepared veterans using the G.I. Bill filled the classrooms immediately following World War II.

After World War II, the growth of the mass media, particularly television, adversely affected reading patterns in America. High school graduation and college entrance requirements were nevertheless raised as a result of the launching of Sputnik in 1957. The push for stronger schools came shortly after the beginning of the space race even though the schools were already trying to accommodate the 1954 *Brown v. Board of Education* decision. Although integration brought huge social upheaval in the schools for several decades, when students were uprooted from their home schools and thrown together with children from a variety of backgrounds, the public exerted pressure to "upgrade" the way reading and writing were taught. About a decade later, the decline of standardized test scores, particularly the SAT scores, became an issue.

In the 1980s and '90s, schools have once again come under fire for their inability to keep up, this time because of concerns in the corporate world that the United States is slipping behind in computer literacy. These concerns were spelled out in detailed studies by the Department of Education (*A Nation at*

Risk), the National Commission on Excellence in Education, the National Endowment for the Humanities, and many others. Their subtexts are fairly similar: as the Cold War winds down and research in space travel becomes a joint effort between the United States and the former Soviet Union, children must study hard so they can compete economically with Japan and other major industrial nations. Thus, American education has been repeatedly shaped by corporate enterprise, national policy, and international conflict.

Psycholinguistics and the Back-to-Basics Movement

Since the 1960s and the arrival of television, computers, and integration in the schools, each faction in the language arts debate has hardened its position. Jeanne Chall, a supporter of the phonics approach, has squared off against Yetta and Kenneth Goodman, the most articulate and impassioned proponents of the whole language approach. Chall attracted her following with *Learning to Read: The Great Debate 1910–1965* (1967), in which she discusses reading for meaning but emphasizes correctness and error-free word recognition and spelling. The primary object of her attack is innovation in reading, a broad category that includes the failed methods of the "linguistic" approach, I/T/A, and look–say (the Sight Word approach), as well as the holistic method that she calls "Language Experience," which did not have a track record at the time she wrote the book.

Chall won the hearts and minds of many readers by raising doubts about any form of innovation. She wrote, "I found some of these young parents to be deeply concerned about providing a proper education for their children, many of whom were still in kindergarten. They were worried that the public schools were not giving pupils a good foundation in the early grades and that as a result these children would not be able to enter a college of their choice" (291). So by using emotional scare tactics, she sounded the alarm about America's schools. More recently, Chall has spoken of the "direct instruction model," a catchall phrase that insists on the systematic instruction of phonics and any other aspects of language that can be reduced to rules and sequential instruction. Chall believes that reading and writing should be introduced in fragmentary developmental stages, rather than by natural methods that whole language proponents advocate. She claims that direct instruction includes features usually associated with whole language reading—that is, the enjoyment of quality literature and the development of lifelong habits in reading—but says that systematized skills should come first. A more extensive discussion on the differences between whole language and her own views appears in Chapter Three.

Yetta and Kenneth Goodman have spearheaded a fundamentally different way of teaching and learning literacy. Kenneth Goodman's book *What's Whole in Whole Language* (1986) has sold more than 210,000 copies and is used in many countries worldwide. Although a more extensive discussion of their work appears in Chapter Three, it should be noted here that whole language does not ignore phonics and other direct instruction. It does always emphasize making meaning and reading authentic texts. Reading and writing are meant for real audiences and real purposes. The whole language philosophy grows out of psycholinguistics research and the work of Noam Chomsky, who explained that language is processed by readers at a much deeper level and with more complex understanding than the surface structures of word order, word endings, and spellings would indicate. The deep structure, or underlying relationships between words, is understood primarily in the context of both the reader's prior knowledge and the rest of the text. Agreeing with Chomsky that language is often open to interpretation because it is inherently ambiguous and often dependent on the situation, psycholinguists have concluded that reading has to begin with the reader's cognition. Like E. B. Huey, they contend that reading is not word-centered but meaning-centered, a transaction between the print and the reader. The best readers bring information to the text, and the least proficient pay too much attention to surface features. Furthermore they agree with the Goodmans that the rules of language are too complicated to teach and therefore most language learning has to take place in meaningful exchanges.

Sociolinguistics also gained prominence during this time, largely as a discipline that examines how culture, race, and economic class affect language acquisition and usage. The findings in this field have reinforced the whole language movement. Out of cultural studies in sociology, linguistics, and education came the social constructivists, who reason that knowledge does not come in units that are distributed from teacher to student. It is situational, associated with the events in which it is learned. Social constructivists argue that we cannot deny the conditioning of the social context of knowledge or the physical environment. Through conversation, reading, and writing, we realign our thinking in light of new knowledge and extend the schemas of what we already think. For social constructivists, knowledge is always in the process of being negotiated and being formulated through linguistic transactions and incoming information.

Process writing as a movement (discussed fully in Chapter Nine) was also influenced by the work of the psycholinguists. Whole language and the writing process share the basic assumption that teaching methods for reading and writing must reflect the way we learn language and speak it. Moreover, they share a common commitment to writing with real purposes for a variety of audiences, and to reading materials that are not artificially composed to serve as a language lesson with a controlled category and schoolbook language. Language experience, primarily a set of practical lessons to develop literacy, helps beginning readers by providing language-making activities for young children, even when they can't read or write many words. Language experience is probably best known for its method of using written transcriptions of the children's own dictated language. Believing "anything I can say, I can write; anything I can write, I can read," teachers write down the stories that children give them orally, and then the children are asked to read the print. The stories are based on their own experiences and discourse. This method was developed by Roach Van Allen in the early stages of the whole language movement.

Chapter Summary

Scientific discoveries in the early part of the twentieth century further sharpened the debate in education that already had been raging for more than half a century. What began as a disagreement about whether to train the child through strict and orderly classroom procedures or to nurture the child's mind through inquiry-based lessons had evolved into a heated argument about competing reading pedagogies for emergent literacy. It became a battle between the advocates of the phonics and progressive approaches. These battles have been waged for more than a century, heating up periodically when an economic upheaval forces schools to rethink their definitions of literacy. During these periods of crisis, the lay public turns to the basic skills for reading and writing, even though the whole-language approach serves the more long-term goals of reading and writing for lifelong purposes.

CHAPTER THREE

The Reading Process: Who's in Charge?

Introduction

The prevailing assumptions about reading instruction that underlie the behaviorist and the psycholinguistic perspectives suggest a tension in the field that flares occasionally into skirmishes and now and then into wars. Before we can begin to sort through the issues of how reading should be taught and how it is learned, it is essential to ask what it is we know about the process of reading and how it is practiced by proficient readers.

Emerging from research in applied linguistics, literary theory, and cognitive psychology over the past two decades has been the growing awareness that reading is a highly complex process involving an active reader who interacts with the text on many levels—using various strategies for decoding written symbols and using her own knowledge, experiences, and assumptions to construct meaning. Psycholinguistic theory, as this theory is called, questions the behaviorist assumptions about reading as a passive activity and asks not only how readers make sense of words on the page but, more politically, how they construct meaning, and whose meaning is being created. The essential question is "who's in charge?" Is the reader controlled by the text, or does the reader play a major role in how a text is read, perceived, and comprehended? Who, in other words, has the power: the text as the writer wrote it or the reader who chooses how to interpret it? To use Louise Rosenblatt's (1978) metaphor, is the spotlight still on the author and the author's text, or has it shifted to focus equally on the reader as a co-creator?

All readers and all teachers of reading operate with a theory about the process of reading, whether that theory is conscious or not, articulated or not. Children who have been taught that sounding out words is the sole means of identifying words and that "sounding out" is an end in itself are likely to have a different theory about how reading works than children who come to school immersed in books and eager to continue the authentic reading learned on a parent's lap. They may see the learning of phonics in school as a confirmation of what they already know or as an activity, bothersome at best, unrelated to the real purpose of reading. Beginning readers are constantly using their home and school experiences to develop and revise their theories of reading. Because the degree to which readers are successful may depend on their internalized theory of reading, we cannot ignore the fundamental relationship between how reading is taught and how readers see themselves participating in the process. The teaching of reading, then, is ultimately political, for it has the power to create readers who are either active thinkers and learners or reluctant, passive, uninvolved learners. In this chapter we will discuss the process of reading as it has been observed in current research. Chapter Four will focus on approaches to reading instruction and their relationship to the processes of reading described here.

The Behaviorist Model of Reading

A mother proudly asks her six-year-old son to read aloud from a newspaper article entitled "Senate Passes Campaign Funding Bill." Jack shyly picks up the article, hesitates briefly, and begins reading. Although he stumbles over a few unfamiliar names, he reads fluently, albeit without much expression. His mother beams proudly as her son finishes "reading." He has "read" words like "politics," "finance," and "government" flawlessly. Meaning, from this perspective, is neither required nor expected. Identifying the words is the primary task.

This popular view of reading suggests that readers pass their eyes over the words on a page, focus on the letters or parts of the words, translate the letters into sounds, and then register the words in the brain. Reading is a passive process involving little mental activity beyond word identification. It suggests that meaning, if important, occurs magically as a byproduct of reading, as an accumulation of bits and pieces of information. Behaviorist theories of learning lend themselves to the view that only that which is directly observable—oral reading or word identification, for example—can be measured, with the result that accuracy and fluent, error-free oral reading become the goals of reading. Comprehension, a mental activity more difficult to "observe," is not easily measurable and therefore less open to direct instruction.

The focus of the behaviorists on observable, testable data led to significant amounts of research on phonics rules and the order in which they should be taught, on word analysis skills for word identification, and on eye movements and reading speed. For example, should the digraph (two letters representing one sound) "ph" as in "phone" be taught before or after "th"? Where in the order of lessons should students be taught the vowels, and how should they be taught? Should they be introduced by the use of diacritical marks such as the use of ⁻ over "long" vowels, or should they be taught by contrasting them with the "short" vowels, such as the difference between "hate" and "hat"? An imposed structure that orders rules from easier to more difficult, from small bits and pieces of written language (sound-letter correspondences) to larger units (words and phrases), with a focus on oral reading accuracy encourages learners to think of meaning as secondary, particularly when the reading materials consist of highly decontextualized language for instructional purposes—lists of words, parts of words, or nonsense words used for phonetic analysis. A mechanistic, linear view of reading reduces the process to learning a set of rules that take precedence over meaning. Primary grades, the theory goes, are for "learning to read"; upper elementary grades later begin to focus on meaning and "reading to learn."

The decade of the 1990s also has its own popular version of reading programs based on behavioral assumptions. Currently promulgated on the nation's airwaves as a quick fix for reading problems, "Hooked on Phonics" claims spectacular success. Other programs available hark back to Rudolf Flesch's *Why Johnny Can't Read* (1955) and its call for a return to the golden age of phonics and basics, a comforting solution for people looking for simplistic answers to the problems of an increasingly complex society.

Behaviorist models of reading that value accuracy in word identification over experimentation with print also concern themselves with the correctness of interpretation under the assumption that comprehension, though not observable, can nevertheless be objectified. In this view, texts, rather than being open to interpretation, contain within themselves implicit meanings that can be discovered by discerning readers. Much time must be spent on helping readers get the interpretation "right," with little allowance for uncertainty and almost none for multiple interpretations. Reading in this view is essentially an uncomplicated, objective process.

Contributing to this behavioral view of literacy is a history that goes back centuries to oral reading behaviors in cultures in which the relatively few people who were literate were privileged to provide translations of texts, specifically Biblical ones, for those who could not read themselves. In fact, well into the early twentieth century, oral recitation was the benchmark of literacy. It wasn't until after World War I, with the realization that many people in the military service had difficulty with the literal interpretation of the texts they were asked to read, that new standards of literacy began to focus on literal comprehension, and it was not until the 1950s that any attempt was made to apply the concepts of literal comprehension and its instruction to the school population as a whole (Myers, 1996).

The Reading Process: A Psycholinguistic Perspective

The theory that complicates these views about the reading process—psycholinguistic theory—offers a more multifaceted view of the reading process and a more complex view of the reader who participates in it. Psycholinguistic theory considers the interplay between a reader's mind and the printed text; it assumes more active participation by the reader in making sense of text. With its focus on the human mind and its interconnections between thought and language, psycholinguistics offers a rich area of inquiry within which to study reading theory. Because reading, as one of the language arts, is a linguistic process, the interconnections among thought, language, and written text are particularly interesting to researchers investigating how children acquire language, oral or written, and how they use that linguistic knowledge when reading.

Goodman, Watson, and Burke (1996) offer a dialogic view of the reading process whose organizing principle is the interaction or transaction that occurs between the reader and the text. As Figure 3–1 illustrates, the interaction of the reader's mind and the author's mind through the printed text occurs because the reader uses various strategies to make sense of the text. Readers, for example, make inferences and predictions about the text and its meanings by sampling information from all levels of the text, from graphic to semantic. In sampling, these researchers contend, readers select the least amount of print information necessary to make inferences and predictions, a process made possible by the

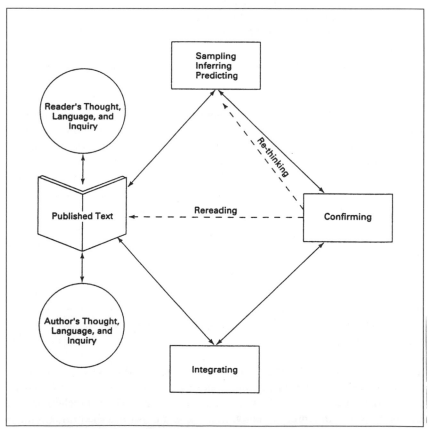

FIGURE 3–1. A Model of Reading

reader's own knowledge and background experiences, largely without conscious awareness. When their predictions are not met, they often correct themselves by going back to the text for more information, a clear indication that the
process is cyclical rather than linear. When predictions are confirmed—when
readers can answer affirmatively the question of whether or not the text makes
sense—they have begun to intergrate the new information with their own
knowledge and experience of the world. The meaning they "get" from the text
is actually a construct shaped by their own understanding and experience.
Rather than a passive accumulation of information, such a process is both active
and necessarily sometimes inexact, for it is a directed search for meaning driven
by each reader's own knowledge, perceptions, questions, and inferences.

Reading as a Linguistic Process

Let's consider for a moment what is involved in comprehending a simple sentence like "The paper is very thin today." What kinds of information does a
reader need to have in order to comprehend this written sentence? Obviously
the reader needs some understanding of the written code, the letters and the
sounds those letters represent, so at one level, at least, the correlation between
letters (graphic information) and sounds (phonemic information) will play a role
in reading. But clearly this information is insufficient and may, in fact, play a
minor role. We have all had the experience of "sounding out" a word like
"transerflying" without getting a full contextual meaning from it. And we can
all identify "thin" in the preceding sentence, though that identification does not
necessarily help us construct the meaning. Obviously grapho-phonic (letter-
sound) information is insufficient because sounding out the word does not provide the meaning, and, in fact, proficient readers go well beyond the boundaries
of letters and words to identify words, as we shall illustrate later.

Another level of knowledge involves an understanding of the meanings
represented by the individual words in the sentence. But word meanings in and
of themselves are limited by the syntactic structures (the grammatical organization of sentences) in which they are embedded. The reader needs to know the
rules of English *syntax,* the relationship among words in the sentence. The individual words in "Is thin paper the very today" can be identified, but in this
order those words have no discernible meaning. Words do not carry the meaning of a text; the syntactic structure provides both a context for meaning-
making and a way of both limiting and opening possibilities of the individual
meaning of words. The meaning of words is always context-dependent.

Even in a nonsense "jabberwocky" sentence like "The skelterhazzle fremyingly prazzled his bangly torpers," readers can construct a limited meaning based
on their knowledge of English syntax. Word order suggests that the sentence
consists of a noun (skelterhazzle) performing an action (prazzled) on an object
(torpers), along with the modifiers of the action (fremyingly) and of the object
(bangly). *Morphological information*—word endings that convey grammatical
information, such as endings like the "ly" on the modifiers, the "ed" on the

verb to indicate the past tense, and the "s" to indicate the plurality of the noun "torpers"—are all syntactic cues that language users/readers use to construct meaning. Readers can even answer a "comprehension" question such as "What did the skelterhazzle do to his torpers?" by using their knowledge of syntax to find the answer: "He prazzled them." Readers may not necessarily "understand" what is happening, but they can use their linguistic knowledge to come up with the expected answer, a not uncommon occurrence in test situations, whether they comprehend fully or not.

But syntax alone, like grapho-phonic information, is also insufficient for word identification. The context of the sentence or paragraph or text, however it is defined, plays a critical role in a reader's construction of meaning. *Semantics* refers not only to vocabulary but also, as Rhodes and Dudley-Marling (1988) describe it, "to the knowledge shared by readers and writers about the world and how the world is represented by language . . . [It refers] to the concepts represented by that vocabulary and how those concepts are organized into schemas, our structured knowledge about the world" (27). We might be able to assign a meaning to "thin," but the information provided in the sentence is too limited for a definitive meaning. We need a fuller context that will provide a sense of the semantic field of the words in this sentence: What kind of paper does this refer to? The paper is thin in what way? If our sample sentence were printed in the context of a conversation between husband and wife, in which the wife is looking for in-depth news about the latest government scandal, the reader would be likely to interpret the sentence to mean that the newspaper had not provided enough information on the topic. If, however, the sentence were in the context of a printing company testing its product, the sentence would take on a very different meaning. How the reader interprets the sentence depends heavily on its linguistic, situational, and social context.

Meaning, in other words, is not directly representational. Readers will construct their own meaning that grows out of their ability to analyze and operate with all four of the cueing systems just described: grapho-phonic, syntactic, semantic, and contextual. As they process print, readers use all four sources of knowledge/information simultaneously. It is not a linear process in which grapho-phonic information leads to word identification, which in turn leads to knowledge of syntax and then finally to a consideration of the context. In fact, if the process of constructing meaning is to occur most efficiently, readers need to begin with a context from the sociocultural situation in which the written text is embedded. A reader who picks up a book in which two characters are discussing world events already has a context for constructing an interpretation similar to the first one described above. The interpretation is not derived from the words and the syntax alone but rather from the contextual knowledge the reader brings to the process itself. "He was struggling to get out of the bunker" will immediately trigger very different meanings depending on whether we're reading a magazine about golf or a novel about World War II. It's not the words that give us the clue to meaning, but the situation in which the words are embedded.

The Role of Context in Reading

Contrary to the popular view of reading, proficient readers actually start with the larger context and work toward the specifics of the print, using word identification via analysis of grapho-phonic information more for confirming predictions than for forming them. Having some knowledge of the context makes prediction about meaning significantly easier, and having some sense of what a paragraph is about makes the identification and comprehension of individual sentences within the paragraph easier. Words, accordingly, are easier to identify when they are embedded in meaningful sentences. It stands to reason, then, that the way to make reading easier is to provide the reader with as full a context as possible. Frank Smith (1994) refers to the process as an inside-out process, with the control of the meaning being within the reader rather than within the text. Other researchers describe it as a top-down, meaning-driven process, rather than a bottom-up, text-driven process. Starting with meaning makes readers' predictions about words and/or letters more efficient. Whichever metaphor the reader prefers—inside-out or top-down—the assumptions are identical. It is the reader who is in charge of the meaning.

One must not be misled, however, into thinking that the context is always going to be sufficient for readers to identify meaning easily. Contextualized language is always easier to comprehend than decontextualized, but the context, though necessary, is not a sufficient basis for meaning.

Take, for example, the words "values," "relation," "variable," and "curve." In the abstract, one can probably provide a common-use definition for each, but a particular technical context might, in fact, complicate and obscure the meaning if one doesn't have sufficient background knowledge to comprehend the following context for these words: "If the known relation between the variables consists of a table of corresponding values, the graph consists only of the corresponding set of isolated points. If the variables are known to vary continuously, one often draws a curve to show the variation." The relationship between the words on a page and the meaning the reader constructs is indeed a dynamic and multifaceted one.

The following newspaper article, with strategic words deleted in a cloze exercise, illustrates the complex relationship between the squiggles on the page and the meaning the reader constructs. Readers are asked to fill in the blanks with single words that are appropriate to the meaning they construct from the passage.

In order to prevent (1) _____ hordes of University of (2) _____ delinquents from (3) _____ Sparty a pair of blue shorts (4) _____ a strategically placed block "M," a paid (5) _____ kept watch on the (6) _____ statue every night last (7) _____ .

Apparently the ploy (8) _____ . MSU Department of Public Safety (9) _____ reported Sparty had a (10) _____ quiet week. DPS paid a student aide (11) _____ $4.00 an hour to stand (12) _____ .

Keeping the guard company (13) _____ several Varsity Club
members, who (14) _____ the vigil before every
MSU-UM (15) _____ as a matter of (16) _____ .
    (17) _____ , there was one scuffle Friday
(18) _____ , police said, when a Varsity Club member
(19) _____ a punch at a (20) _____ heckler.

To be able to fill in the blanks successfully, the reader must have knowledge of the syntactic structure of English, an understanding of the morphological system, appropriate vocabulary to express the notion suggested by the context of the article, and an understanding of the semantics and the meaning of the
passage vis-à-vis background knowledge about the football rivalry between
these two Michigan universities. Linguistic, discourse, and contextual knowledge are all required to read the passage successfully.

Reading this passage is not a linear process; to determine the appropriate
word choice for number 8, for example, the reader needs to read ahead to
determine whether the endeavor was successful or not. Readers regularly read
ahead and then go back to pick up, confirm, or modify original predictions.

When higher-order knowledge exists, i.e., conceptual rather than simple
word knowledge, that knowledge will influence the processing of lower-level
linguistic elements. For example, knowledge of semantics affects the degree to
which syntactic predictions will operate efficiently. Knowing that Sparty is a
scantily clad Spartan statue suggests the preposition "with" rather than the conjunction "and" in blank 4. And knowledge of semantics and syntax will make
word identification more efficient. For example, knowledge of the sports rivalry
between the University of Michigan and Michigan State University, which
reaches its peak the week before their annual football game, will dictate the
word "week" rather than "month" or "year" in blank 7. Identifying appropriate words for any of these blanks will be considerably more complex without
this background knowledge. Students from other countries who good-
naturedly try to complete this cloze passage struggle considerably more with it
than native Michiganians, not because their knowledge of English isn't as
sophisticated—although that is a factor in some cases—but because they are
unfamiliar with the tradition being described in the article. Their lack of higher-
order knowledge of U.S. football culture has a negative impact on their ability
to process information at lower levels of word analysis.

The Role of Prediction in Reading

Readers' ability to provide the appropriate responses in the exercise above
evolves not from their ability to use graphic information so much as from the
wide range of knowledge—linguistic, semantic, conceptual—that they bring
with them to the reading process. Instead of identifying every feature, every
letter, or even every word, readers select the most salient features of letters,

words, phrases, and sentences, depending on the background knowledge they bring to the reading, as the basis for sampling, predicting, confirming, or correcting.

Psycholinguistic reading theory has received tremendous support from research on eye fixations and information-processing, going back to Huey (1908), as discussed in Chapter Two. Frank Smith's particularly cogent discussion (1994) suggests that because the brain can process a limited amount of information per eye fixation, that is, can "take in" only 5–7 bits of information per single glance, the amount of nonvisual information the reader brings to the page is critical. In a single glance the brain can process either 5–7 *unrelated* bits of information or several more bits of *related* information. If a row of unrelated letters is flashed before a reader's eyes in a split second, the reader will be able to identify no more than 5–7 letters. If the row of letters consists of five unrelated words, the reader will be able to identify two of those words, comprising 10–12 letters, a significant increase because the letters are organized into a discernible order. And if the line of print consists of five related words in a meaningful sentence, the reader will be able to process the entire sentence, comprising 20 or more letters, because the line of print is organized into meaningful words within a meaningful syntactic context. The difference in each case is not that the brain is taking in more information but that the brain is using existing nonvisual, schematic information to make the visual information go further. For example, there are no patterns, no meaning in the following line of print, so that the observer is capable of identifying only 5–7 letters, perhaps those in the bracketed area:

R Z N [T K L P S D] M J C B

There are word patterns in the following line of print, so that the observer is capable of processing two of the words:

STREAM NIGHT [TREES EAGER] HAPPY RUNNING

In addition to word patterns, there is whole meaning in the following line of print:

[YOU CAN READ THIS EASILY.]

In this example, the reader uses syntactic and semantic knowledge, not available in the first two examples, and can therefore identify the full sentence. Although the eye can take in only 5–7 bits in each of these three cases, the knowledge of syntax and the semantic relationships found in the third example enables the reader to process a full sentence containing 20 letters. From her own store of nonvisual information she has filled in to make predictions based on limited graphic information.

When readers have considerable background knowledge, prediction is more likely to be meaning-based. When readers have limited knowledge, prediction may occur on the basis of words or phrases, likely with less accuracy because the basis of prediction is narrow.

Prediction, of course, is a strategy we use in all aspects of our lives, although we may not be conscious of the significant role it plays until a prediction we have unconsciously made is suddenly exposed as incorrect. When we unexpectedly find a door closed as we walk from the bedroom to the bathroom in the middle of the night, a nasty bump into the door makes us aware that our prediction, for the most part unconscious, has not been met. Or the sign on the shoe store may get registered as "Payless Shoe Store" instead of the actual commercial name, "Payless Shoe Source." (In fact, when we ask our college students to fill in the blank for us in Payless Shoe _____), the majority respond with the prediction they've always made: "Store." Some doubt our word that it is actually "Source" and insist on checking it out for themselves.

For proficient readers, predicting during reading is rarely conscious, until we come to the first part of a hyphenated word at the end of the page, as in Frank Smith's (1994) example: "The captain ordered his mate to drop the an- _____ ." Before turning the page, we may mentally run through a couple of possibilities that are both syntactically and semantically appropriate. Several words could appear here—answer, anemone, antibody, anchovy—but several others would not even occur to us because they are neither syntactically nor semantically appropriate: anticipate, annoy, animate. But if we know something about captains and ships, we are more likely to predict "anchor," which fits the structure as well as the meaning. If prediction is the unconscious elimination of unlikely alternatives, as Smith suggests, it is the result of knowledge so well-learned that readers require little conscious effort to apply it (Goodman, 1967).

If proficient reading involves prediction, the process is necessarily inexact. A focus on accuracy in oral or silent reading, where "mistakes" are construed as negative, may impede strategic construction of meaning and efficiency in reading. Readers too strongly tied to accurate word identification may not feel comfortable making the more global predictions that will encourage their use of the knowledge they bring to the reading.

Notice the kinds of predictions you make as a reader when you read the following passage:

The Fish That Got Away

As Joe walked back to the lodge, his friend met him, wondering what Joe's story would be this time. "How was the fishing, Joe?" he asked. "Not bad," Joe said, "except that I let the big one get away. It ripped a a hole in the net and swam right though it. It would have been one of the the biggest fish I ever caught."

Even our college readers, proficient though they are, often fail to see the two consecutive "a's" or the two "the's." The majority, on first reading, read "though" as "through" because their linguistic sense and their search for meaning leads to a syntactically and semantically logical prediction. When, as readers, we focus on the construction of meaning, we necessarily pay less attention to the details of the text that a proofreader would be expected to focus on. Our linguistic, semantic, and global knowledge allows us to make predictions about meaning and structure, and encourages us to overlook the features that don't fit into our predictions. Unfortunately, too much of the traditional reading instruction asks young readers to read like proofreaders rather than like meaning-makers, and consequently reading proficiency, fluency, and meaning suffer. In fact, the most proficient readers among us are more likely to overlook these mistakes because we are intent on constructing meaning.

Print is most predictable when all aspects of the language system—graphophonics, syntax, semantics, and situational context—contribute to a reader's construction of meaning. If a reader's background knowledge of variables and graphs and mathematical concepts is limited, the predictions will need to be made more on the basis of individual words and syntax rather than on semantics. This suggests that children learning to read need predictable materials—familiar stories, poems, and rhymes—that will help them make predictions about words and phrases based on the familiarity they have with the story or poem. At the secondary level, students needs accessible materials as well—materials to which they can relate, materials with enough familiar concepts and familiar styles of writing, materials that help them connect their own experiences to those being represented in the text. If the materials do not adequately supply what students need to comprehend the text, the teacher must help students fill in the background knowledge they will need in order to understand the text.

The Role of Schema

Reading, then, is less a matter of the information on the page than it is of the information already in the reader's head. Frank Smith refers to this in-head knowledge as "behind-the-eyeball information" (1973, 6). Without some preexisting knowledge of the subject we are reading about, comprehension of the text is virtually impossible. We have all had the experience of trying to read difficult material on a subject about which we know very little. The words in the text may seem simple, the syntax may be straightforward, but the concepts are so foreign that we cannot comprehend them. Reading, says Smith, is largely a nonvisual process. Of course, it's true that we can't read with the lights out, we can't read if the text is not accessible, but at the same time the mere presence of a text is not sufficient for comprehension. We must use what we already know to make sense of the printed page. Smith describes the relationship between the visual and the nonvisual information as a trade-off: the more nonvisual information the reader has, the less visual information is required. And the converse is also true. The less nonvisual information the reader brings to the reading task, the more visual information is required.

Readers who have some experience with the topic at hand have a *schema* for the reading, a cognitive structure that has developed from the reader's direct or vicarious experience with the topic. Rather than storing random bits of information, our systems of knowledge consist of well-organized, hierarchical structures of knowledge with intricate connections among them. These schemas allow us to operate cognitively and perceptually, to make sense of the world in which we live. Schemas are instrumental in forming our worldviews, in making predictions about our world in general and the world of texts in particular.

Many readers, for example, have first-hand experience with flying as a means of transportation. They're either flown themselves or have heard numerous accounts about flying. Their *content* schema includes knowledge of how airports operate, how frequent flier points work, how baggage is checked and handled, and what the ticketing procedures are. Their *structural* schema includes knowledge of how airports are organized—where the check-in counters, flight information screens, and baggage claim areas are located. When they approach an airport to meet a friend at the plane or to fly to Acapulco for a vacation, their content and structural schemas help them make decisions about what to do once they enter. For people with almost no experience with airports, the decision-making becomes more difficult. They may need to ask about location or procedures. Or they may wander on their own, trying to figure out the process of checking in, checking baggage, and finding out flight information.

Readers operate in a similar fashion when they approach a text. Those with some content knowledge of the topic will have an easier time negotiating the meaning; those with less knowledge may find it more difficult. Readers also have rhetorical, structural, and linguistic schemas as part of their repertoire for comprehending texts. Knowledge about the genre itself—whether poetry or fiction, textual material or expository essays—will provide a basis for how to approach the text. Readers whose knowledge of text organization and rhetorical structure is strong will use that structural knowledge to negotiate meaning and will need to do less "wandering around" in the text in an attempt to make sense of it.

Both content and structural schemas are to some degree socially and culturally determined. The Western tradition of argumentative essays, with the major point stated in the beginning and supporting points following consecutively, is not a universal rhetorical style. Arabic readers, for example, are more likely to expect that supporting points will lead to the major point at the end of the essay. In a similar way, socially determined structures in storytelling set up different expectations in different speech communities in the United States. White middle-class readers usually tell topic-centered narratives; African-American children often use a topic-chaining format that is less linear and direct, a storytelling structure that is unfamiliar to most middle-class Anglo-Americans (Byers and Byers 1972). Socially and culturally determined schemas will affect the differences in expectations for the text and in how texts are processed, an issue that becomes important when students' expectations for print and storytelling differ from school instruction and teacher expectation. (For a more detailed discussion of linguistic/cultural differences in reading, see Chapter Four.)

Miscues and the Negotiation of Meaning

Readers make mistakes when they read because their assumptions about the meaning and structure of a text—their schemas—provide the framework for their perceptions, and their assumptions may differ from those of the author.

Where the assumptions of the reader differ from those of the author, we are likely to find mistakes, or "miscues," as we prefer to call them. Developed by Ken Goodman to study the reading process through oral reading, miscue analysis provides a window into the kinds of strategies—predicting, confirming, correcting—that readers use. Unlike traditional reading programs, in which a mistake is treated as an error and therefore assumed to be negative, miscue analysis treats a mistake not as a random error but as a deviation from the text triggered by the reader's predictions or associations. One measure of reading proficiency, therefore, is the quality of the miscues the reader makes. A miscue that does not change the meaning is of a higher quality than one that distorts the meaning in a significant way. Some miscues, in fact, reflect a reader's strength. Our students' reading "source" as "store," for example, illustrates a high-quality miscue that is grammatically and semantically acceptable and does not change the meaning.

In the following passage from a short story, "The Weapon" (Figure 3–2), most of the miscues that Sarah, a seventh-grader, makes are semantically and syntactically acceptable in the context of the selection and therefore neither change the meaning nor indicate loss of comprehension. (It is important to stress that good oral reading is not necessarily an indicator of good comprehension. Following any oral reading of this type, it is important to ask the reader to retell the story in his own words as a check on the comprehension that has taken place.) Substitutions are indicated by the word written in above the text word, omissions are circled, corrections are underlined and indicated by C, and unsuccessful attempts at correction are underlined and indicated by UC.

Sarah reads fluently and operates efficiently with strategies for constructing meaning. Going well beyond using grapho-phonic information to identify words, she samples the text information and makes predictions based on her search for meaning. She doesn't always correct because correcting a miscue that is already high quality has little impact on meaning. Her miscues, for the most part, are of high quality, retaining both an acceptable syntactic structure and an acceptable semantic sense. Her ability to operate at the level of meaning allows her to make inferences and intuitive leaps not possible if she were reading at a word level. She's constructing a version of the text that makes sense within her own schematic framework. Sarah's retelling of the story after reading further confirms a high degree of comprehension of the story. She retells the major elements of the plot and clearly understands the intent of the story.

Debbie, on the other hand, has more difficulty (Figure 3–3).

Debbie's miscues are less acceptable both syntactically and semantically. They often do not make sense in the context of the story and suggest a focus less on meaning than on word identification. Her predictions are at the level of letters and words rather than meaning. She creates sentences with non–English structures ("And how you ride it should and take chances . . ." "I know not have a chance of getting away.") that result in sentences devoid of meaning.

Do Sarah and Debbie have different conceptualizations of reading? Their miscues suggest that they do. How they approach texts and the strategies they

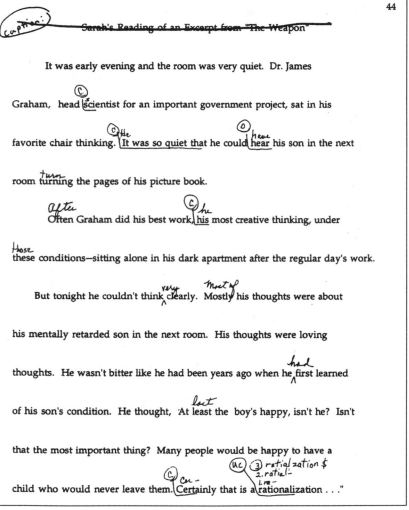

FIGURE 3–2. Sarah's Reading of an Excerpt from "The Weapon"

use are certainly different: Sarah's predictions are based on an active search for meaning, Debbie's on sounding out at the expense of meaning. We have little evidence that Debbie is constructing a meaningful text from the intersection of her background knowledge with the information in the text. Debbie, unlike Sarah, fails to engage in the interactive process that Goodman claims for proficient readers.

The oral reading patterns of readers often indicate their level of comprehension. However, sometimes readers' difficulty with oral reading masks a surprisingly high level of comprehension. For example, when Althea, a sixth-grader, read "Space Pet" aloud for the first time, she made several puzzling

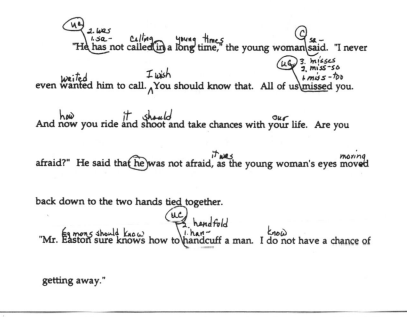

FIGURE 3–3. Debbie's Reading of an Excerpt from "Hearts and Hands"

miscues that represent the complexity in text comprehension (Figure 3–4). The story is about Claribel, the canary, smuggled aboard a space station, whose fainting because of an insufficient supply of oxygen alerts the people on board about the oxygen depletion and thereby saves their lives.

Althea is confronted with the word "canary" three times in this short passage. The first time her substitution of "carrot" for "canary" fits syntactically but not semantically. We don't know why Althea made that substitution—whether

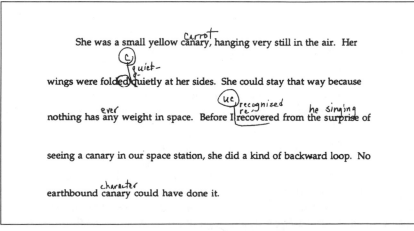

FIGURE 3–4. Althea's Reading of an Excerpt from "Space Pet"

she was reading more on the basis of first letters and/or sounds of words or whether she had little knowledge of canaries—but her prediction is not what we would call successful. The second time she identifies it accurately, but the third time she substitutes another word, "character," which makes sense in the context of the story. Later in the story, she rejects the accurate word and uses nonsense words: "$calnens" and "$carenon."

Only once, in other words, does Althea say the word "canary" and then she abandons it for two nonwords at the end of the story. Although the negotiations that readers are engaged in can only be inferred from the reading they do and are rarely directly observable from the reading itself, one is likely to assume from Althea's oral reading that she has not processed the concept of Claribel being a bird, let alone the concept of the species canary. But when we listen to her retell the story, we are confronted by the fact that readers are able to make intuitive conceptual leaps that are unexplainable from simply listening to the story being read aloud. Asked to tell everything she could remember about the story, without any information being supplied, she talks about "Charabel" the bird and what happened to the bird, and when she is asked what kind of bird it was, she replies, "A canary."

How do we account for her miscues while reading, in contrast to her understanding of the story at the end? We can only speculate that she may have been unfamiliar with canaries and lacked confidence about Claribel's identity. And perhaps as she was retelling the story, the pieces began to fit together, and only at that point was she willing to commit to her "text" that was being created. Whatever else she was doing, as she was reading, Althea was constructing her version of reality vis-à-vis the story, trying out assumptions and modifying them, and finally emerging with a picture of the story somewhat akin to the author's. She negotiated the meaning by pitting her own knowledge against the textual information, and what emerged was her story construction. The meaning that is constructed is never simply an artifact of the reader's mind in isolation, nor of the writer's text; it is a carefully negotiated construction that is the third text—the reader's—as it has emerged from the dynamic interplay between the reader's schema and the author's text. Althea was able to bridge conceptual gaps in the text by using her own knowledge and life experience. Texts as written by writers are never fully explicit; they always contain gaps—structural, conceptual, linguistic—that readers must bridge or fill in. And when readers are encouraged to read for meaning rather than for accuracy in word identification, they often demonstrate an uncanny ability to comprehend, despite their surface miscues.

The Nature of Texts and Readers' Interactions with Them

Predictions operate at the macro level of meaning as well as at the micro level of words. All texts have a degree of openness that allows for personal interpretation, even the text that Althea was reading as she imposed her own linguistic and conceptual structures on it, although other texts allow for far more openness than "Space Pet." Literary texts, particularly poetry, are more open to interpretation than referential or informational texts. In her transactional theory of reading literature, Louise Rosenblatt (1978) distinguishes between "open" texts, or those that are likely to elicit an aesthetic response, and referential texts, which are meant to convey information more than produce an emotive response. In Robert Frost's poem "Stopping by Woods on a Snowy Evening," the meaning of "promises to keep" and "miles to go" in the last stanza is frequently debated.

Is the last stanza to be read literally? Is it meant to suggest the need to do much more before old age and death occur? What does Frost mean by promises to keep? What is the significance of the lovely dark woods? We could go back to the author to ask him what he intended to mean (in fact, critics did, but Frost refused to say), or we can begin to accept the notion that readers must, in effect, create their own meaning, their own texts. Literature forces us to fill in the blanks where loaded vocabulary, double entendre, unexplained fragments, unexplored suggestion, surprising constructions leave things unexplained. Thus a literary work of art, pregnant with possibility for understanding, tends to be more "open" in the sense that the kinds of responses—both affective and interpretive—may be open-ended, and the "third text," the one the reader constructs in response to the literary text, is interpreted more through the cultural, historical, and personal lenses that a reader brings to it than through the author's intended meaning.

Referential texts, the category into which we place most content area reading, tend rather to be more direct in their statements and therefore make fewer demands on the reader's use of inferences. Unlike literary texts, referential texts make deliberate attempts to communicate more directly by lessening the numbers and kinds of reader response through the style and structures of the writing. A case in point might be this paragraph from a Harper and Row reader:

> Without maps or instruments to guide them, some birds fly thousands of miles without help. Birds usually travel by the same paths, or flyways, that their parents and grandparents did. These air highways are very broad and irregular. (Evertts and Van Roekel 1966, 240–241)

Although the authors here employ some metaphors to carry the reading—the comparison between the child's family tree and the bird's and the analogy of flyways to highways—the passage is meant to convey information, and so the material is less open to varying interpretation. Textbook authors, especially those writing in the natural or social sciences, history or civics, and foreign languages, make a conscientious effort to organize their information and select key ideas to fit a format that is accessible to their readers.

Even so, there is always some slippage in any text, even in referential texts; that is, readers always construct some idiosyncratic meaning that only partially overlaps the author's intended meaning. Although textbook authors generally try to safeguard against widely variant readings, their readers will nevertheless bring to these texts some ideas that have been influenced by the differing historical, social, and economic conditions under which they read, as well as their individual backgrounds and interests. A child reading the above passage may not have seen a highway and can only imagine in her own way what the bird's flight pattern might be like. Similarly, the extent of the reader's open-mindedness, or the stance the reader might take toward the text before opening the book's covers, may alone determine much about the text's meaning. Today's astronomy student is likely, for instance, to take Ptolemy's descriptions of the earth-centered universe more as a piece of fiction than as scientific discourse, whereas most tenth-century readers approached the same astronomical observations as fact. A piece of American history may likewise be read as revisionist fiction or as fact, depending on the reader's perspective. Even "factual evidence" may elicit variant readings, depending on the cultural and historical context.

Although the intellectual history of the text's formation does much to shape any reader's stance and expectations, the reader's use of it ultimately dictates the meaning of the third text. Comprehension takes place when the text answers the reader's questions. Students accommodate the information, either by reconsidering and adjusting preconceived ideas or by adding to schemas already in place. This is true whether the reader has misconstrued the material or not. A naive reading carries the same significance for the reader as an informed one. Young readers may therefore overlook information that tells them they have misunderstood something in the text. Worse yet, they may twist facts to fit their "theory of the world in their heads," and there is often little in the text, especially a literary text, to prevent this from happening. The author's intended meaning and the meaning the text might have for others therefore become secondary to the uses any single reader will make of it.

The point here is that so much of the reading experience occurs privately between text and reader. Teachers have less influence on what their students make of the readings than they like to admit. This has always been true, but it is all the more undeniable in the multicultural classroom, where students can hold widely divergent interpretations of the text. Even the most seemingly factual texts may elicit surprising student responses, particularly for the teacher who is removed in age, gender, race, religion, or other experiences from her students. For example, a civics teacher may face students who do not want to be reminded of public responsibilities and are quite apathetic about aspects of the Declaration of Independence that inspired students of an earlier generation. Or a science teacher may have to allay fears about unknown implications of recent technological discoveries in genetics. Or a literature teacher may be surprised to learn that *The Adventures of Huckleberry Finn*, regarded by some as racist, has become controversial to teach. Recent responses to Twain's work are quite different from those expressed in the classroom even a few years ago and register that change in thinking. To keep up, many teachers conduct ongoing assessments of student attitudes so that they are continually re-educating themselves about shifting opinions. This is important for leading discussions that help everyone arrive at a mutually respectful understanding of the material, an understanding that takes the students' views into account as well as the teacher's.

A Social Constructionist View of Reading

Implicit in much of the previous discussion is a view of reading that pushes at the edges of personal experience by focusing on the larger social and cultural contexts of reading. Because readers and knowledge are socially constructed, how readers respond to and make sense of texts is a direct result of how the society and the culture shape their responses. Reading and comprehension occur within a broad cultural context of social issues and attitudes that predispose readers to read in certain ways. Readers, like writers, create meanings that evolve from their individual perspectives based on class, race, gender, and religious and economic backgrounds. Readers do not read "objectively," in the sense that a text is imbued with knowledge that is understood or comprehended in a "pure" form. Every reading, the third text, is a reflection of the reader's own sociocultural perspective.

For example, comprehension of a passage about marriage customs in other cultures is going to vary depending on the reader's own cultural experiences. Some readers may have difficulty comprehending an article with feminist overtones because of their own belief systems, and others will produce very idiosyncratic interpretations that enable them to avoid questioning their own belief systems (Wilson and Thomas 1995; Thomas and Wilson 1993). Readers are rarely even conscious of their own cultural values that encourage them to read texts in particular ways.

The author's text, like the reader's interpretation, is socially constructed and culture-bound and represents "truth" only as the writer sees it. More often than not, readers are encouraged to comprehend and understand what they are reading. Rather than question a text, they are urged to assume its authority, a perspective that encourages acceptance without questioning, passivity over active reading. Textual authority, deeply entrenched in our educational system for generations, has roots in the religious and cultural traditions of Biblical authority and the sacredness of the text. To question the text is to commit heresy. Whether readers are conscious of it or not, the same attitude prevails toward secular texts. If it's in print, it must be true, and if they are printed often enough, even blatant lies take on a degree of truthfulness—a phenomenon witnessed repeatedly in the willingness of readers to accept at face value the stories in *The National Enquirer* and the claims politicians make in their campaign literature.

Psycholinguistic reading theory has evolved a perspective on reading that suggests that constructing meaning necessitates reading *against* the text (Scholes 1985) if readers are to make literacy work for them. The tendency to believe that a point must be true if it's in print has led to the mindless, unquestioning acceptance of ideas ranging from the innocuous conviction that one's horoscope is going to determine one's daily experiences to the insidious belief that the Holocaust never happened. The process of reading/comprehending (for these two concepts are ultimately synonymous) must engage the reader not only in a conversation with the author but in an oppositional dialogue that moves the reader beyond simple comprehension to critical reading of the text. Each reader must decide for himself as he constructs his own meaning how much or in what way to accommodate the worldview of the author and the author's reality into his own thinking (Brent 1992). More broadly conceptualized, comprehension insists that readers consider the cultural context of what they read and that they read the subtexts—the hidden agendas—of the texts in order to understand the author's particular political perspective and agenda. This extends to questioning a magazine ad's subtle implications that women enjoy being sex objects and to critiquing the subtle and not-so-subtle agendas of television advertising and TV talk shows. Readers must learn to separate their own views from the author's. Lessons on bias and opinion, on implicit and explicit expression, on taking a skeptical stance, and on setting criteria for making judgments are therefore crucial to effective critical reading strategies. Only then will readers see themselves as participants in the construction of knowledge, not as mere recipients of someone else's views.

A political perspective on reading is not necessarily popular in the educational mainstream. Students who question too much, who aren't willing to accept the "truth" of the text, whose interpretations contradict the status quo, are not always welcome in tightly controlled classrooms. But teachers who discourage or fail to allow time for serious inquiry and questioning in favor of "safe" responses to texts are shortchanging students and limiting their intellectual growth. When definitions of comprehension include the ability to question, to disagree, and to use reading and writing as instruments of power, real change in readers' attitudes and patterns of behavior is possible. Understanding that literacy is not politically neutral is the first step in developing a sense of independence as literate human beings. Changing the status quo is more possible if readers feel collectively empowered to critique texts and the assumptions implicit in them. When a community of readers and writers uses their literacy for these purposes, there is the potential for liberation.

Conclusion

So now we come back to our original question: Who's in charge? In collaboration with the text, the reader is in charge. The reader must be. Given what we have said about the nature of meaning and how it is constructed, the role of schemas and prediction in the construction of meaning, and the role of sociocultural-political influences on reading, it is clear that the reader is as important as the author's text in this dynamic interchange and the construction of meaning. Traditional approaches to literacy that stress the functional and mechanical aspects of learning reading will no longer do. What is needed in reading instruction is a vision of the power of print to change lives. When the instruction provides students with opportunities to become active participants in the process, to question and critique, readers become empowered. They no longer look for the one right answer; they begin to trust themselves as thinkers and learners, they start questioning authors and the content of their texts, and they begin to use their literacy for asserting themselves in their own educational, social, and political lives.

The chapters that follow discuss in some detail the implementation of a theory of reading that draws on psycholinguistics, sociolinguistics, and the social construction of meaning. Such a philosophy can be implemented in a range of classrooms from elementary to secondary, across a wide span of content areas, and with readers whose backgrounds diverge widely. It is a view of reading that encourages readers to recognize their roles in the process and to become empowered by it.

CHAPTER FOUR

Influences on Language and Literacy Development and the Teaching of Reading

Chapter Three discussed the nature of reading as a psycholinguistic process in which meaning is constructed through the reader's transaction with the text on all its many levels, including graphic, syntactic, semantic, and conceptual. Extending our view of reading as a psycholinguistic process, and providing a framework for our discussion of sociocultural influences on language and literacy development, we will first argue in this chapter that just as the process of reading is language-based, so is the acquisition of the process. A child learns to read by using the same psycholinguistic strategies she employs in learning to speak and comprehend oral language, demonstrated both in her developing reading ability and in her emergent writing, and the child's experimentation in both reading and writing supports the further development of these processes. Classroom practices employed to aid students' developing literacy must reflect these principles.

Within this framework we go on to argue that, although the processes of becoming literate are similar across speech communities, the language patterns, sociocultural assumptions, and literacy practices may differ from one cultural group to another. This section of the chapter moves from a discussion of the principles of dialect variation and the myths and misconceptions about dialects to the degree to which these dialect differences do or do not interfere in the acquisition and practice of literacy. Central to the discussion is the negative impact of differentiated instruction based on social class and dialect that is practiced in many school systems. The discussion moves on to the cultural differences among young readers that school systems must accommodate and finally to recommendations for overcoming linguistic and cultural stereotypes in literacy programs that will support the literacy development of students representing a wide range of backgrounds, cultures, and abilities.

Universal Principles of Literacy Development

The complexity of language precludes the learning of language either by direct instruction or through mere imitation of adult language. Instead, with an innate predisposition for acquiring language, all children, regardless of the speech community in which they live, observe patterns of speech and form hypotheses about word meanings, syntactic structures, and units of meaning. Once these hypotheses are formed—e.g., that modifiers precede the nouns they modify, or that negative markers consist of "no" or "not" and appear early in negative phrases—they test their hypotheses. They say things like "big dog," "owie finger," and "allgone milk," and they utter phrases like "no want spinach" and "not go." These structures are not fully adult-like, but they fit patterns that the child has observed, and as the child tests these hypotheses by using them and getting additional language data and feedback from other language users, he modifies and refines the original hypotheses and moves them closer to the adult system of rules. Soon he realizes that some modifying phrases follow nouns ("the milk is *all gone*") and complex syntax must be used to make some sentences negative ("I *don't* want *any* spinach"). But almost none of these rules are learned through imitation or direct instruction. Language learners are active, creative, thinking minds at work, constantly gathering data, developing hypotheses about rules, testing and revising them, and integrating them into a linguistic system that in its phenomenal sophistication is far too complex to have been learned by mimicking. When kids focus on the meaning, they acquire an understanding of the linguistic rule system used to convey that meaning. Language is learned most easily when the language itself is not the focus of attention. Instead, the focus is on the meaning that the child is learning to construct.

The process of becoming literate involves the same principles and strategies. Children who have been "reading" books on their parents' laps and who have developed a sense of story and an intent to find meaning from the books they read don't shut off their active, meaning-making brains when they come to school and begin instruction in reading. Just as they hypothesize a rule system for oral language in an attempt to communicate with parents and siblings, so they hypothesize the rules of written language as they make sense of print. As with oral language development, children use the forms and structures of written language in the service of meaning-making.

The questions to consider include the following: What kinds of support structures can instruction provide to foster these language-learning skills? What is the most proficient, logical, sensible way to help children become literate? Is it by teaching them phonics and a set of rules about the form and structure of written language, or is it by giving them meaningful structures and predictable stories to read that provide opportunities for them to hypothesize the rules of written language? Is reading instruction best served in whole language classrooms in which young readers and writers are reading trade books of their own choice to themselves and to each other, discussing favorite stories in small groups, writing their own stories for class publication, using invented spelling in their writing, and experimenting with written language? Or is it best served in classrooms where phonics lessons are organized in sequential order, from easiest to most difficult, and where meaning is secondary to acquiring knowledge of phonics rules? And finally, are these approaches to reading instruction always mutually exclusive?

Direct Phonics Instruction

We have already discussed the history of reading instruction in this country in Chapter Two, along with an explanation of the controversy between whole language and traditional reading programs. But one point that bears a fuller explanation is the role of phonics in learning to read.

Even though this topic appears to have little direct bearing on the teaching of social studies, science, math, or geography, some students in these courses may concurrently be enrolled in a developmental reading course operating on principles of remediation in reading. Other students may have difficulty with the material because they are products of unsuccessful reading instruction or they are simply reluctant readers. Any deficiencies in early reading instruction may need to be remedied in our secondary classrooms, and other more successful practices can be supported and encouraged.

Furthermore, the central issue in the phonics vs. whole language conflict is a larger issue of learning theory, of which reading theory is just one part. Understanding the theoretical issues involved in the debate strengthens our own language and literacy instruction.

Much of the debate so central to our work as teachers operates on a simplistic understanding of the nature of reading skills and the ease with which phonics can be taught. When teaching phonics, teachers are inclined to teach from simplest to most complex, in a seemingly logical order. However, what seems easiest and most logical for the teacher may be antithetical to the way in which oral and written language is learned and used because the movement from part to whole often precludes the use of context. Word lists rather than meaningful language units become the unit of instruction, and texts used for reading instruction contain artificially constructed sentences with vocabulary controlled for the specific phonics rules being taught. What seems logical and simple to the teacher organizing the lesson may, in fact, seem meaningless to the child operating with the assumption that reading is supposed to make sense.

Further difficulties with systematic phonics instruction include the large number of rules, the complexity of rules that seem simple and straightforward on the surface, and their conceptual abstractness. Based on an analysis of the 5,000 most common words in elementary reading materials, Frank Smith (1994) cites the existence of a minimum of 166 phonics rules that deal with sound-symbol relationships, plus the 45 or so exceptions, for a total of 211 rules. In addition, given the fact that many common words defy regularization—such as "off" and "of" (same letters, different sounds); "have," "gone" and "come" (violation of "silent e" rule making the preceding vowel "long"); "above," "cap," "call," "cape," "father" (different pronunciation of each "a") and must therefore be learned individually as sight words—the phonics lessons become increasingly complex and unwieldy. Learning these words and rules in isolation, when the reader has no meaning or language context to provide support for word identification, complicates the process of reading, a conclusion reached by Ken Goodman (1965) in his seminal study that demonstrated that words are easier to identify within context than without.

What makes language concrete and accessible is its meaning. Bits and pieces of language—isolated words, isolated letters and sounds—are the most abstract aspects of language. Why is it that we ask beginning readers to focus on the abstract, when in fact the concreteness of language lies in its meaning, its wholeness? A word makes concrete sense when embedded in a familiar, meaningful whole, not when it is isolated for microscopic study.

And finally, meaning is not simply the product of word identification. A strong emphasis on phonics misleads readers into assuming that word identification is the ultimate goal of reading. Reading is not the act of successfully sounding out words but rather the complex act of processing grammatical and semantic information beyond the word level to construct meaning.

Emergent Literacy: Print Awareness

Despite the complexity of sound-letter correspondences, grapho-phonic information is one of the cueing systems we use as proficient readers. At issue here is how children acquire this information. As we have just argued, the rules are often developed through reading meaningful texts rather than through isolated phonics lessons. The preschool reading "texts" that children use to familiarize themselves with print include environmental print—signs, labels, advertisements—and connected texts—beginning readers' storybooks, magazines, and picture books. Many children already understand the alphabetic principles and have developed their phonemic awareness of sounds by the time they get direct reading instruction. At the most, the direct teaching of sounds and letters may simply reinforce what they have learned from the environmental print that surrounds them daily.

Few three-year-olds fail to recognize the golden arches of McDonald's or the Coke label on the soft drink bottle. Three-year-old Michael recognizes the macaroni and cheese label on the blue and yellow box, and then says, "That's like the M in my name. M says 'macaroni' and M says 'Mike.'" When three-year-old Timmy asks his father what that bottle is on the table, the father replies, "It's a bottle of glue." Timmy picks up the bottle, looks at the Sears logo, and says, "Oh, where America shops!" Apparently he is not able to read the S-e-a-r-s label in its traditional cursive form, but he recognizes the label holistically and assigns a meaning to it. Kids recognize early in signs and on billboards the letters of the alphabet that appear in their own names, and they begin to associate sounds with certain symbols, a first step in connecting the phonemes of oral language with the orthographic symbols in print.

In the early stages of print awareness, children often focus on the generic meaning of symbols. The M of McDonald's signals hamburgers, the Coke label signals soft drink. When asked what the word says, the three-year-old is likely to say "pop" or the acceptable word in the child's own linguistic system. Only later is the child likely to name the correct label. "Crest" in the early stages may get identified on the basis of its function—"brush teeth"—and then later as the generic "toothpaste," and still later as "Colgate" or "Crest" or "Aim," depending on the child's familiarity with the particular brand.

We should not assume that the words that children begin to recognize as part of environmental print are without a context. The word "STOP" on the stop sign is used within a wholly meaningful context—the situational context that includes the placement of the sign, its shape, and its color. Some young children may momentarily hypothesize "SLOW" as "stop," but they soon learn to "read" the color and the placement as significant factors in meaning. Young children rarely read the sign above the Baskin-Robbins ice cream parlor as "Camera Shop," or vice versa, because the full situational context precludes those interpretations.

The basic principles about print with which these young readers operate include the assumption that reading is active, that it is an attempt to make sense of print, and that it involves taking risks, guessing, and predicting. Caregivers have realistic expectations, and in response to children's "reading," they provide positive feedback that focuses on meaning: "Yes, that's what that says," or "No, it says. . . ." To use Vygotsky's (1978) terms, rather than providing direct instruction, caregivers provide the scaffolding, the support and feedback that children need to figure out the rules or patterns themselves. For the most part, children and adults expect to experiment and make errors in every stage of development as a natural part of the process of developing rules.

Emergent Literacy: The Writing-Reading-Literacy Connection

Writing as part of learning to read encourages greater familiarity with letters, the sounds they represent, and the relationship between written symbols and meaning. Instead of withholding real writing opportunities from students until they can master the correct spelling of words and the construction of complete sentences, successful reading teachers recognize that many children begin "writing" long before they can form letters and long before they understand the alphabetic principles of the writing system. In a social environment where children see writing occurring along with reading, the process of writing helps solidify their understanding that writing, like reading, is making meaning.

Like children acquiring the rules for oral language, young writers go through a series of stages that includes scribbling, recognizing letter-like features as part of written language, and making connections between specific written symbols and sounds. In the scribble stage, often dismissed as unconnected to reading and writing, children, in fact, already demonstrate their awareness of written language and the functions of writing by scribbling markings that reflect the written language of their culture (Harste, Woodward, and Burke 1984). Children from different cultures produce scribble writings distinctively different from each other, as illustrated in the samples in Figure 4–1 (Harste and Carey 1979). In this study researchers collected writing samples from three four-year-olds with different language backgrounds attending a preschool program. Each child has gleaned from her own culture's writing system the style, conventions, and features of the script and has reproduced them in scribble writing. These are four-year-olds internalizing aspects of their own writing system—the directionality of print, the meaning intent of writing, and the shape of characters and letters, examples that clearly demonstrate that there is literacy before schooling and that children literally learn to write and to read by writing and reading, using their culture's writing system as the model for their own development.

The process of writing and coming to understand the nature of print becomes increasingly more sophisticated with experience and continued experimentation. As evidence of early literacy development, Weaver (1988) cites four major stages in children's developing awareness of print symbols: prephonemic, early phonemic, letter–name, and transitional.

In the *prephonemic* stage the child recognizes a connection between letters and oral language/meaning, but there is no recognition that the letters represent specific sounds. Letters at random are often strung together to form a message without a phonemic value. In contrast, in the *early phonemic* stage the child is beginning to use letters to represent sounds, with each word typically represented by one or two letters. Bissex, for example, in GNYS AT WRK (1980), cites the example of her four-year-old son Paul trying to get her attention by writing on a piece of paper the following message: RUDF? (Are you deaf?)

In the *letter-name* stage, the child is operating in a more sophisticated way with phonemic representation. Vowel letters are now being used to represent

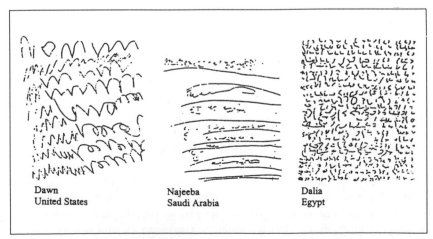

Dawn
United States

Najeeba
Saudi Arabia

Dalia
Egypt

FIGURE 4–1. Uninterrupted Writing Samples from Three Children, Age Four

vowel sounds, and more of the sounds in a word are consistently being represented by letters. The choices young writers make to represent sounds often include letters whose names sound most like the sound they're trying to represent (Weaver 1988). The following example of the letter–name stage was provided by Annie, age five, in a note to her mother away at a conference, as she writes: DE MOM I OP DAT U GT THER SFLY I L U VERY MH. (Dear Mom, I hope that you got there safely. I love you very much.)

The characteristics associated with the letter–name stage represented here include more accurate letter representation; the use of "d" to represent "th" in "that," which was how Annie pronounced it at the time; still a predominance of consonants but also some vowels; and the use of letters whose names (H— "aitch") sound most like the sounds they're trying to represent ("much").

Children who "write" their own stories will also incorporate the conventions of discourse, as Annie does: salutations in letters, formulaic introductions and conclusions ("Once upon a time," and "They lived happily ever after," etc.), and other discourse features of the stories they are familiar with—yet one more example of their ability to use familiar stories as a model for their own.

In the following example of a kindergartner moving from the letter–name stage to the *transitional* stage, in which spelling inventions are fewer and more consistent with standard orthography, the young writer's invented spelling is highly individualized and unique, but also very consistent with the general developmental patterns of writing observed in research studies:

"WEN the suN cumPs a raBO isoNas I cat bleVE it is so PRite I wat to see a RaBO" (When the sun comes up a rainbow is so nice I can't believe it is so pretty I want to see a rainbow.)

With its mixture of upper-case and lower-case letters and its use of letters to represent oral pronunciation, this example illustrates how children learn the rules of written language through experimentation when given the opportunity and encouragement to write freely without fear of error. Typical of young writers, this child has systematically eliminated the nasal "n" before consonants, in "rainbow," "can't," and "want," a characteristic that Charles Read (1975) discovered many years ago in his highly respected study of children's spelling patterns.

A considerable body of recent research strongly underscores the efficacy of invented spelling in whole language classrooms. For example, Gunderson and Shapiro's (1987) study of the writing of first-graders using invented spelling drew the conclusions that these young writers used far more vocabulary words in their own writing than they would have encountered if they had been using the traditional basal reading series, their own writing included high-frequency vocabulary remarkably similar to that found in the basal readers, and their invented spelling revealed that they understood phonics relationships very well.

Implications for Early Reading Instruction

Children rarely come into primary-grade reading programs as blank slates without any knowledge of print, letters, or the relationships between letters and sounds or between words and meaning. Most have already experimented considerably with writing, and a number have already become quite sophisticated in their reading and writing abilities.

Take our friend Annie, for example, who loved from an early age to experiment with written language. She wrote grocery lists, letters to grandparents, her own short "autobiography" modeled after her older brother's middle school assignment, and her own stories, but when she was confronted with a very strict phonics program in the first grade, she became confused. These phonics lessons, focusing on sounding out words and making diacritical marks over vowels to indicate their pronunciation, were an exercise in nonsense. When Annie was asked to write a story, she said to her mother, "I can't. I don't know how to make the marks above the letters." In a few short weeks, a confident, developing reader and writer had become a nonwriter, convinced that she no longer knew how.

When the reading instruction contradicts what children do naturally as language learners and ignores what children already know about language, young readers and writers run into deep trouble. Annie did survive as a reader and writer, but not without a struggle that could have been avoided had her classroom instruction not ignored or contradicted her developing knowledge of reading and writing. Classroom methods must work with, not against, the natural tendencies of children to deal with print.

A review of the research on reading instruction strongly suggests that if there is any advantage in direct phonics instruction, it is an advantage only if the instruction occurs within a meaning-based whole language context. In short, phonics lessons are most effective when they are presented at the moment of need rather than removed from meaning-based authentic reading. Essentially, readers learn to read proficiently when their reading instruction includes authentic texts and real stories in which meaning and enjoyment are the focus. A recent review of research on systematic phonics instruction admits finally that "approaches in which systematic code instruction is included *alongside meaning emphasis, language instruction, and connected reading* are found to result in superior reading achievement overall" (emphases ours) (Adams 1990, 49). Good reading programs provide access to information about sound-symbol correspondences when the child needs the support in reading meaningful texts, not as a substitute for those authentic texts.

The grapho-phonic system is one of the cueing systems readers use for word identification and meaning, but it cannot be used in isolation or taught as the only system for learning to read. Quoting Heilman, Artley (1977) says, "In the final analysis, the *optimum* amount of phonics instruction for every child is the *minimum* that he needs to become an independent reader" (Heilman 1972, 280). That's why a simplistic approach to reading instruction rooted in phonics and word analysis to the exclusion of a fully contextualized, meaning-based approach will not do. P. David Pearson, in his review of reading research, says:

> Recent work (Winsor and Pearson 1992) suggests that in whole language classrooms in particular, invented spellings may be the medium through which both phonemic awareness . . . and phonics knowledge . . . develop . . . as the

consequence of, rather than the cause of, success in authentic reading experiences (Pearson 1993, 507).

Classroom instruction can further support phonics knowledge that the child has developed from authentic reading and writing experiences, but the lessons must be appropriate to the child's needs, presented within a whole language context, and must work in concert with the patterns the child is already developing.

The Role of Language Variation, Dialect, and Culture in the Acquisition of Literacy

We are arguing that learning to read involves similar strategies for children across cultures and across speech communities, but this is not to suggest that linguistic and cultural variation have no effect on literacy. To the contrary, the linguistic system that speakers of English bring with them to the classroom may have a strong impact on the nature of the instruction they are given. Even though the topic is often ignored in the literature and in textbooks on reading instruction, assumptions about linguistic variation and its impact on reading are deeply embedded, though often unarticulated, within materials and classroom approaches to reading. The following sections illustrate the assumptions about linguistic and cultural differences that affect the patterns of instruction and therefore the quality of literacy development as well.

Dialect Variation in Oral Language

There is ample evidence, anecdotal as well as empirical, that people are judged by linguistic yardsticks—the linguistic features that mark them as members of a particular speech community. If we were to create a character for a TV sitcom who is not very bright, what kind of "accent" would we give that character: a British accent, a Boston accent, a Michigan accent, or a Mississippi accent? It's unlikely to be the first two (unless it's a Cockney or a South Boston dialect), most likely to be the last. Why is it so easy to agree on this question? We've built up stereotypes based on language, usually at unconscious levels. A colleague of ours who grew up in Kentucky and went to graduate school in Wisconsin talks frequently about his need as a graduate student to eliminate his Kentucky dialect if he expected his peers to take him seriously. The belief that speaking a certain dialect of English reflects a lack of education at best, or lower intelligence at worst, has led many people, including well-intentioned educators, to negatively stereotype speakers of a dialect whose speech patterns differ from standard language patterns.

All speakers of a language speak a dialect of that language. "Dialect" is not a pejorative term. It simply denotes that all speakers speak a particular variety of the language that includes geographical, ethnic, class, and gender features. One writer of this text spent her early years in Minnesota before moving to Michigan, her ethnic background is Dutch, she grew up in a lower-middle class home, and she is a female: all these factors affect her particular speech patterns or dialect of English. She uses the flat /æ/ sound in "can," sometimes referred to as the midwest nasal. She used to use the phrase "too yet" in a sentence like "I have to do that too yet," until she realized that this remnant of her ethnic background was being judged negatively by others. She often says "bring" when she should use "take," a grammatical feature she's never quite gained full control of, and her language is filled with hedges and qualifiers such as "It's *probably* necessary to consider . . .," a reflection, perhaps (another example), of her gender. Furthermore, she occasionally finds herself saying "icebox" instead of "refrigerator," a definite reflection of her age and her upbringing. Her dialect is a mix of many different influences, although she is considered by most to be a speaker of northern "standard" speech patterns. Dialect, then, is a set of speech patterns, most of which are shared by other members of the speaker's speech community(s). All English speakers speak a dialect of English, including those midwesterners who tend to think that everyone else speaks a dialect but them.

The notion of "standard" needs to be addressed here because of the common assumption that there is some kind of "standard" dialect against which all other dialects are measured—and invariably found wanting. Linguists, whose business it is to study language, agree that there is no "standard" dialect and that it is much easier to explain what is *not* standard than what *is*. In reality, linguists insist that a standard doesn't exist. At the most, maybe a claim can be made for regional standards: what is "standard" in New Orleans is not "standard" in Bangor, Maine. Even then, within any region people are hard-pressed to define a set of standard features upon which there is full agreement. Nevertheless, the fact that it really doesn't exist doesn't lessen our fears of falling short of its expectations (but that's another story).

The most we can say about "standard" features of language is that they are the ones we pay least conscious attention to because they don't call attention to themselves; they tend to be those features that are not stigmatized—those that do not mark a speaker as a member of a particular socioeconomic class. If readers are looking for the definitive list of standard features, no such list exists.

Dialect variation can and usually does involve all aspects of the linguistic system: phonological or pronunciation differences, such as how a speaker pronounces the vowel in "roof" or whether a speaker pronounces the "r" in "yard"; lexical or vocabulary differences, such as whether the speaker sits on a "couch," a "sofa," or a "davenport"; and syntactic or structural differences, such as "she is working" or "she be working," or "he shouldn't do that" or "he hadn't ought to do that." Regional dialect variations tend to be phonological (related to pronunciation) and lexical (word choice), while social and ethnic dialect variations tend to include more syntactic (grammatical) differences. Many of the features are likely to occur with greater frequency in spoken language than in written.

A brief comment about dialect vs. grammar. Some seemingly grammatical problems found in many working-class communities such as the use of double negation ("I don't have no . . .") or subject-verb agreement ("They was . . .")

are really examples of social dialect features that bridge geographical areas, ethnic communities, and gender and age differences. They include such features as "I could have went . . .," "I seen . . .," or "anyways," usages that are the most severely stigmatized, most likely to be considered "nonstandard," and to be eradicated when speakers consciously attempt to standardize their language.

One speaker's rule system will vary from another's, and the one that deviates from the "standard" rule system is more likely to be considered "ungrammatical." We are not taught these rules consciously, but they evolve in our earlier years from the speech patterns of our parents, and in childhood and adolescence from the speech patterns of our peers. When Sally says, "I done it," she is operating with a verb rule that differs from Sam's, who says, "I did it." And when Jake talks about "the argument between John and I," and Jan refers to the "fight between my boyfriend and me," they are each probably operating with a rule consistent with the patterns they've learned from family or peers or friends. (Incidentally, Jake's use of "between John and I" is the less standard usage.)

All dialects are linguistically valid, fully grammatical systems of language whose speakers are fully capable of complex thought and expression. Speakers of British English, midland Appalachian, African-American Vernacular English, and northern English all operate with a set of rules that govern their use of language, even though the rule systems vary. Every dialect is an intricate, rule-governed system of phonological, semantic, syntactic, and lexical rules that enables its users to communicate effectively and fully. Some varieties or dialects may be more socially prestigious than others, but they are no less capable of enabling speakers to express complex thoughts or of providing for a full range of linguistic functions and purposes. The deficit notion of language—that some dialects are less well-structured, incomplete, illogical, substandard, or impoverished versions as measured against an ideal language system—is patently false. Dialects are simply *different, not deficient* systems of language.

Many speakers and writers are capable of shifting from one dialect to another, particularly those who live in multicultural, multidialectal communities. Speakers who use multiple negation ("I don't have no time") in an informal setting may use standard negation ("I don't have any time") in a more formal one. Their bidialectal ability comes from living, working, and socializing in multicultural circles. Such shifting can occur on many levels. A truck driver uses a trucker's linguistic register on the job but not necessarily in more formal situations. A speaker with southern roots who now lives in a northern metropolitan area, and whose dialect has shifted in the direction of northern dialect features, may shift back to using more characteristically southern features when visiting family and friends in South Carolina. A speaker of African-American Vernacular English may adjust her speech patterns when she discusses business with her real estate agent. All language users, in both oral and written discourse, shift among various levels of formality depending on their purpose and audience.

Children's and adolescents' language is very much subject to shifting as they refine their linguistics rules, learn more complex rules, and acquire new structures and usages gleaned from the linguistic systems of their peers. Most of language is acquired in this way, from the people in those groups with whom we most closely wish to identify. Undoubtedly the most successful teacher of language and usage is the peer group with which we want to be identified.

When speakers of any age, including adolescents, function within several speech communities, they easily adjust their speech patterns as they move from one group to another. Our adolescent children operate with a different set of linguistic patterns around the family dinner table than they use in gym class. Sometimes they slip, and when they do, their parents roll their eyes and ask them please not to use that language at home. "Me and Costa are going to 7-11" has been corrected by the speaker's father so many times that the son now uses it deliberately as a way of tweaking his father. Sometimes the correction works, sometimes it doesn't, and sometimes it's deliberately ignored, all depending on how deeply embedded the usage is in their linguistic system and how much they want the approval of their parents.

This brings us to another point. How much correction of grammatical patterns that are not deemed "standard" in traditional terms should teachers attempt? Making students aware of other rules that are considered "standard" is part of our job because it provides alternatives for students when they need to use them. But there is a difference between punitive public correction of stigmatized forms and more private, positive correction when the student indicates a willingness to accept it. When teachers understand the validity of all linguistic systems and the complexity involved in changing dialect patterns, perhaps the shift from punitive to positive correction can be made. A more positive, supportive approach to change is ultimately going to be more successful. Furthermore, the fact that adolescents are, for the most part, already operating with different rules for different social situations suggests that the more traditional, standard forms are not far from their consciousness, and once they see the need for alternatives and learn that they can and do operate with multiple sets of speech patterns, their resistance to using standard forms will decrease. Resistance is strongest when the speaker assumes that one set of speech patterns must be substituted for another and that the teacher's goal is to eradicate the less standard one.

Because most speakers are bidialectal at some level and operate with different speech patterns for different social situations, reading a text written in standard poses little difficulty. Even speakers who shift dialect less than others still have an ability to comprehend and understand spoken and written forms of other dialects, whether or not they can speak them. Listening and reading are *receptive* language systems in which listeners and readers can understand another variety of language without having to produce it. People who live their entire lives in the upper Midwest sound foolish and feel awkward when attempting to produce southern English features because these are not a natural part of their speech, even though they can understand and comprehend southern features with a little effort within the context of a conversation. Needless to say, sometimes a word, phrase, or pronunciation may temporarily impede comprehension, but usually the difficulty is short-lived. Speakers' receptive language abilities are always greater than their productive abilities. This fact plays an important role for all dialect speakers in the comprehension of meaning during the process of reading because it enables them to understand features they themselves would not produce.

To some extent the features of written dialect reflect the lexical and syntactic features of spoken dialect, although the written language has its own particular features that cross dialect boundaries and obscure regional or social class differences. Social dialect features that abound in oral language are often greatly diminished in written language.

Research on Language Variation and Reading

It is true that if the reader's linguistic system is sufficiently different from that in the text, the reader may have some difficulty with comprehension. For example, speakers of Australian English might have difficulty comprehending some American English vocabulary. We have all had the experience of being momentarily befuddled by a dialect feature we are unfamiliar with in someone's speech patterns. When President Clinton said that one of his detractors didn't know him from "Adam's off ox," the majority of Americans might have had trouble understanding that he referred to the ox on the right side in a team of oxen. An Arkansas dialect has features uniquely its own that are not always accessible to outsiders. It stands to reason, then, that sometimes dialect features in print may be momentary impediments to comprehension. But dialect differences, says Carolyn Burke (1972) have minimal effect on comprehension: "The linguistic circumstance which mitigates this distance [i.e. the distance between the child's dialect and the dialect represented in the text] is the fact that reading is a receptive language process which makes use of a well-developed system of redundant cueing" (91). A reader whose oral dialect regularly deletes the final "s" in a consonant cluster like "ks" may also regularly delete the plural "s" from "books" in her oral reading of the phrase "the three books." She has most likely not misunderstood the intent of the author, for in this short phrase there are two cues that signal plurality: "three" and the "s" on "books." Although she has made a deviation of the text in her oral reading—a miscue—she has not likely misinterpreted the author's intended meaning. Oral and written language repeatedly offer this kind of redundancy. Burke goes on to cite several instances in which the text dialect and the reader's dialect differ and where the reader, in oral reading, uses a word substitution or a pronunciation pattern that reflects the reader's own dialect, rather than the text dialect, without loss of comprehension, as determined by an oral retelling of the story following its reading. Readers, like listeners to oral language, pay attention to a wide range of cues in language to construct meaning.

Furthermore, written English is not exactly like any system of oral language. Writing is, in fact, a dialect of its own. Readers from a wide range of dialect backgrounds have expectations for print that include use of "bookish" language, lack of informal oral features like "Y'all" or "youse guys," and certain linguistically complex syntactic features that are almost exclusively found in written English, such as the use of nominative absolutes: (*Her homework finished,* Samona went for a bike ride). Included in these expectations are the "standard," nonmarked forms of English usage. Regardless of their own oral speech patterns, readers expect a certain degree of standardization in the texts they read.

Types of Dialect Miscues

1. *Phonological Miscues.* The largest percentage of dialect-involved miscues involving dialect are phonological variations. The child in Boston who reads "playing in the park" as "playing in the pahk" or the third-grader who reads "library" as "libary" are making phonological miscues that represent different dialect pronunciations but will not result in a loss of comprehension. Unfortunately, teachers do not necessarily judge all such pronunciation miscues to be equal. An African-American reader's substitution of "wif" for "with" or "aks" for "ask," like the earlier ones, are predictable miscues that reflect the pronunciation patterns in the speaker's language system— miscues that will have no appreciable effect on the comprehension of the material. Yet these latter miscues are more likely to be corrected by misinformed teachers than are the former, on the biased assumption that African-American Vernacular English presents a greater impediment to comprehension than do other dialects of American English. However, the very fact that these readers are translating the text words into their own linguistic systems suggests that comprehension is actually occurring. One can logically assume that a more careful attention to the "standard" pronunciation may very well result in a loss of comprehension rather than an increase because it diverts the reader's attention from meaning to pronunciation.

   All readers, in fact, make these kinds of phonemic translations while reading orally, and they are rarely even conscious of it. The African-American child who reads "hold" as "hol" is operating with the same /d/ deletion as the Anglo child reading "bread and jelly" as "bread 'n' jelly"; neither may be conscious of the deletion and both are comprehending the word. Which child, though, do you suppose is most likely to be corrected?

2. *Lexical substitutions.* Lexical or vocabulary substitutions happen less frequently than the phonological miscues described above, and only when the lexical substitution changes the text meaning need there be any question about legitimacy. "Bucket" for "pail" or "wait a minute" for "wait a moment" merely substitute the reader's natural lexical preference for the text word and do not involve meaning change. Although lexical substitution is much less frequent than phonemic variation in oral reading, it occurs with some frequency among both developing and proficient readers and usually indicates that the readers are predicting and anticipating meaning as a natural part of the reading process, a valuable strategy that should be encouraged rather than criticized.

   In the short story "Poison," by the British writer Roald Dahl, many of our undergraduate students impose their own American dialect on the following sentence from the text as they read it orally or as they try to construct the text verbatim after reading it silently: "I switched off the headlamps of the car so that they wouldn't shine into the window and awaken Harry Pope." Many readers read "headlamps" as "headlights," the lexical item most common in their own dialect. And because their focus has been on comprehending the text as they predict and anticipate meaning, most of these students are unaware that they have even made a miscue.

3. *Syntactic miscues.* Syntactic or grammatical miscues involve a structural change in the text sentence. Often readers impose a different structure, usually more akin to their own syntactic system, on the sentence in the text. Sarah, the proficient reader with excellent comprehension described in Chapter Three, made the following miscue in the story she was reading (see Figure 3–2): "Most of his thoughts were about his mentally retarded son in the next room."

For this reader, "most of" is a more common syntactic structure than "mostly." On the basis of what was syntactically and semantically familiar, she predicted a structure that, while syntactically different, was nonetheless semantically identical and resulted in no change in meaning. Other common syntactic miscues are different verb forms, such as "was" for "were" or "seen" for "saw," and hypercorrections, in which the reader uses two grammatical markers of the same type, such as "likeded" for "liked" or "helpeded" for "helped."

None of these miscues results in a semantically unacceptable reading, and they all retain the meaning of the text and reflect the speakers' own syntactic systems at work. Syntactic miscues, in fact, suggest that readers are processing language on a syntactic level beyond sounds and words, moving from a focus on smaller elements to a focus on larger units more directly related to meaning.

4. *Phonologically induced syntactic miscues.* These miscues are triggered by a pronunciation rule in the speaker's oral dialect that affects the surface syntactic structure of the sentence. Speakers who use a rule that allows for the deletion of a final consonant in a consonant cluster (deleting the "k" in "desk" or the "d" in "hold") may also delete grammatical inflections in words in which the inflection is represented by a final consonant in the cluster. For example, in "walked" the cluster is /kt/ with the past tense represented by the final /t/ ("ed" in the spelling). Readers who operate with this rule may read past tenses of verbs by deleting the final "ed" or read plurals by deleting the final "s" using the phonological rule in their dialect that allows the deletion of that consonant. "What happened?" may be read as "What happen?," "wings" and "sides" as "wing" and "side." The reader who deleted the past tense inflection in "happened" and the plural inflection in "sides" had no difficulty understanding either the tense or the number. These phonologically involved syntactic miscues rarely change meaning, for readers in their oral reading of such texts merely delete the final consonant because of the existence of that deletion rule in

their own oral dialects, not because they do not comprehend or "see" the past tense or plural forms. These miscues most clearly relate to the inflectional system of English—the grammatical markers for plural, past tense, possessive, and third person singular—and are among the most common syntactically involved dialect miscues among African-American Vernacular English (AAVE) readers. Reading "walk" for "walked," "John" for "John's," or "des" or "deses" for "desks" is not uncommon among AAVE speakers.

The examples above offer overwhelming evidence that oral dialect variation has an influence on oral reading, but they in no way suggest that that influence interferes with reading proficiency or with reading comprehension. In fact, the ability to translate print language into one's own familiar language patterns is strong evidence that comprehension is occurring.

If dialect variation itself does not interfere in the developmental process of reading and comprehension, why is it that many nonmainstream students struggle in the development of literacy? Interference sometimes occurs because bias against less prestigious dialects and speakers of those dialects is institutionalized in the methods and materials used for reading instruction. Phonics- and sound-centered programs are likely to insist on the correction of all dialect miscues. The programs and tests of reading ability often force teachers to make instructional decisions that may contradict what they intuitively know about language and reading comprehension. When textbook instructions stress accuracy in oral reading at the expense of meaning, readers are getting the message that surface accuracy is more important than comprehension. When reading tests include items that ask readers to read lists of words that focus on accurate pronunciation and word identification, irrespective of meaning or without context cues to meaning, readers begin to build an internalized model of reading that may ultimately be detrimental to their development of reading proficiency. When reading materials and tests ask readers to "sound out" words on the basis of a "standard" dialect, these materials have considerable potential to distort the task of reading and to interfere in the construction of meaning.

Instructional materials and measures of evaluation can also implicitly favor certain dialects over others in terms of what is accepted as the accurate response. Teachers may be encouraged to accept the Boston sixth-grader's "pahk" for "park" but not the African-American's "aks" for "ask." It is a natural part of the speakers' own respective dialect systems to pronounce these words in this way, and yet teachers often restrict their support for dialect miscues to those dialects that have greater prestige. If one child's pronunciation is going to get corrected, it is far more likely to be the one that reflects a class or ethnic feature rather than a geographic one. Perhaps the most insidious message for those readers whose dialect features are stigmatized is that only "standard" English or more prestigious dialects of English are valued as legitimate vehicles for reading and literacy development.

The Issue of Correctness

All this theory may be very well and good, you may be thinking, but shouldn't teachers help readers overcome their dialect miscues by pointing out the correct pronunciation or word or structure? After all, isn't there some virtue in correctness?

First, let's consider the virtue-in-correctness issue. It is true that most teachers correct kids' mistakes, and most kids expect parents and teachers to correct their mistakes. But we'd like you to think about your own oral reading for a moment and remember those times when you've had to "perform" in front of an audience: reading the Biblical scriptures in a church service, reading round-robin in the "Bluebirds" reading group in third grade, reading a few of Ophelia's lines from *Hamlet* in your English class. Were you concentrating on the meaning when you were reading orally, or was your thinking centered on reading the passage correctly? Were you thinking about the complexity of Ophelia's relationship to Hamlet, or were you more conscious of your sweaty palms and your fear of making a mistake? It's a fact of information-processing that we can't do both of these tasks simultaneously. If a reader is overly concerned about correctness, attention to meaning becomes difficult. This is particularly true if we're reading a text with linguistic features different from our own. As teachers, do we most want our students to comprehend the concept of "peanut butter 'n' jelly" or to be conscious of articulating every consonant in that cluster? Ultimately we need to ask ourselves which is more important: reading for surface accuracy or reading for meaning? Where do we want our students' attention to be?

The next question is, of course, whether or not correction should always be avoided. The answer is that correction may sometimes be appropriate. If the miscue results in a difference in meaning and is not a dialect miscue, some correction may be necessary, although if readers are reading for meaning, they are likely to self-correct if they realize their reading is not making sense. Jumping in too soon makes readers too teacher-dependent.

The dilemma about helping kids "correct" and change their dialects is a philosophical issue that transcends the educational one. First, do we have the right to try to change someone's personal means of self-expression? Even if we think it is educationally advantageous to speak a "standard" dialect, do we have the right to impose it? And how do we decide which dialects to change—the southern features? the African-American features? or the British features of the daughter of the Fulbright scholar from London? Furthermore, how successful are we likely to be in imposing linguistic structures on students whose language patterns are deeply ingrained and for whom the home dialect is the comfortable one? (After all, one of us, rather highly educated, is still trying to master "bring" vs. "take.") Because peer groups determine more about the dialect we speak than does the classroom, our overt corrections may have limited effect unless the speaker is open to that kind of correction.

And finally, even if we wish to encourage kids to use a standard dialect for the advantages it will afford, is the reading lesson the place in which to insist on it? If the focus on accuracy distracts the reader from reading for meaning, the answer must be a resounding "No!"

Cultural Patterns and Literacy Development

Beyond readers' self-concepts and experiences with reading instruction lies another sphere of influence on literacy development that has only recently received the attention it deserves: the cultural influences on assumptions about literacy and their impact on student achievement. The cultural differences that make our classrooms challenging as well as interesting and lively go well beyond the linguistic features that differ from one speech community to the next. They ultimately represent differences in ways of making meaning and ways of learning that may be contrary to traditional school expectations about literacy.

Shirley Brice Heath's ethnographic study (1983) of three communities in the Piedmont area of North Carolina highlights the differences between school/teacher expectations and the language-learning patterns and assumptions found in different cultural groups: Roadville, a white working-class community; Trackton, an African-American working-class community; and the townspeople who are mainstream African Americans and Anglos of the region. The study suggests that in schools, the mainstream language values and skills were expected of all students, mainstream and non-mainstream both, but that the individuals from Roadville and Trackton brought different language values and skills to the classroom (Heath 1983, 4).

Roadville children from an early age participate in the family dialogue. Their parents speak to them frequently, they are encouraged to name objects and "say" words as a means of learning language, and they are taught to respect authority and to speak to an adult authority figure only when spoken to—all processes of language socialization that fit well into mainstream classrooms. Although these cultural behaviors are expected by the schools, particularly answering questions about objects and remaining silent in the presence of authority figures unless spoken to, they may work against children in other respects. Roadville children often end up passive in a school setting that values volunteering answers and asking questions (Kutz and Roskelly 1991). Furthermore, because Roadville children seldom use written texts in their homes to get new information, and they rarely discuss written texts, they are likely to run into some difficulty in a school culture that values the creation of stories and the discussion and interpretation of literature. Texts in this culture, often of a religious nature, are viewed as immutable sources of finite, definite knowledge, and truth is literal rather than metaphoric (Farr and Daniels 1986, 30–31). Storytelling is suspiciously like lying, a response that is usually at odds with traditional classroom practice.

Trackton children, on the other hand, are encouraged to engage actively with adults in conversation and to learn the discourse patterns of language through complicated rules for turn-taking. They are rarely encouraged to name objects or answer questions that the adult already knows because talking with children is not consciously for the purpose of "teaching" language, as is often the case in mainstream and Roadville homes. This kind of unspecified open dialogue enables Trackton children to learn language easily and fully, but it creates difficulty for them when they must conform to the authoritative classroom where the open interaction with adults that they've been used to is now frowned upon. For starters, they must begin to answer questions that the teacher already knows—a rather artificial language event from their perspective. Another complication for Trackton children is that literacy is a shared event in their culture. Silent reading and individual seat work are foreign experiences to children raised in a culture where literacy is embedded in collaborative oral practices, a problem exacerbated by the school's view of reading as a competitive rather than collaborative event (Kutz and Roskelly 1991, 76-77). As Kutz and Roskelly suggest, "Children from both Roadville and Trackton end up being seen as academically deficient, not because they can't think but because their home practices around language and literacy are so different from the school's" (77).

Native Americans, like African Americans, experience marginalization in classrooms resulting from differing sociocultural expectations. Susan Philips' (1977) study of Native Americans' differing expectations about class discussions suggests a mismatch between the expectations of the students and those of the teachers in teacher-directed discussions during reading lessons. Many Native Americans fail to participate verbally in classroom interactions where the teacher is directing the discussion, not because they fail to understand the instructions or requests but because a response is not imperative within their own sociolinguistic rule system.

> [T]hey show relatively less willingness to perform or participate verbally when they must speak alone in front of other students . . . [and] they are relatively less eager to speak when the point at which speech occurs is dictated by the teacher, as it is during sessions when the teacher is working with the whole class or a small group. They also show considerable reluctance to be placed in the "leadership" play roles that require them to assume the same type of dictation of the acts of their peers.(380)

Philips raises the question of whether teachers need to change their modes of instruction or whether the students need to learn to accommodate themselves to a different style of learning. Particularly in classrooms where cultural diversity exists, it is important, she maintains, to allow a "complementary diversity in the modes of communication through which learning and measurement of 'success' take place" (393).

In the KEEP program with Polynesian children in Hawaii, those children who were allowed to speak out without being called on and to chime in even when another child was speaking performed better in their reading lessons. With the stress on comprehension in the discussions following story-reading, the discussions gradually took on an overlapping-turn structure similar to that common in ordinary Polynesian conversations (Cazden 1988, 71), and the students in the reading discussions who were allowed to use this form of overlapping speech achieved higher scores than those who had to abide by more traditional classroom turn-taking rules. In such classrooms, discontinuity between home and school is less problematic, and successful learning more easily occurs.

Cultural Discontinuity

These cultural differences, labeled as "cultural discontinuity" (Au 1993, 8) suggest a potential mismatch between the culture of the school and the culture of the home that results in misunderstandings between teachers and students in teacher-student interactions, in assignment-giving, in classroom structure, and in the institutional practices that promote the status quo. In its most innocuous form it merely encourages passivity in students and a disconnection from learning, but in its most insidious form it denies students their right to be culturally different, marginalizing them and reinforcing their attitudes about themselves as social and academic misfits. Teachers' own assumptions sometimes unconsciously reinforce these self-images, and the eventual result is a cultural group alienated from learning.

Cultural discontinuity is both subtle and pervasive, and it is often ignored in schools. Because many of the language and learning patterns described above differ from mainstream cultures and from school expectations, they are ignored, misunderstood, and rejected by educators who assume that their own experiences are the norm. Heath and Mangiola (1991) suggest that the expectations we all have about language and learning patterns and about how people learn and what information is shared are largely culturally determined and may differ sharply depending on our cultural group. "The rub," they say, "comes because these expectations seem to us so 'natural' that they are virtually invisible" (15). And if we can't see them and remain unaware of their existence, we will continue to perpetuate the notion that one way—*our* way—of learning is the only way. Becoming aware of culturally different ways of knowing, differing preferences for classroom interaction, and the legitimacy of those variations may help alert us to the disjunctures between student expectations and teacher expectations that create barriers to learning.

Most of our discussion here questions the overemphasis on phonics instruction, but we must also be cautious about assuming that whole language instruction without structured lessons on particular skills is necessarily effective for all students. Delpit (1995) suggests that teachers consider the needs of individual students whose learning styles and needs may differ, and she cautions about too readily assuming that all children will benefit from whole language instruction. We believe that a whole language program, in order to be appropriate for all students, must accommodate the individual learning styles of students and must address the need for skills within a whole language framework. Our view of whole language does not preclude instruction on sound-symbol correspondence and word identification but rather incorporates that focus within a context of meaningful language.

Differentiated Reading Instruction

The bias inherent in materials and instructional practices that favor one dialect over another or one cultural group over another is not limited to the variations of surface structure features in language. As our previous discussion suggests, more deeply embedded in classroom practice is the notion that these surface features represent inherently different and sometimes inferior ways of learning that may be particularly limiting for nonmainstream children. In classrooms where language differences are judged on qualitative terms, the operational perspective is that difference equals deficit. Although reading instruction rarely perpetuates social class stratification intentionally, it nevertheless does so through the kinds of theoretical assumptions that result in questionable classroom practice. *Ability grouping* or "tracking" for reading instruction, for example, can work to the detriment of students placed into lower tracks. Ability-group placement is often accomplished through the use of standardized test results, despite other contradictory evidence about student reading ability. Even when teachers question test scores, they usually make grouping decisions based primarily on the scores themselves (Shannon 1992). To compound the problems inherent in grouping, considerable evidence suggests that grouping often occurs on the basis of social class (Shannon 1992; McDermott and Gospodinoff 1981). Those with nonmainstream dialects are more likely to end up in lower groups because of negative attitudes toward those dialects. Furthermore, ability grouping rarely provides opportunities for movement from one group to another, particularly for students in low ability groups to move up. Once in a low ability group, almost always in a low ability group. Some kids may escape by adjusting their reading habits, but the majority of kids in the lower groups tend to fulfill teachers' prophecies about them, brought on by teacher attitudes or by the kinds of instruction they receive in their reading groups, as we discuss in the next section.

One of the most insidious results of being placed in a low ability group is the kind of differentiated instruction that is provided. High and low reading tracks differ as much in instruction as in variation in ability because of negative institutional practices and attitudes based on deficit models of language (Allington 1983). For example, Allington reports that teacher interruptions for error correction during the process of oral reading vary dramatically from high groups to low groups. Teachers interrupt kids in low ability groups two to five times as often as they do kids in high ability groups, regardless of the type or quality of the miscue. A miscue is considered more serious—a mistake that needs correcting—far more often when the reader is in a low-ability group, even when the miscue is of high quality. One result is that readers begin to assume that all miscues are "mistakes" and are all equally negative and that reading is primarily a matter of getting the words right. Another result is that kids are given less time and fewer opportunities to correct themselves and to continue reading for further information, which might lead to self-correction. Students become hesitant readers, relying on the teacher for help, reluctant or unable to monitor their own reading (Shannon 1992).

In another study (Allington 1983), two-thirds of the miscues of poor readers were corrected, but fewer than one-third of good readers' miscues were corrected. One might assume that the quality of miscues was higher among the high reading group, but in a related study, only one-tenth of the semantically acceptable miscues were corrected for good readers, while more than one-half were corrected for poor readers. And in another study, 78 percent of dialect errors were corrected, while only 27 percent of nondialect errors were corrected (Cazden 1988), a practice that sends a clear message about the need to avoid those kinds of miscues, even if it means focusing less on meaning than on surface accuracy. In bilingual programs often nonnative pronunciations are mistaken for miscues, and teachers subvert the children's progress in reading comprehension for the sake of a pronunciation lesson.

The amount of reading and type of instruction are also differentiated between low and high groups. Much greater time is spent on phonics instruction in low ability groups, a practice that encourages readers to assume that functional word identification is all they need. In a study of fourth-graders, Gambrell, Wilson, and Bantt (1981) found that students in low ability groups worked on phonics in isolation twice as often as students in high ability groups, they spent only half as much time on reading in context, and half of their time during reading lessons involved activities unrelated to reading, compared to one-third of the time for students in high groups. Readers in high groups read more per lesson because they are interrupted less. They have greater opportunities for sustained reading and for silent reading, which helps build reading fluency and comprehension. Given the organization of reading groups, the very students who need the sustained, uninterrupted reading time to build fluency and to help them focus on meaning are the very ones who are least likely to get it.

It is clear that the way to avoid developing negative, counterproductive habits of reading and assumptions about the nature of reading is to avoid being placed in a low reading group. Readers placed in high groups get better; readers placed in low groups are likely to be struggling readers for a lifetime because they are seldom given real opportunities to develop their proficiency. Self-correcting abilities are inhibited, with students remaining teacher-dependent readers who focus on form rather than on meaning, who come to value surface-accuracy at the expense of comprehension. And when one's dialect, social class, or cultural group in part determines the placement, many Hispanic, Native American, or African-American kids, regardless of initial ability, start out behind and frequently never catch up.

Instituting Change

We would like to interject a cautionary note here. Once we recognize the differences in learning patterns among our students, we need to make decisions about our classroom instruction: do we continue what we are doing and work to make our culturally diverse students less resistant to our approaches, or do we make changes in our approach to material and instruction? Many nonmainstream children resist traditional instruction because they don't see the advantages that the dominant culture ascribes to literacy and education, nor do they believe the result will be positive changes in their lives. Even more problematic, when school-based discourses and learning patterns conflict with the values and viewpoints in some nonmainstream community discourses, children must make difficult adjustments and decisions. Our secondary classrooms are populated with students who find the conflict too great—who fear the change that literacy might bring, who fear the gulf that may develop between their family values of language and literacy and the school's values. The cost, in other words, may simply be too high. Those students act out, tune out, reject instruction, and pretend not to care. Some minority students, according to Fordham and Ogbu (1986), often engage in resistant behaviors that the researchers term "cultural inversion," resisting the culture and the cognitive styles that are identified with the dominant group.

One study, for example, found that the use of African-American Vernacular English (AAVE) increased as children got older and as their peer-group participation increased (Labov and Robins 1969). Another study found that the first-graders who used AAVE increased their use of dialect proportionally to how much they were hassled for their use of the dialect. "The more their speech was corrected, the more they used dialect, and in such classrooms, reading scores were low. In classrooms in which the children were allowed to express themselves and read orally in dialect, the use of dialect did not increase and their reading scores were higher, with many children above the norms (McDermott and Gospodinoff 1981, 218). At the very least, these subordinate groups have an ambivalent relationship with mainstream education, according to Edelsky (1991): "Deliberate success in school—learning the ways of The Man—is often perceived as both an opportunity and a betrayal" (131). Cultural assimilation may be part of successful literacy development for some minority students, but cultural assimilation pressed on minorities against their wishes may encourage them to actively oppose it in order not to have to give up their distinctive identities and cultures (Gibson 1991).

A better school policy, according to Gibson, is one that sustains and supports multiculturalism, one that encourages accommodation and acculturation but not assimilation:

> Such a policy, if embraced by the schools, could help minority students to
> view the acquisition of academic learning and proficiency in the dominant

language and culture as additional sets of skills that would lead not to a replace-
ment of their minority cultures but to successful participation in both mainstream and minority worlds. A policy of *additive acculturation* would help students distinguish the acquisition of academic skills and proficiency in the ways
of the wider society from their own social identification with a particular ethnic group. (375)

She goes on to say that the process of accommodation and acculturation must be
a two-way street, a shared process, an interethnic reciprocal process of learning.

Implications for Reading Instruction in Secondary Classrooms

The success or failure experienced by developing readers and writers lays the
foundation for reading and writing behaviors in secondary classrooms. The kin-
dergartners in Ribowsky's study (1985) who had more positive attitudes toward
reading as a result of their whole language instruction will more likely continue
to be positive about reading, as compared to the students in phonics programs
whose attitudes were less positive. As Weaver (1990) discusses, Stice and Bertrand's (1989) study of first- and second-graders in whole language classes, compared with students in traditional reading programs, showed that the whole language students had a significantly higher view of themselves as readers,
suggesting that children reading authentic books, who are immersed in meaningful reading and writing experiences, and whose own culture is validated in
the classroom are more likely overall to develop greater independence in both
reading and writing. When children view themselves as capable readers, and
when their interest in reading increases with positive attitudes toward pleasur-
able reading experiences, the likelihood of their developing into competent,
confident adult readers increases significantly.

Negative attitudes toward literacy also develop because students perceive
reading as a meaningless academic exercise. Annie, as a first-grader, resisted having to deal with nonsense. Contextualized reading made sense to her; sounds and
letters in isolation did not. Secondary students and adult learners are no different.
In some high school classrooms only the levels of nonsense change. History texts,
full of names and dates, that don't provide enough background information or
connections to students' life experiences feel like nonsense. SRA kits (color-
coded cards with short passages on a wide range of subjects that increase in
reading difficulty) do little to foster reading interest or provide sustained, meaningful reading experiences, and phonics programs and fill-in-the-blank exercises
in adult literacy programs merely reinforce the adults' feelings of inadequacy.

For teachers, becoming aware of their own reading processes is the necessary first step toward helping students change their perceptions of what reading
is and of themselves as readers. Bringing out into the open the myths about
reading and the misunderstandings about language variation in the process of
reading may avert poor self-concepts and help readers develop sound reading

strategies. And discussing with students the issues of ability grouping and how early reading experiences may have affected their reading habits could redirect young readers' assumptions and reading practices.

In an attempt to change the patterns of student-teacher interaction to accommodate different cultural expectations, teachers have options that will help empower students, including the following:

- Integrating multicultural literatures into literature classes, not the token poem or novel written by a minority person but the inclusion of significant pieces of literature from a wide range of cultures.
- Giving more than a token nod to the history of various ethnic groups in this country in history classrooms.
- Discussing inventions by women and minorities in social studies and science classrooms.
- Affirming differences rather than ignoring them.
- Providing opportunities for all students to become critically literate, to use their language and literacy resources to critique the society that exercises the power. Only when students feel that their literacy can be used for critical as well as for economic power will they see its full value in their own lives.
- Allowing full disclosure and discussion of the limits of literacy—that literacy is no guarantee of power and that literacy can fetter rather than liberate if it is misused and granted only to certain segments of society.

Several "best-practice" classroom approaches will be discussed in successive chapters, but four in particular deserve focus here as examples of putting the theory of literacy acquisition into practice for students of all linguistic and cultural backgrounds in secondary classrooms.

1. *A reading/writing workshop.* Establishing reading/writing workshops as part of the ongoing experience in an English language arts program helps students develop the skills they need as readers and also encourages them to take ownership of their own reading and writing. Rick B. bases his middle school workshop on Nancie Atwell's model (*In the Middle: Writing, Reading, and Learning with Adolescents,* 1987). As Rick sets it up, the workshop includes mini-lessons on reading and writing strategies and on issues of language variation, shared reading, writing in response to reading, and publication of written work.
2. *Personal anthologies.* Another high school English teacher (Sullivan, 1988) asked her unmotivated readers to develop their own personal anthologies of readings that particularly appealed to them, all from outside sources— a mixture of poetry, nonfiction, short fiction, journals written by others, and a children's book. The authors they included had to range from someone not yet graduated from high school to women and minority writers, historical as well as contemporary. Before compiling their collected materials into a portfolio, the students wrote reflective pieces on the process, on what

these selections meant to them personally, and on what they learned from doing it. What they discovered was a renewed interest in reading a variety of genres and a greater awareness of the range of cultural reading material available.

Similar notebooks on science topics such as medicinal herbs or ecological issues, on math topics such as architecture or statistical trends, or on music topics such as performances and concerts would be excellent ways of personalizing topics in content areas.

3.   *Skinny books.* Because the range of reading ability is broad in the average secondary classroom—from third or fourth grade reading level to college level reading—the task of meeting the needs of all students is indeed a difficult one. When reading material is too conceptually difficult, readers choose not to read. Teacher Erik M. counteracted this problem in his ninth grade biology class. He found several articles written for lay audiences and related to the course content he wanted to cover, put them in vertical files, and made them available to his students in place of some of the text material. In many cases, because the articles were more interestingly written and more conceptually accessible, they provided a way into more difficult reading. James T. tried this strategy with his government class, and current newspaper articles became his "skinny books." Sometimes students went on to read the more difficult text, but often these materials served as the center of the reading and enabled students to see the relevance of the course content to current issues.

4.   *Experimenting in the discourse of the discipline.* Readers must also be immersed in the disciplines of various content areas in order to learn their particular discourse patterns: the chronological structure of a history text and the cause-effect discourse patterns employed by historians; the poetic forms of writers in literary study; the systems of analysis and classification in science writing. Students acquire knowledge of the discourse by reading in those disciplines. When the content is accessible and the focus is on making sense of the text, they learn those patterns as they read. Like young children acquiring their initial understanding of written code, older students learn the codes of discourse structures, for the most part, by reading. Sometimes calling attention to the discourse patterns helps reinforce that knowledge by making it more explicit, but readers largely begin to understand these patterns intuitively as they muck around in the discipline—doing science experiments, reading different historical accounts of an event in history and comparing them, reading and writing poetry and playing with language themselves. Suggested here is the need for experimentation, risk-taking, and creative/imaginative thinking about the expression of ideas in a variety of formats. The ninth-grader who attempts to parody a Shakespearean couplet or the sixth-grader who writes a letter from the point of view of Rosa Parks is experimenting with the discourse of the discipline in similar ways to a first-grader using invented spelling to write a story.

The very nature of traditional schooling will need to change as well, beyond the kinds of instructional decisions teachers can control. Unless the pervasive inequalities implicit in traditional school structures—tracking, testing, and traditional patterns of teacher-dominated instruction—are changed, students from diverse backgrounds are likely to be prevented from achieving high levels of literacy (Au 1993, 11).

Whole Language as a Framework for Developmental Programs

Another population of students often ignored in the phonics–whole language discussion have specific literacy needs that cut across linguistic and cultural boundaries: the "at-risk" students who function at the margins of the system and for whom school and literacy have little value. These students, who may be enrolled in your content area classrooms, may also be taking courses in developmental or "remedial" reading, and their unique situations as developing readers need to be addressed. It may be easier to acknowledge the role of whole language experiences in regular secondary content area classrooms than in reading programs for developmental readers because of the behavioral approaches to remediation deeply embedded in those programs. "Remediation," unfortunately, has regularly consisted of the bits-and-pieces approach to learning to read—the one-more dose-of-phonics-ought-to-do-it mentality—most likely because the assumption is that smaller pieces are more manageable. Instead, developmental reading programs need to provide positive connections to print and reading suggested by whole language programs that support multicultural strategies. Adolescents and adults, like children, are whole language learners, and adolescents and adults in developmental reading programs, more than any other learners, need to have that learning validated.

One study of adult illiterates seeking help with their reading found that all the adults had very limited experiences with the pleasure of reading:

> Not one person could recall ever hearing stories or being read to at home or in elementary school . . . Many of those interviewed did not connect meaning with print . . . The adults believed that sounds or words hold the secret to reading; none looked for meaning or mentioned the author as part of the process . . . When asked how to improve reading instruction in school, they consistently recommended more phonics, more work on sounds, more work on words—more time doing what has not worked. In spite of their own failure to learn, more than half of the respondents believed that no change was needed in teaching of reading. (Rosow 1988, 122–123)

Because they had turned their negative attitudes toward reading against themselves, they believed that they were to blame for their inability to read.

How would a developmental reading course be organized in order to implement whole language principles? In addition to the suggestions listed for regular content area classes, the following brief ideas may spark other imaginative ways of organizing a developmental reading program based on the principles of reading as a psycholinguistic process.

1. *Using self-selected, independent reading.* Some part of each week could be devoted to the independent, self-selected reading of materials beyond the textbook: young adult novels, appropriate magazines, nonfiction, mysteries, science fiction, books by minority writers. Bring in pamphlets, manuals (car, driver's education, etc.), and other high-interest materials. The independent reading time for self-selected reading mirrors reading in the real world.

2. *Sustaining independent reading.* The day before each of those reading periods would be an opportunity for short class discussions to help sustain the independent reading. Topics could include the following, each revisited several times over the semester:

    • What is there to read? This discussion could involve the teacher and students sharing the interesting reading they have done, making recommendations to their classes about what is available.
    • Myths and misconceptions about reading. Opportunities to talk about dialect variations in reading, miscues, the nature of the reading process, and how comprehension happens encourage greater self-awareness that strengthens students' use of proficient reading strategies.
    • Problems I'm having in reading. Such a focus could engage students in talking about reading difficulties experienced in other classes, what makes reading difficult or easy, what can be done to make reading easier. Here the teacher can provide brief mini-lessons on strategies for handling more difficult texts. Atwell (1987) suggests talking about popular authors—Richard Wright, Lois Duncan, S. E. Hinton, Chris Crutcher, etc.—and reading together short selections of their works, which leads to rich discussions about reading and writing processes, how texts are read and reread, and how authors come to write as they do.
    • Current issues in education related to reading. What are the difficulties in reading tests, why are they given, what uses is the information put to? Do speed-reading classes help develop proficiency? What are the state requirements for proficiency tests in reading for graduation? How is functional literacy defined, and is functional literacy adequate for success in the workplace? Are students being asked to settle for something less than full literacy, and what are the political ramifications? Students in developmental classes may find these topics challenging, but they speak directly to their lives and are worthy of consideration and discussion.

Such discussions help to sustain the independent reading that follows, and they provide opportunities to make readers more conscious of the issues related to reading proficiency and availability of materials.

3. *Reading aloud to students.* It is sometimes helpful to model the process of reading for students by selecting the most important sections, stopping often to summarize or comment, providing examples of the kinds of issues and questions that engaged readers focus on. Reading aloud is also a means of drawing students into the reading and, as such, has no age limitation. We have found that our college students share, with young readers, an interest in being read to.

4. *Writing rather than worksheets and short-answer drills.* Worksheets on reading skills and worksheets on content area materials have little carryover to students' reading or comprehension. Instead it is much more productive to provide meaningful writing experiences that ask students to respond to the issues in the text in personally meaningful ways. (Several suggestions for using writing as a aid to comprehension are included in the following chapters.)

5. *Rewriting texts.* Asking students to put material in their own writing is an excellent way of helping them focus on key issues and on main ideas and topics, and it also helps them decide which supporting material is important and how to make connections between ideas. More accomplished students might rewrite some material for less accomplished readers or for younger readers whose conceptual abilities are less sophisticated.

6. *Additional suggestions.* Other ideas include providing activities that encourage self-expression in response to reading, such as painting, scrapbooks, making book jackets, writing stories; planning some group activities; organizing reading groups around common topics of interest; and encouraging dramatic activities in response to reading, such as readers' theater or skits.

These approaches to developmental reading provide stronger motivation for reluctant readers to adopt reading habits and attitudes that will encourage positive lifelong connections with reading. Whether students are adolescents or adults in developmental reading programs, isolated phonics instruction that hasn't worked in the past is even less likely to work at this point in their lives.

Literacy is too often defined in terms of phonics mastery or fluency in oral reading. In reality, true literacy is meaning-centered. Students who are not fully literate can only be taught through a meaning-centered curriculum, not through a program focused on isolated, meaningless skills and drills. Adolescents or adults reading at a fourth-grade level need the same opportunities for meaning-making as preschool children and college seniors do.

Conclusion

It is too simplistic to blame reading failure on teacher expectations based on race and class. Rather, school failure is usually the result of a constellation of wider sociocultural factors implicit in traditional school practice and in public educational policy. As Nieto (1992) explains, to the extent that expectations play a role, it is the expectations of the society as a whole, mirrored in the classroom, that are implicated. When George Bush, while running for office, visited Garfield High School in East Los Angeles, the school made famous by the efforts of Jaime Escalante (the subject of the book and movie *Stand and Deliver*) and others in producing an unusually large number of students going to college in spite of poverty and discrimination, his speech to the student body indicated governmental and society attitudes and expectations:

> Rather than build on the message that college was both possible and desirable for its students, he focused instead on the fact that a college education is not needed for success. He told the largely Mexican-American student body that "we need people to build our buildings . . . people who do the hard physical work of our society." It is doubtful that he would have even thought of uttering these same words at Beverly Hills High School, a short distance away. The message of low expectations to students who should have heard precisely the opposite is thus replicated even by those at the highest levels of a government claiming to be equitable to all students. (Nieto 1992, 31)

And as the population of U.S. classrooms becomes increasingly multicultural and multilingual, it is imperative that those in power begin to change attitudes and policies in order to make classroom practice reflect the literacy needs of all of its students, not just those of the mainstream majority. The real impediments to comprehension are the attitudes toward, and ignorance of, linguistic and cultural differences—attitudes that are institutionalized in reading materials, approaches, and instruction. If we want to expand literacy rather than restrict it, we need to value the differences among all students, both the linguistic and the cultural. Valuing differences rather than resisting or ignoring them may not solve all the problems of low performance in literacy, but it is a necessary first step in the process of reconceptualizing student potential.

CHAPTER FIVE

Selecting, Assessing, and Introducing Texts and Materials

In many content area classrooms, the course text is the primary reading material and may even be the major source of new information for students. In order to make the best use of the text when constructing the course curriculum, a teacher must first evaluate the text, determining its suitability for the students who will be taking the course. Course planning can then make the best use of the good features in a text or circumvent its flaws through supplementary materials and teaching strategies.

Text assessment is also imperative when text selection committees review new texts. These decisions become increasingly important as school budgets tighten while text prices skyrocket, and numerous publishers vie with each other to produce competitive texts that will ensure them a piece of the profitable school text market. In addition, text decisions are long-term commitments: The text chosen in 1997 will most probably still be in use ten years later, and in some schools and districts even fifteen or twenty years later or more. For all of these reasons, teachers should understand the various factors involved in text assessment and be familiar with several standard methods for evaluating texts and ascertaining that the match between text and students is appropriate.

Teachers must also select and assess instructional materials beyond the core text to provide a varied and information-rich learning environment designed to meet the needs of all students. This includes such materials as additional readings in both fiction and nonfiction, original documents, news media, and computer information. Finally, students must be introduced to the course text and other materials in ways that will ensure maximum use and comprehension.

This chapter centers on text materials, using this term in its broadest sense to include the many types of reading materials and texts in other formats available for today's classrooms. It will cover the following: (1) assessing texts; (2) introducing students to the core classroom text; (3) selecting reading materials beyond the text; and (4) broadening the concept of "texts" to include new technology.

Evaluating Texts for Classroom Use

Although we don't recommend that teachers lock-step their students through a text page by page, covering the material as it is laid out by the textbook publisher, we do recognize that a well-written text can be a tremendous asset to a course. Conversely, a poorly designed or outdated text can put more of a burden on the teacher, who must develop strategies to overcome the text's problems. Teachers must, therefore, select suitable texts for their students and understand the potential problems their students might have with the texts they are using. For these reasons, text evaluation is crucial for both day-to-day and long-range planning. The in-depth text assessment that can be most useful to the classroom teacher involves evaluating the text in several different ways, which are described in the following sections.

Quantitative Factors in Text Assessment

Readability formulas provide a relatively quick and efficient method for estimating the difficulty of a text. Based on the simple idea that short words and sentences are easier to read than long words and sentences, these are numerical formulas based on word and sentence length. Their greatest strength is that they present an objective and quantifiable measure; their greatest weakness is not taking into account such features as style and concept load. Nevertheless, classroom teachers may find it useful to know how to apply readability formulas to get a rough estimate of the difficulty of a text as long as they also understand their limitations. The grade level assigned to a text by the publisher is often calculated using a readability formula. In fact, some publishers go so far as to manipulate word choice and sentence length to achieve the desired grade level.

Many readability formulas are available for teachers to use. Among the best known are the Dale-Chall (1948), Flesch (1951), Fry Readability Graph (1977), the SMOG (McLaughlin 1969), and the Raygor Readability Estimate (1977). Several word processing programs exist that will apply different formulas to the same passages typed in from a text, but it is not difficult to apply a formula by hand. We find the Raygor Readability Estimate (Figure 5–1) reasonably reliable and easy to use to get a quick estimate of a text's reading level, accurate plus or minus a year.

The Raygor Readability Estimate

The Raygor formula uses three 100-word passages from the beginning, middle, and end of a text. It is based on the number of sentences and the number of words with six or more letters in each passage. The activity below will give you practice using the Raygor Readability Formula with one 100-word selection from this book. Follow the directions and fill in the blank slots with the information requested.

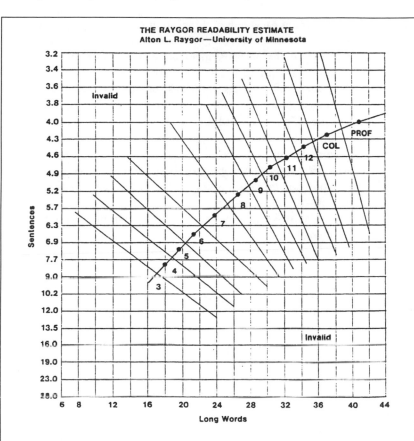

THE RAYGOR READABILITY ESTIMATE
Alton L. Raygor—University of Minnesota

1. Count out three 100-word passages at the beginning, middle, and end of a textbook selection. Count proper nouns but not numbers.
2. Count the number of sentences in each 100-word passage, estimating to the nearest tenth for partial sentences.
3. Count the number of words with six or more letters.
4. Average the sentence length and word length measures over the three samples and plot the average on the graph. The grade level nearest the spot marked is the best estimate of the difficulty of the selection.

(Raygor 1977. This graph is not copyrighted.)

FIGURE 5–1.

1. Turn to the opening paragraph of this chapter on p. 73, which starts with "In many content area classrooms . . ." Count the first 100 words and put a slash mark (/) at that spot. Remember, count proper nouns but not numbers. The 100-word passage ends with the word _____ .

2. Count the number of sentences to the nearest tenth of a sentence. (Note: The last sentence of the 100-word passage has a total of 36 words, but only 4 words are part of the 100-word passage. To find the nearest tenth, divide 4 by 36, e.g., 4/36 = .1.)
    The 100-word passage contains _____ sentences.

3. Put a check mark over each word with six or more letters and total these. The 100-word passage contains _____ words with six or more letters.

4. Find the spot on the Raygor chart where these two numbers intersect and note the reading level.
    The approximate reading level of this 100-word sample is _____ .

With three 100-word samples you would do steps 2 and 3 for each passage, then average the three sentence lengths, average the three word lengths, and enter the averages on the Raygor graph to determine the approximate reading level for the text.

To check your answers, see Appendix A at the end of this chapter.

Other Readability Formulas

The widely-accepted Fry Readability Graph (1977) is similar to the Raygor, but based on counting the number of sentences and number of syllables in each passage. Because it is often difficult to agree on the number of syllables in a given word, there is more margin for error and two users of the formula may come out with different readings. Baldwin and Kaufman's study (1979) comparing the Fry with the Raygor found the Raygor as reliable as the Fry, but easier and faster for teachers to use.

McLaughlin's SMOG readability formula (1969) requires the use of a square root table or calculator with a square root function. Instructions are as follows:

1. Count three sets of ten consecutive sentences each, near the beginning, middle, and end of the text (thirty sentences total). A sentence is defined as any string of words ending with a period, question mark, or exclamation point.

2. Count the number of words with three or more syllables in these thirty sentences.

3. Determine the nearest square root of the number of words with three or more syllables.

4. Add three to this square root to give you the readability level of the text.

The SMOG formula is designed for material that students will read without the teacher's support or explanation; therefore, the readability level is based on the reader's understanding of 90 to 100 percent of the material. The Raygor and Fry, which assess material used for classroom instruction assuming teacher support and explanation, give readability levels based on students understanding 65 to 75 percent of the material. For this reason, the SMOG will usually yield a higher readability level than the Fry or Raygor. McLaughlin's score yields "the reading grade that a person must have reached if he is to understand fully the text assessed" (McLaughlin 1969, 640) within one and a half grade levels.

Limitations of Readability Formulas

The linguistic surface features of sentence and word length do influence readability, but this is only one factor in text assessment. Other factors may be much more important in selecting suitable reading material for the classroom. However, a quick use of a readability formula may illuminate problems students are having or are likely to have with a text. A science teacher in one of our reading methods courses was struggling with the beautiful new text the school had chosen for its eighth-grade general science course. When the Raygor showed it was written at the college level, she understood her students' complaints.

Although readability formulas can give rough estimates of text difficulty, the teacher can't rely solely on them because concept load and unfamiliar vocabulary are significantly more important text features. For example, the children's picture book *Veronica* by Roger Duvoisin (1961) tells the story of *Veronica*, the *conspicuous hippopotamus*. The repetition of these three long words makes the story appear much more difficult than it really is on a readability formula; yet the repeated use of *conspicuous* in numerous contexts eventually makes its meaning abundantly clear. Conversely, the simple language of a writer like Ernest Hemingway belies the difficulty of the subtle meaning that needs to be read "between the lines." Take, for example, the following passage from "The Short Happy Life of Francis Macomber" (1936):

> "We're going after buff [buffalo] in the morning," he told her.
> "I'm coming," she said.
> "No, you're not."
> "Oh, yes, I am. Mayn't I, Francis?"
> "Why not stay in camp?"
> "Not for anything," she said. "I wouldn't miss something like today
>   for anything."

The linguistic features alone fail to account for the wife's nasty allusion in the last line to her husband's anticipated cowardice. The abstract ideas and metaphoric language of literature and poetry are a good example of the limitations of readability formulas. Nor do these formulas accurately assess the difficulty of symbolic meanings in math or science or the heavily technical vocabulary of a computer manual.

In addition, readability formulas are based on the assumption that short sentences are easier to read than longer ones. But short sentences alone don't make for easy reading because sometimes a longer sentence shows relationships, making the ideas easier to comprehend. Take, for instance, these three short sentences:

Rain fell every day for a week. The dam broke. The town was flooded.

Showing the relationships among these ideas, illustrated in the sentence below, makes for easier comprehension even though the sentence is longer and the syntax more complex than in the three short sentences:

The town was flooded because the dam broke when rain fell every day for a week.

Style, another critical component of text readability, is also not taken into account in readability formulas. Compare these invitations to write, from two different composition texts:

1. Are you ready? Is your writing hat on? Are your writing juices flowing? Let's write!
2. The five main steps in writing a composition are listed below in the order in which they are performed. Write a 500-word theme following these steps.

Nor do readability formulas consider the organization of the material or its coherence, or the reader's prior knowledge of the subject, interest in it, and background of personal experience, factors that strongly influence the text's readability. For all these reasons, we recommend that teachers include a readability measure as one aspect of text assessment, but rely more heavily on an analysis of the text for its qualitative features.

Qualitative Features of Text Assessment

Aware of recent reading theory, publishers continue to make a concerted effort to produce readable textbooks. What we hope they will emphasize is how to help readers better understand the material by designing "user-friendly" texts that are interesting, informative, and easy to comprehend. Unfortunately, these commercial enterprises often think first in terms of an attractively designed layout because the sales of these books are big business. Publishers want to create products that are appealing to students and teachers alike. As a result, they have researched and selected readable fonts, graphics and layout that have visibly improved the appearance of the material. Where plain black and white type once filled page after page, today's texts use bold facing, color, and paragraph indentations marked by bullets and numbering to highlight key ideas. Extensive use of graphics and photographs also makes today's texts more visually appealing. Texts often come now with a wide assortment of "teacher-proof" materials that may include teachers' manuals, workbooks, overheads, videos, and CD-ROMs. In some cases this teaching package dwarfs the actual classroom text and may even compound the problem of covering the material because so much more is available with little guidance as to what is worth concentrating on. Finally, although many of these texts have proved a great improvement over older texts, in too many cases publishers have paid little attention to the content, often recycling old material, and their textbooks have turned into expensive mistakes for schools. For all these reasons, it is important for teachers to examine classroom texts for what Singer (1986) calls their "friendly" and "unfriendly" features.

"Unfriendly" Texts

Here are some features that may contribute to the unfriendliness of textbooks:

- Writing style. Despite recent improvements in the visual appeal and readability of texts, the typical textbook writing style is still often stiff and stripped of expression, as though it were written by committee (and some texts are!). Attempts to limit the vocabulary make the text sound artificial, and simplifying the syntax leads to a sameness that dulls the very points that should be highlighted. Many textbooks are "voiceless," lacking any sense of the author's enthusiasm or involvement with the topic. When considering a text for classroom use, read a whole chapter of it at one sitting and read a few sections aloud to hear the writer's style. Is the language fluent, inviting, stylistically pleasing? Does it hold your interest?

- "Dumbing down." In an effort to simplify content to make the material accessible to a broad range of students, textbook authors may resort to shortened explanations that gloss over complicated issues and fail to develop any context or background for the reader to understand the significance of the discussion. This is especially a problem in some mathematics textbooks, which leave most of the explanations and demonstrations up to the teacher, giving only brief explanations in words before turning to the symbol systems of math to convey information. Math books thereby become mainly workbooks, useful only for their practice exercises and examples. This puts a heavy burden on the teacher to convey the meaning of the material in its entirety. Foreign-language texts may have the same problem, failing to give adequate explanations and applications in English before turning to the foreign language.

- Facts v. concepts. Some texts dwell on isolated facts and long lists of detailed information, rather than provide underlying principles or concepts that bring some coherence to the material. Social studies texts are especially guilty of this approach. One chapter in a commonly used American history book, for example, gives as much space to Thomas Jefferson's bedroom slippers as it does to the Monroe Doctrine, and it reduces the War of 1812 to the description of a few skirmishes and a short anecdote about Frances Scott Key writing "The Star-Spangled Banner." Another popular eighth-grade text covers history from the beginning of time to the present of every major country in every continent of the world. How many eighth-graders are able to absorb such a panoramic and comprehensive view of history?

Faced with such a plethora of detail, most students have little idea how to decide what is important and what can be skipped. We are reminded of an experience one of our own children had in an American history class. Stephanie was studying for a multiple-choice final exam in this eleventh-grade course when she burst into tears. One column-long paragraph in her text was nothing but a list of names of all the women whom the authors considered important in the women's movement. Although her parents recognized most of the names and could put them in context based on their own experiences (Elizabeth Cady Stanton and Betty Friedan, for example), Stephanie had no context for these names. For her, it was like memorizing a column of names in the telephone directory—a source of enormous frustration to a committed student.

Students relying on such texts never really understand trends and movements. Unfortunately, they lose sight of the lessons that history has to teach us today.

- Excerpts, abridged editions, and expurgated versions. English textbooks also have their problems, mostly because some publishers resort to anthologies with excerpts of famous works in lieu of whole pieces in the hope that students will be more likely to read the short pieces. The aesthetic sense of the piece may be lost under these circumstances. Literature is reduced to a mechanical quest for plot or, worse yet, to a search for the answers to the questions at the end of the selection.

Some anthologies print abridged or expurgated versions of texts in an attempt to make a difficult author, such as Chaucer or Shakespeare, more accessible to young readers, or to remove potentially problematic sexual allusions. We have seen texts that give students no indication that the original version has been altered in any way, thus robbing them of a true reading of the classics. One of us remembers the shock of discovering that Charlotte Brontë's *Jane Eyre* was not the short 150-page gothic horror story that she had read in high school but rather a complex, descriptive novel over 400 pages long of a young woman's growth from adolescence to maturity. "Unfriendly" texts and anthologies deprive students of the full appreciation of language as a work of art.

- Ineffective organizational patterns. Some texts may be organized in outmoded patterns that don't reflect contemporary approaches to the material. For example, some English textbooks are still based on traditional categories, with units on plot, setting, character, tone, irony, and other elements. Not only is this approach long outmoded as a critical tool, but it tells students that literary conventions and devices are more important than the content of the literature and its relevance to human lives. Few students remember whether or not there was irony in Shirley Jackson's short story "The Lottery," but they will remember whether it was a good read and what it tells us about mindless and cruel ritual.

We have also seen foreign-language texts based on a skills-and-drills approach to the subject rather than the current approach that stresses language as a meaning-making activity. Such texts often offer isolated and unrelated bits of information and exercises in each chapter, with the material becoming increasingly more complex as the book progresses, but the material is never put together as a coherent whole for the student. For instance, a single chapter might include one or two points of grammar accompanied by a set of exercises, a bit of dialogue to memorize, a paragraph to translate into the foreign language, a paragraph of the foreign language to translate into English, some cultural information, and several photographs of places of interest in the country being studied. None of these sections will have any relationship to the others; they are ostensibly gathered together into one chapter according to their level of difficulty along whatever progression the text author is using. This puts a heavy burden on both teacher and student to create a coherent view of the language and culture from the text's myriad bits of information.

- False assumptions. In some cases, textbook authors assume that their young readers have stronger backgrounds in the field than they do or that students will naturally draw on prior knowledge to make sense of new material. For example, some science texts assume that students think like scientists and neglect to explain some of the most fundamental premises that make scientific knowledge meaningful: why biologists would want to classify all plants and animals or why scientific notation is necessary. Science texts may also assume more math background than many students have and fail to give the kind of math instruction necessary for a full understanding of how and why certain computations are required, so students end up memorizing formulas instead of understanding concepts.

  Many textbook authors also depend on students to remember the basic concepts from chapter to chapter and fail to tie information together, treating each new chapter as if it were discrete and separate from what preceded it. Another problem with "unfriendly texts" is that they overlook opportunities to make real connections between students' lives and the text material, presuming that students will see these connections themselves. Or they may overlook the wide assortment of backgrounds of their multicultural readers.

- Political pressures. Finally, too many textbooks today are being revised due to the pressure of political action groups—conservative and liberal—that dictate the content of the material using an ideological agenda. There is plenty of blame to go around. Since the 1940s publishers of science texts have been pressured by groups who want to omit any mention of evolution or who want to promote creationism. Likewise, there have been heated discussions by parent groups about the inclusion or exclusion of material that would lead to classroom discussion about human reproduction, and too many parents are drawing up unreasonable lists of readings that they believe should be banned from anthologies and school libraries.

In history and social studies, similar pressures have come from groups who suggest alternate versions of history with more emphasis on race, ethnicity, and gender. Attempting to meet these demands, some text publishers may go overboard, distorting historical information to ensure that every group's story is told. One recent revision of a "famous old high school history book" incorporating more multicultural information was criticized for "the allocation of space and emphasis [that] pushes the book toward a kind of affirmative action history" (Leo 1994).

Friendly Texts

Fortunately, many texts, especially those published in the last ten or fifteen years, have taken full advantage of the new understanding of reading that has emerged in the past decades. Authors have become more aware of the importance of building in structural devices that lead readers to and through new information and have included aids to understanding throughout the text. Here are some positive text features to look for when assessing texts:

- Chapter and section introductions that draw on students' prior knowledge of the material, link forthcoming information to material studied in previous chapters, set forth clear goals for what lies ahead either as a list of information to be covered or a set of questions that will be answered in the chapter or section, and provide motivation for studying the material to come. Some texts also provide definitions of key vocabulary words at the start of each new chapter.
- Chapter and section conclusions that review the material just presented, summarizing key points, reviewing important new vocabulary, and pointing ahead to applications of the information and linkages to the material to come in following chapters. Suggestions for further reading and for activities that extend learning are also useful concluding materials.
- A consistent pattern of opening and concluding material so students learn to rely on these comprehension aids as they read and study.
- Use of "metadiscourse" to bridge the distance between text and reader by talking directly to the reader (Crismore 1984). The author can remind students of material studied in previous chapters, suggest ways in which they might have encountered this material in their own lives, and discuss useful ways to study the information. This type of informal conversation with students can do much to make a text more accessible. Here are examples of metadiscourse from a "friendly" middle school grammar and composition text (Olsen, Kirby, and Hulme 1982). Notice the use of the personal pronouns "you" and "we," the questions put directly to the reader, and the references to material from previous chapters or the student's own life.

> This is a book about writing. Before you say, "So what," look through the book. It may look like an ordinary English book, but we hope you will find it

surprisingly different. We hope you will find the activities interesting and even inviting. This book can help you improve as a writer, if you are willing to work at the job. (3)

So far you have been learning to write by practicing writing. The free writings, the strong verbs practice, and the revision work you have done in the first chapter are important steps in becoming a better writer. In this chapter and throughout the remainder of the book you will also practice building and combining sentences. . . . The exercises are designed to give you more options in your writing style so that you can vary your sentence length and surprise the reader. (20)

Have you ever wondered what you will be like as you grow older? Have you ever looked at an older person and tried to imagine yourself at that age? . . . Write a short poem beginning with the line "If I were older . . ." (81)

- A constant focus on central ideas and key points, providing a coherent framework for whatever is being presented. Details and examples should develop the central concepts, not just provide endless pieces of information to be sure that every possible point is covered.
- Introduction of new vocabulary in ways that don't swamp students with new words and technological terminology, and a consistent pattern for defining new words as they are encountered in the text and for redefining important ones as they recur in subsequent chapters.
- Liberal use of introductory and transitional words and phrases that signal specific meaning to the reader and show relationships among ideas: first, second, third, finally; on the other hand; furthermore; therefore.
- Use of visuals that support the main ideas of the text and offer additional information rather than just make the page more attractive.

Using a Checklist for Qualitative Assessment

A checklist focusing on qualitative features of texts that aid comprehension is a good way to assess text elements that readability formulas ignore. Below is a checklist designed to help teachers assess both the strengths and weaknesses of any content area text. It includes the items discussed above as "user-friendly" plus numerous other aspects of a text that lead to successful use for both teacher and student. Applying this checklist and the Raygor Readability Estimate to a text will give teachers comprehensive information about the text's readability.

Checklist for Qualitative Text Assessment

Textbook Title _____

Author(s) _____

Publisher _____ Copyright Date _____

Directions: This checklist is designed to help you evaluate the readability of your classroom text through an analysis of its qualitative features. If possible, rate the text based on your knowledge of the classes and students who will be using it. After responding to the items below, you will be asked to describe the strengths and weaknesses of the text as an aid to planning for instruction.

Use the following rating scale in responding to each item. Put the appropriate number in the blank to the left of the item:

3: Excellent; evidence of this feature throughout; yes.

2: Average; adequate use of this feature; present to some extent; OK.

1: Poor or unacceptable evidence; does not apply to this text; no.

GENERAL ANALYSIS

_____ The book is recently copyrighted and the contents are genuinely up-to-date.

_____ The contents of this text are suitable for achieving the course objectives.

_____ The text is considered appropriate for its intended students according to the _____ readability formula that places it at the _____ grade readability level.

LINGUISTIC AND RHETORICAL FEATURES

_____ Language is clear and direct; it is easy to read.

_____Vocabulary choice and methods for introducing new words are appropriate.

_____ Key words are highlighted, italicized, in boldface, or underlined.

_____ New vocabulary and technical terms are defined when encountered through the use of context clues, synonyms, margin guides, footnotes, or at the beginning or end of the chapter.

_____ Tone, writing style, manner of presentation are appealing to young readers.

_____ Metadiscourse is used to bridge the distance between text and reader.

CONCEPTUAL FEATURES

_____ Chapters emphasize central concepts and principles, are not encyclopedic collections of facts treated as if all information were equal.

_____ Facts support and enhance central ideas.

_____ Explanations of ideas include many examples, illustrations, analogies.

_____ Material is presented in a coherent pattern; ideas build on each other; relationships among ideas are made clear.

_____ Connections between chapters, sections, and central principles are explicitly indicated as the book moves forward, not left to be inferred.

_____ Subject matter is developed logically within chapters and sections as well as across the text as a whole.

_____ New concepts are introduced by relating them to previously learned ideas.

_____ Appropriate assumptions are made about students' level of prior knowledge of concepts and new information.

TEXT ORGANIZATION AND FORMAT

_____ Chapters can be outlined easily.

_____ Transitions assist logical movement from one paragraph and section to the next.

_____ Explicit signals are given to readers about organizational patterns, e.g., "There are three reasons for . . ."; "We will now compare . . ."

_____ Headings, subheadings, and italic and boldface type are used to help students identify major ideas by presenting a quick overview of a chapter's contents.

_____ Graphic aids such as illustrations, maps, graphs, charts, diagrams, and tables occur on the same page or facing page as the discussion and are clearly described by captions.

_____ Text interprets graphs, maps, charts, diagrams, or tables.

_____ Graphics clarify or extend main ideas; they don't simply decorate the page.

_____ Cover, print size, graphics, layout, and other text features are appealing to young readers.

LEARNING AIDS

_____ Table of contents shows a meaningful progression of ideas and information.

_____ Index is adequate for locating information in the text.

_____ Glossary defining important words is included.

_____ Appendix contains useful additional information for readers.

_____ Each chapter, unit, or section begins with an overview that may include objectives, a brief summary, questions to be answered, a list of what the student can expect to learn, or a set of purposes for reading.

_____ Each chapter, unit, or section concludes by reviewing the main points just covered with review questions, a chapter summary or a list of main ideas.

_____ Suggestions are given at the ends of chapters, units, or sections for supplementary readings, writing topics, projects, and other extension activities to stimulate interest and enrich learning.

_____ Questions and activities are appropriate to the developmental level of the intended age/grade level.

_____ Questions and tasks draw upon varied levels of reasoning: literal, interpretive, associative, evaluative, analytical, problem-solving.

_____ Questions and tasks draw on students' affective, aesthetic, and personal responses, not their cognitive abilities alone.

TEACHING AIDS

_____ Teacher's manual has appropriate suggestions and strategies for using the text, not just overheads and master sheets of workbook-type exercises and study guides.

_____ Teacher's manual suggests ways to use writing, collaborative learning, whole language approaches, and other strategies to encourage student interaction with the text and discourage passive learning.

_____ Manual offers suggestions for special needs students such as poor readers, advanced students, and slower learners.

OTHER FEATURES

_____ Whenever possible, the text relates information to students' lives and experiences.

_____ The text applies material to practical, real-life situations.

_____ The book contains a fair representation of various ethnic groups and men and women in its content, illustrations, and examples.

_____ The text is free of sexual, social, or cultural bias and makes an effort to present role models for all readers.

_____ The text has the following additional features worth noting:

_____

_____

_____

SUMMARY

Go back and review your ratings for each of the above areas, assessing the text's relative strengths and weaknesses. Then summarize your findings below. Strengths of this textbook are:

Weaknesses of this textbook are:

As a teacher, I will have to do the following when using this text:

(This checklist has been derived from similar text evaluation checklists by Irwin and Davis 1980; Readence, Bean, and Baldwin 1989; Vacca and Vacca 1989; Moore et al. 1994.)

Student-Centered Factors in Text Assessment

Information about a text's qualitative and quantitative readability is not enough to assess the book's appropriateness for the classroom because these assessment measures are all text-based. It is also critically important to evaluate the match between text and student because students' interests, reading ability, and prior knowledge of the subject all influence their interaction with a text. As part of text evaluation, teachers should ask the following questions about the match between text and students:

1. Do my students have sufficient prior knowledge of the subject to use this text as it is designed or will I have to build a knowledge base first? Does the text attempt to build a bridge between what students already know and the new information of the course?

2. Does the text draw on my students' interests and make the material relevant to their experiences and the multicultural backgrounds they bring with them to the classroom?
3. Do the linguistic demands of the text match the language and reading abilities of my students?
4. With appropriate classroom instruction, will the text be accessible to the majority of students who will be using it?

Cloze Procedure

Some information in response to the questions above can be gained by comparing the text-based assessments to what a teacher already knows of his student population. However, no text assessment is complete without input from students. The cloze procedure, a relatively simple text assessment tool for the teacher to design and administer, adds the final piece of information necessary for selecting appropriate classroom texts. In the cloze procedure, words are systematically deleted from a passage in the text being assessed and students are asked to fill in the missing words.

Originally created by Taylor (1953), the cloze procedure is designed to evaluate the match between a particular text and the student's reading ability. It does not indicate a student's general reading level, nor can it predict how well an individual student will learn from the text since so many other personal factors come into play. However, administering a cloze test to the group of students who will be using the text can show whether or not the text is appropriate to the range of reading levels in the class.

Using a cloze procedure entails the following steps: (1) selecting a passage, (2) systematically deleting words, (3) preparing the test handout, (4) preparing students to take the test, (5) administering the test, (6) scoring the responses, and (7) analyzing the results.

The following activity is designed to show you how to create, administer, and analyze a cloze procedure. You can then use this as a model for creating a cloze test on a text you are assessing.

A Recipe for Cloze Testing

A. Constructing the Cloze Test
   1. *Select passage.* From the content textbook select a passage of approximately three hundred words of continuous text. The passage should be representative of the readability level of the entire _____ . The material must not_____ been previously read by _____ students. Complete paragraphs should _____ used.
   2. *Identify words to* _____ *deleted.* Approximately 25 words _____ be left intact as _____ lead-in to the selection. _____ underline every fifth word _____ 50 words have been _____ . These words will comprise _____ missing words to be _____

by the students. Words _____ after the fiftieth deletion
_____ be left intact.

3. *Prepare* _____ *test.* Type the selected _____
using double-space format, leaving _____ for the words previously _____ . Care should be taken _____ make
all blanks of _____ length.

B. *Administering the Cloze Test*

Duplicate the test _____ distribute one duplicated copy
_____ each student. Emphasize the _____ oral
directions to your _____ .

1. Supply only one word _____ each blank.
2. Encourage guessing, _____ students should attempt to
_____ all blanks.
3. Misspellings will _____ scored as correct as _____ as
they are recognizable.
4. _____ cloze test will not _____ timed.
5. Before beginning, silently _____ through the entire test.
_____ will then read it _____ to you before you
_____ .

C. *Scoring the Cloze Test*

Determine each student's raw _____ in the following manner:

1. _____ only exact replacements as _____ . Synonyms are incorrect.
2. Misspellings _____ the only exception to _____
above rule. Do not _____ the student for spelling
_____ .
3. Inappropriate word endings are _____ .
4. The raw score will _____ the number of correct
_____ for each student.

D. *Classifying Student Performance*

It _____ generally been found that _____ who
score between 40 _____ 60 percent would benefit
_____ use   of   that   textbook. _____
scoring at this level are said to be performing at their instructional reading level. The textbook might be too difficult for those students scoring below 40 percent. It may be too easy for those scoring above 60
percent.

To check your answers see Appendix B at the end of this chapter.

The following considerations will be useful for teachers using the cloze
procedure with their students.

Passage choice is one of the most crucial factors in using cloze successfully.
Select a continuous passage about three hundred words long from a very early
part of the text so that students do not have to draw on knowledge from previous chapters to understand it. This must be a passage students have not yet read.
It should start at the beginning of a new paragraph, and it should not contain a
large number of technical terms, proper nouns, numbers, or specific dates,
although including one or two of these items is acceptable.

A lead-in of one or two complete sentences will give students a sense of the content, vocabulary, and style before words are deleted. Likewise, a lead-out of complete sentences about twenty-five words long gives closure to the material. Leave a blank space of exactly the same length for each missing word so as not to give clues about word length; fifteen spaces per blank is recommended to give plenty of space for long words. The entire blank, all fifteen spaces of it, must be on the same line or students will misinterpret it as a two-word blank. If you can't fit all fifteen spaces on one line, leave a long space at the end of the line and put the full fifteen underlined spaces at the beginning of the next line.

For ease in reading, type the test double-spaced and leave plenty of white space around all four sides. Do not try to cram the entire passage on one side of a page if it does not fit comfortably. Leave enough space between lines for students to write in their answers.

Before students are ready to take the test, two problems must be addressed: (1) their probable lack of familiarity with the cloze procedure, and (2) their unfamiliarity with tests that encourage guessing instead of filling in the one right answer. For these reasons, it is important to prepare students by modeling how to tackle a cloze passage. Some students may be familiar with the cloze procedure from the commercial pads of MadLibs in which readers fill in missing words to create silly, funny (or even vulgar) stories.

One good way to introduce cloze procedure is to use a few sentences of a song or a well-known fairy tale with every fifth word deleted, encouraging students to fill in the missing words. Once students see what cloze entails, a few textbook sentences should be used to demonstrate how to make reasoned guesses based on content and on the syntax of the sentence. The teacher can put a few sentences on the board with every fifth word deleted, elicit responses, and discuss with the whole class what clues led students to fill in the blanks as they did. A final step might be to have students work together in pairs or small groups filling in missing words from another short selection and coming to consensus about the words within the group. These activities do not take much time, ensure student comfort when the actual cloze test is administered, and also serve as a review of the unconscious reading skills we all bring to bear as we read. Throughout this preparation, the teacher should stress guessing and assure students that it is not necessary—indeed, it may be next to impossible—for them to get every word right.

We find it useful to tell students that the cloze procedure is *not testing them* but is instead *testing the textbook* for its suitability in their classroom. It also relieves their anxiety to tell students they may get over half the answers wrong, which is far more than acceptable for other kinds of tests.

To administer the cloze test, supply students with oral directions on how to take the test and then allow them to read through it silently. Next, read the test aloud to the class so they hear it before they are left on their own to fill in the blanks. Finally, since the test has no time limit, the teacher should provide an activity for students who complete the test while others are still working.

In scoring the test, only the exact word is counted as correct. Minor misspellings are the only exception to this rule. It is tempting to accept synonyms, but this only creates problems and unnecessary decision-making about whether or not to accept a specific synonym. When only the exact word is counted as correct, scoring can be objective and fast. The scoring classification system described below takes into account the fact that only the exact word is accepted. Once the raw score of correct answers is calculated based on a total of fifty blanks, multiply the raw score by two to get the percentage of right answers for each student.

The teacher must keep in mind that the cloze procedure is an informal assessment measure, designed to help teachers make reasonable judgments about classroom texts. On the basis of test scores, teachers can accept or reject a text, or begin to plan classroom instruction with some knowledge of the interaction between their students and the course text. Instruction can always be modified once the text is in actual use. The following chart classifies cloze scores by independent, instructional, or frustration level:

Cloze Test Scoring Guide

Reading Level	Percent Correct	Comprehension Level
Independent	100 to 59	Too easy
Instructional	40 to 60	Acceptable for teaching
Frustration	0 to 39	Too difficult

Students who are able to fill in over 60 percent of the blanks correctly will most likely be able to read and comprehend the text independently. If this is the only classroom text, these students will benefit from supplementary reading materials at a higher reading level and independent projects to challenge them. Those scoring in the 40 to 60 percent range will be able to learn from the text with guidance from the teacher; for these students, the text is at an adequate instructional level and teachers can be reasonably sure that the text is a good match for students' reading abilities. Students scoring below 40 percent are likely to have difficulty with the text despite classroom instruction and cannot be expected to learn from it independently. These students may need additional help in the form of carefully structured materials to guide them through the text, individual attention, or texts that provide the same information at an easier reading level.

The Maze Technique

Similar to the cloze, the maze (Guthrie 1974) offers students three alternatives for each blank space, which makes it easier for students to take, but harder for teachers to prepare. Because students are not guessing at the missing word but are instead choosing a word from the three possibilities, teachers may believe this is a more accurate method for assessing the match between text and student. The maze technique is especially useful as a test for foreign-language classes. To create a maze test, just follow the directions for the cloze except that three words are inserted at each blank space. The student is directed to circle the best word. Guthrie recommends giving the following three alternatives:

1. The correct word
2. An incorrect word that is syntactically acceptable for that slot (same part of speech) but is incorrect in terms of content
3. A word that is neither syntactically nor semantically acceptable

Care must be taken to vary the position of the three alternatives so the student does not learn to depend on the same position for the correct word. As with the cloze, the maze draws on students' abilities to use context, content, prior knowledge, and syntactic information to fill in the missing word. Figure 5–2 is an example of a brief passage altered for a maze test. The correct response is circled for each deleted word.

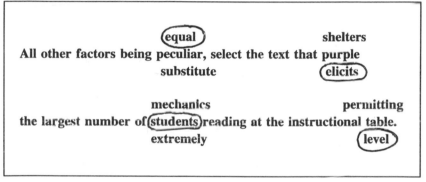

FIGURE 5–2. A Maze Test

Because the maze test is easier for students, scoring is much more stringent. Here is the scoring guide for the maze test:

Maze Test Scoring Guide

Reading Level	Percent Correct	Comprehension Level
Independent	100 to 90	Too easy
Instructional	70 to 89	Acceptable for teaching
Frustration	Below 70	Too difficult

The cloze or maze procedure has a decided advantage over readability formulas because it allows the reader to demonstrate knowledge of the relationship between language and meaning, while readability formulas are based solely on text language. The cloze or maze takes into account not only the syntactic structure of the text, but also how that structure meshes with the reader's conceptual knowledge of the material; therefore, it matches student and text in ways that readability formulas can't.

When used with a careful qualitative analysis of the text plus the grade level score from a readability formula, the cloze or maze procedures can give teachers enough important information to begin planning for classroom instruction and to decide what kinds of additional materials or special assistance is needed for successful teaching and learning with the given text.

Informal Observation and Assessment

The final key to success with the core classroom text is a teacher's informal observation of students as they use the text in class and for homework assignments. The evaluation techniques described above are an important start to aid in instructional planning, but we recommend that teachers deliberately create classroom activities and assignments that permit them to observe students' actual interaction with the text. Moore (1986) suggests three types of naturalistic text assessment in the classroom:

1. Observation of students as they work with texts and participate in discussions
2. Reading conferences in which the teacher discusses with students what they have read and asks questions to determine comprehension
3. Collection of work samples to see if students are able to make good use of text material as they respond to assignments

A teacher's informal notes in each of these three areas can pinpoint the special needs of some students for additional help or supplementary material. Naturalistic, in-class assessments can also help a teacher use a text more effectively or elect to switch to an alternative text if this one presents obstacles for too many students.

For the classroom teacher, the best text assessment process combines multiple methods of evaluation since no single tool gives a totally reliable measure of a text's readability in a given classroom with a particular student population. It is only through a combination of both formal and informal assessment, and continuous monitoring of students' responses, that a teacher can make the most useful judgments about the suitability of a text for his classroom.

Putting It All Together for Text Selection

Combining the formal text assessments described above—readability formula, qualitative checklist, and cloze or maze—can help text selection committees for a department, school, or district make appropriate text choices based on student factors as well as text features. Given the high cost of classroom text sets and their probable longevity, it is worth spending whatever time and effort is necessary to review thoroughly each text under consideration.

We suggest that a text selection committee do a Raygor Readability Estimate on each text, followed by a qualitative analysis of each text that is within an appropriate reading range for the classes that will be using it. Finally, a cloze or maze test should be created from each of the texts still under serious consideration. If at all possible, the test for each text should be given to two or three classes of students who are likely to be using the text once it is selected and the results for each text compared. All other factors being equal, select the text that the largest number of students are able to read at the instructional level.

Introducing Students to Texts

The following pages will discuss ways to introduce texts to students and prepare them to use the texts with maximum benefit. Active learners interact with their text and know where to look within it for answers to their questions. One way to encourage an interactive approach to the core classroom text is to give students a structured activity that provides them with a "guided tour" through the book before they begin to use it. The following sections show two different ways to introduce students to texts: the text preview, a general form that can be used with any text, and a treasure hunt created for a specific text.

The Text Preview

The text preview is an activity designed for a class period early in the semester to familiarize students with the text's predictable organizational patterns, text aids, and other special features that students can rely on when reading and studying. A text preview like the one below guides students in reviewing the salient features of any textbook. The teacher can work through this preview with the entire class, guiding their responses and answering questions. However, we suggest a more collaborative approach in which pairs of students work together at responding to the text preview items while the teacher circulates, giving help as needed and informally observing students' interactions with the text. This is a stress-free way to introduce students to collaborative work, especially if it will be a prominent classroom strategy. The teacher also benefits from this chance to do some informal assessment of students' prior knowledge of texts.

A Text Preview: Getting Acquainted with Your Textbook

Title of textbook _____

Author(s) _____
  Credentials (qualifications they have for writing this textbook):

  _____

Most recent copyright date _____

Publishing company and place of publication _____

1. Read the Introduction, Preface, or Foreword. The author usually uses these opening statements to discuss the purpose of the book and what it will cover. Briefly summarize what it says:

_____

_____

_____

2. The Table of Contents gives an overview of all the topics to be covered in the book plus the learning aids that are included. Examine the Table of Contents and answer these questions:

How many sections, parts, or major topics is the book divided into? _____
Name one of these major sections _____
How is this book organized? Does the organization seem logical? _____
Describe the organizational pattern of this book _____

_____

3. The Glossary is a dictionary of important terms used in the book. Does this book have a Glossary? _____ If it does, what page is it on? _____
List three words from the Glossary that are new to you and give their definitions:

1. _____
2. _____
3. _____

4. Find the Index to this book. On what page does it begin? _____
The Index lists all the topics and names of people covered in the book. It is a quick way to find the information you want. Select two topics you know will be included in the book and list them below. Look these up in the Index and add the page(s) where information on these topics can be found.

1. _____ page(s) _____
2. _____ page(s) _____

5. Bibliographies are lists of books used by the authors when writing the text or suggestions for additional reading. Bibliographies can be found at the ends of chapters, at the end of the book, or in both places. They can be useful for locating more information about material covered in the book. Where are bibliographies located in this textbook? _____
List several books from the bibliographies that you might want to read.

_____

_____

6. The Appendix is a section at the end of the book that contains additional information not included in the text itself. Does your book have an Appendix? _____ If so, on what page does it begin? _____
List two or three items located in your book's Appendix: _____

_____

7. Now examine the way each chapter in your book is organized.
First, look at the opening pages of several chapters or sections and answer YES or NO to the following questions:

Are there questions at the beginning of chapters? _____

Are there objectives at the beginning of chapters? _____

Are there summaries at the beginning of chapters that explain what each chapter includes? _____

Second, look at the end of several chapters or sections and answer these questions:

Does each chapter end with a summary of what was covered or a list of key points from the chapter? _____

Does each chapter have questions to help you review the material? _____

Does each chapter have suggestions for additional readings, independent projects, and other activities you could do to learn more about the topic?

_____

Does each chapter have practice exercises or suggestions for writing to help you apply the new information and think even more about it? _____

Finally, look at the way your text signals important information or new topics.

Does it guide your reading with clear headings for paragraphs, topics, and sections? _____

Does it use boldface headings? _____

Does it use large, bold letters or italics for new ideas? _____

8. How does your textbook help you with new vocabulary words?

Where are new words defined besides the Glossary? _____

Is there a pronunciation guide for new words? _____

9. Now examine the pictures, illustrations, diagrams, graphs, charts, and maps that support the written text and give additional information.

Are these clearly labeled or described so you know their purpose? _____

List three visual aids, their page numbers, and describe the purpose for each:

1. _____

2. _____

3. _____

10. What other features does your text have that you think will be useful to you as you read, study, and learn? _____

_____

_____

11. What seems to be the most interesting section or sections in this book? Why do you expect to find them interesting? _____

_____

_____

(Two sources provided ideas for this text preview: Brozo and Simpson 1991, p. 323; and Readence, Bean, and Baldwin 1989, pp. 71–75.)

A Treasure Hunt Through the Text

An alternative method for introducing students to their core classroom text is to send them on a "treasure hunt" to answer a list of ten to twenty-five questions whose answers can by found by hunting through the text (Bryant 1984). This may take time to prepare, but a special benefit of this approach to the text preview is that it can be designed to provide an overview of the material to be covered during the semester. In preparing a treasure hunt, be sure to include questions that require students to look up words in the text's glossary, use the index, preview the table of contents, and make use of other text aids they will need to rely on when studying. Below are representative items from a treasure hunt on a secondary school American government textbook:

Sample Treasure Hunt Questions

1. When was this text first published?
2. How many times has it been revised?
3. What is the "franking privilege"?
4. How does the second paragraph of the Declaration of Independence begin?
5. What does the thirteenth amendment to the Constitution guarantee?
6. How many members are in each branch of Congress today?
7. Who was the first woman to serve in Congress?
8. What are the three qualifications for the Presidency set out by the Constitution?
9. If a reader wants to learn about interpreting political cartoons, where can this information be found in this book?
10. In the diagram "Audiences Reached by Leading Media," what percent of the audience is reached by TV?

When using a treasure hunt, the teacher should first give the class a brief introduction to the text's features—glossary, appendix, index, etc.—and review the purpose for each of these reading aids. Students can then be set the task of finding answers to the questions. This can, of course, be done independently, but once again we recommend that it be a collaborative activity for the reasons discussed earlier.

The purpose of both the text preview and the treasure hunt is to be certain that students understand all the features of the text that are there to make learning easier—to know where they are in the text, what they have to offer, and how to use them. Once students have completed their preview activities, it is useful to review what they found and to discuss how the various features of the text can help them as they read and study throughout the term.

Selecting and Using Reading Materials Beyond the Core Text

Even if your core classroom text is a model textbook according to the assessment measures described above, there are many reasons for expanding students' knowledge with additional readings and other materials from the wide variety of resources available. A textbook is designed to present a great deal of information in an organized fashion; it necessarily aims at "coverage." Often, the personal content of any field gets lost in the textbook author's effort to present as much information as possible. In addition, many core classroom texts are seriously flawed, and all of them present information preselected and preorganized by the text authors. The teacher can compensate for these problems by providing a classroom environment filled with multiple resources and designing instructional activities that promote their use. She can also incorporate a wide variety of print and nonprint materials—trade books, newspapers, magazine articles, poetry, videos, films—into daily classroom planning.

As the title of this book indicates, we strongly support a view of learning that builds knowledge holistically through the gathering and sharing of information within a community of learners. This approach presupposes using multiple materials to encourage students' independent interests in the topics being studied and to offer them opportunities to explore beyond the text. Within a collaborative classroom community, the knowledge any individual or small group of students amasses and shares then becomes part of the classroom knowledge base. This suggests that when students learn from varied resources rather than from a single text, the knowledge and understanding of the entire class is enriched.

Incorporating a broad variety of texts into the instructional program also addresses the "multiple voices" of the students, providing resources that will meet the needs, interests, and abilities of a diverse classroom body. Students benefit from an in-depth look at a subject and the many perspectives that a variety of resources can provide.

Benefits of Using Multiple Materials

This section will present a rationale for including a wide variety of print and nonprint materials in classroom instruction, followed by an overview of available resources and suggestions for their use.

To Add Focus and Depth

Readings beyond the text deepen students' understanding of course material and permit them to focus on areas of special interest. Consider a class studying World War II. The classroom text can provide background, principles, causes, names and dates and battles, statistics, and the historical events of the war. Supplementary materials allow students who are military buffs to delve into uniforms and weapons, or to spend time absorbed by such books as David Cooke's *War Planes of the Axis* and *War Wings: Fighting Planes of the American and British Air Forces*. Fiction lovers can read *Friedrich* by Hans Peter Richter, the story of a young Jewish boy in Germany during the persecution of the Jews; James Forman's *My Enemy, My Brother,* the story of a teenager who survives the Holocaust; or *Night,* by Elie Wiesel, fiction based on his own nightmarish WWII experiences. Anne Frank's *The Diary of a Young Girl* and Judith Isaacson's *Seed of Sarah* offer two very different autobiographies of the Holocaust: Anne Frank's is the story of a family hiding in an attic in Amsterdam for three years until finally discovered by the Nazis, and Isaacson's the experience of a young Hungarian girl in the Auschwitz concentration camp. *Never to Forget: The Jews of the Holocaust,* young adult nonfiction by Milton Meltzer, describes Nazi treatment of the Jews before and during the war. Students reading at an adult level might enjoy *D-Day: June 6, 1944,* Stephen Ambrose's account of the war and its subsequent impact on American society. These varied approaches offer different points of view about the war and greatly expand students' knowledge and understanding.

To Fulfill Personal Interests

Students are motivated to read when supplied with multiple resources and given choices over what they select. This ownership of their learning provides intrinsic motivation to read and learn, especially if they are not "tested" on this work in the traditional way but are instead given alternative ways to present their learning such as oral presentations, drama, collages, book talks, or writing of their own. The use of multiple materials in the classroom promotes lifelong reading and learning.

To Provide for Individual Reading and Learning Abilities

The range of reading abilities in any given class may be as wide as six to eight grade levels, which is problematic for teachers using only one text for all students. An approach to the classroom that includes opportunities for students to choose their own reading materials for independent work on specific topics permits all students to find interesting material written at their own independent reading level. For example, a unit designed to examine race relations in the United States could offer *Roll of Thunder, Hear My Cry* by Mildred Taylor for students reading at middle school level, Harper Lee's *To Kill a Mockingbird* for high school level readers, and Maya Angelou's *I Know Why the Caged Bird Sings* for mature readers. Although these three choices are based on different time periods and view race relations from different perspectives, all three offer invaluable insights into the destructive forces of racism and offer students the opportunity to adopt an insider's view of racial issues.

To Add a Multicultural Dimension

Introducing a wide variety of reading materials into a course promotes a more multicultural understanding of the course than a textbook can with its limited opportunities to digress, add depth, and provide a variety of perspectives.

Students can choose to read about people from their own ethnic background to gain a stronger sense of identification with the topics of the course. Or they can use their readings to approach a topic from different perspectives and gain a broader view of the topic. The next section of this chapter includes a list of resources teachers can refer to when searching for multicultural materials to use with their classes.

To Stimulate Independent Thinking

Independent reading outside the text encourages critical thinking and also draws on more than just cognitive abilities; often a reader's aesthetic, affective, and personal response to these outside readings helps make the material much more accessible than just working through a series of textbook assignments. Class discussions of these readings and other opportunities for students to share their thoughts with peers offer unique occasions for independent thinking and critical response to new material.

To Promote the Field

Most of us chose to teach the field we are in for sheer love of the subject. We are ardent readers of fiction and poetry, or we remember playing with math puzzles even as children, or we were the only child in the neighborhood to ask for a chemistry experiment kit for a birthday present instead of a Nintendo game. An important goal in any classroom is to share our own enthusiasm and build students' interest in the field: to encourage them to share our passion for the subject. The classroom text just won't do it! Students deserve to be immersed in good, readable, highly motivating material in every content area they study. For one thing, they must make career choices themselves in the near future; learning about a subject from an autobiography or a nonfiction trade book may open up a whole new field of interest and suggest career options. But beyond the merely vocational, classrooms flooded with topic-centered trade books and other materials are more likely to develop lifelong interest in a given field than a classroom environment focused on one text-based source of information. If we want students to become "insiders" in our field and to appreciate the excitement of studying it, multiple resources beyond the text offer this opportunity.

Broadening the Concept of Text

A wealth of materials exists for use in classrooms, from the standard encyclopedias that students learn early to draw on for reports, to the array of trade books, both fiction and nonfiction, that are sold in bookstores everywhere and fill most shelves in the library. Given this ever-increasing supply of interesting and valuable nontextbook reading material, it is astonishing that so many classrooms seem to be built entirely around one textbook. Students often don't even know how much other material is available and would benefit greatly from a chance to browse through the stacks in a good library or spend a free reading period examining the resources in a well-supplied content area classroom.

We recommend that teachers add all of the following types of resources to their classroom reading lists for students and also develop ways to incorporate these materials into daily lessons and unit plans.

1. Fiction, especially young adult novels with teenage protagonists. These now span a wide range from historical fiction and science fiction to novels dealing with contemporary issues of family and society.

2. Poetry. Using poetry about any topic under study can add a new dimension to the straightforward information of the textbook and may even stimulate students to write their own poetry about the field. Sometimes a quick scan through a poetry anthology with a topical index can yield numerous poems suitable for content areas: animal poetry for science classes, poems about emotions or athletics for health education classes, historical poetry from the wars the United States has been engaged in for social studies courses.

3. Nonfiction, which has an even wider range than fiction. Students can be given wide latitude of choice here, especially if the books are screened in advance by the classroom teacher and the school librarian.

4. Biographies and autobiographies of well-known or interesting people. This genre is now growing to include people not necessarily famous, but important for the role models they present or the lives they lead: ethnic minorities, women, the ordinary person who represents the experiences of a group or historical period.

5. Works by and about women. The contributions of women are often overlooked in school textbooks and literature anthologies, a factor that has done untold damage to our society in its hidden message that women's voices are either not there or not worth including. Many teachers today recognize the need for both boys and girls to be made aware of the role women have played in history, science, math, literature, and all other fields. Textbooks, especially the older ones still used in many schools, are often dominated by male voices. Trade books, videos, biographies and autobiographies by and about women ensure that women's voices are also heard.

    For teachers who wish to include more women in their courses, Whaley and Dodge's *Weaving in the Women* (1993) provides resources and teaching ideas primarily for secondary school literature courses, but many can be adapted to other fields and units of study. The recent Public Broadcasting Service (PBS) series on contemporary women scientists, now available on video, provides role models of women in the sciences designed to encourage young women to enter these traditionally male-dominated fields.

6. Multicultural readings. Texts have made an effort in recent years to include minority information and perspectives on every topic they discuss. However, these are often superficial, sometimes merely there to ensure a minority presence in the text. Multicultural readings in fiction, nonfiction, biography, and autobiography give minority students a chance to see themselves in the context of the field being studied and give all students a chance to understand a topic from the multiple perspectives that

are difficult to cover in a textbook.

The following annotated bibliographies of multicultural materials for secondary students are useful resources for teachers in all subjects.

Kaleidoscope: A Multicultural Booklist for Grades K–8, edited by Rudine Sims Bishop (1994), reviews nearly four hundred books focused on people of color including African Americans, Asian American, Hispanic Americans/ Latinos, and Native Americans.

Native Heritage: American Indian Literature, edited by Carter Revard (1993), presents literature by and about American Indians.

Eileen Oliver's *Crossing the Mainstream: Multicultural Perspectives in Teaching Literature* (1994) provides an extensive annotated reading list of authors and titles from a variety of cultural groups.

Multicultural Voices in Contemporary Literature: A Resource for Teachers by Frances Ann Day (1994) presents the lives and works of thirty-nine authors from different cultures.

The list of annotated bibliographies at the end of this chapter includes more multicultural resources.

7. Newspapers and magazines. We suggest teachers keep an ongoing file of newspaper clippings pertaining to their field. Students can be encouraged to help with this, too, by bringing in newspaper articles they come across that relate to the work in your classroom. Browsing through a folder of recent newspaper articles about your subject lends an immediacy and relevancy to the study of any field that is impossible for students to get from a textbook alone. Magazines can offer an even fuller picture of current information in a field of study, often including photographs, interviews, and other recent material that brings textbook information up-to-date and stimulates student interest by presenting information in a popular format. Richardson (1991) and Stoll (1990) offer descriptions of magazines appropriate for use in the classroom.

8. Reference materials and encyclopedias. Most students are familiar with encyclopedias but they may not know about all the other reference materials they can find in the library: biography indexes, book reviews, government pamphlets, etc. These can make stimulating reading for the right student, or important research tools for students doing independent projects.

9. Art and music. Art and music can add an aesthetic element to the classroom, from the soaring music of *2001: A Space Odyssey* for science classes to spirituals, jazz, and blues music to deepen understanding of the era under study in a history class. Discussion of the mathematical underpinnings of music can lend a new dimension to a math course, computer classes can study the basis for computer music, and physics classes can explore the structure behind the music of a synthesizer. Art can also stimulate interest in content area classes by enriching students' aesthetic sense and building a

fuller picture of whatever is being studied. Books on crystallography and subatomic particles contain stunning pictures for use with science students, and the art of any era under study in a history class adds a new dimension to students' appreciation of that period. Just as Crick and Watson were amazed by the beauty of the DNA molecule when they uncovered its shape, described in Watson's *The Double Helix* (1968), art can help students discover the beauty inherent in every field.

10.   Videos and films. Showing movies in class used to be the mainstay of the "burned-out" teacher or the way to fill up those difficult days before vacations. But in recent years the growth of these visuals for the classroom has made it possible for teachers to integrate them more fully into any field of study. Many "classics" read in American and British literature courses and almost all the plays of Shakespeare are now available on videos, as are discussions of contemporary literature by such writers as Alice Walker, Toni Morrison, and William Stafford. Several award-winning PBS series are now available on video: the history of baseball, *Art of the Western World*, *The Civil War*, and *Normandy: the Great Crusade*. Videos no longer need be a digression from the syllabus or an add-on; the right video can be used as an alternative to the textbook in presenting information central to a course. Most important, films and videos can help make course material more accessible for those students struggling to keep up with the textbook.

To help you find material appropriate for your content area, the end of this chapter has a list of annotated bibliographies of trade books, magazines, videos and films appropriate for use in the classroom. These bibliographies are often organized by topics or content areas for quick access to materials in your field.

Methods for Use and Presentation

Materials other than the textbook are most beneficial in the classroom when they are not seen as supplementary materials but are incorporated right into the course structure as an integral part of the information load. Here are several ways to do this that will work well in almost any content area class.

• Oral reading. The teacher can read a selection or entire book aloud to the class in conjunction with a topic or unit of study. People of any age enjoy being read to, and this gives the teacher an opportunity to coordinate reading materials with the topic under study, extending concepts, or using the supplementary reading to make the material relevant to students' lives. Since only one copy is needed, the cost is minimal for this powerful opportunity to engage students' interest and expand their understanding.

   For instance, Isaac Asimov's *Fantastic Voyage* is an excellent piece of science fiction to accompany the study of the body in science. The teacher can read selected portions of the voyage that mirror factual accounts of human anatomy as they are studied in class. Music teachers can read excerpts from biographies about composers of the works being played in orchestra to give the musical pieces more relevancy or as a lead-in to discussions of what the composer might have been trying to achieve in a given piece. A high school literature teacher can introduce novels or stories by reading authors' statements about their own work or biographical material. For students with reading difficulties or those who just don't take the time to read on their own, this is a significant way to enrich their curriculum.

- Assigned reading. The teacher can assign a selection or book for everyone in the class to read instead of, or in conjunction with, the core classroom textbook. Inexpensive paperback copies of young adult novels and other appropriate reading material make it possible for an entire class to read the same book related to a period or concept under study. Once the teacher decides on the central concepts he wants students to understand within a unit, he can then select an appropriate reading to expand their understanding.

   For instance, the Interactive Math Program (IMP), a new approach to high school math, has students reading and studying Edgar Allan Poe's short story "The Pit and the Pendulum" for clues about the length of the pendulum, its rate of descent, and how long the protagonist had to escape (Long 1995). A fictionalized or autobiographical account of an era or a particular war can be assigned to add a personal dimension to the study of history: *Johnny Tremain* by Esther Forbes or James Lincoln Collier and Christopher Collier's *My Brother Sam Is Dead* when students study the American Revolution; Irene Hunt's *Across Five Aprils* or Milton Meltzer's *Voices from the Civil War: A Documentary History of the Great American Conflict* when they study the Civil War; *Fallen Angels* by Walter Dean Myers or *When Heaven and Earth Changed Places: A Vietnamese Woman's Journey from War to Peace* by Le Ly Hayslip when they study the Vietnam War.

   At the University of Michigan–Flint, fiction regularly accompanies history courses, adding another dimension to historical fact. Students taking History of Women in the United States read Louisa May Alcott's *Little Women*. When students study the Industrial Revolution in Western Civilization, they are assigned Mary Shelley's *Frankenstein*, a gothic horror story that also illustrates many prominent nineteenth-century issues, among them fear of science and technology.

- Independent reading combined with a performance, presentation, or report. As part of a unit of study students can be given wide latitude in selecting an appropriate reading based on the unit's work. Everyone in the class might read a different book or magazine or multiple copies of several texts might be available for students to choose among. Students can be given a week or two to complete their reading and then offered a choice of ways to present their information, perhaps as a concluding activity toward the end of in-class work on the unit. This type of individual reading serves several purposes: students develop an in-depth understanding focused on the topic of their independent reading and the whole class, including the teacher, gets to benefit from the combined information of the presentations. Here is a list of twenty-one alternatives to the traditional book report in content area classes.

1. Put together a display of illustrations, photographs, and artifacts representing the piece you read; make a class presentation describing the display.
2. Make a three-dimensional diorama from the reading using a shoe box or small carton; this can represent a historical era, illustrate an event from the reading, or demonstrate scientific facts and understandings.
3. Dramatize an episode from the reading; first write it and then perform it.
4. Make puppets based on the reading and perform a puppet dramatization.
5. Interview a character, historical or fictional, from the reading; this can be a written interview or a "live" interview performed for the class.
6. Present a TV or radio newscast using facts and events from the reading.
7. Write a news article about one character or event, or create a newspaper based on the era, events, and characters of the reading.
8. Make a collage based on the reading; use photos, and pictures from magazines; words, quotes, titles, and phrases from the reading; symbols representing key features.
9. Take a series of photographs illustrating the reading; add captions or quotes from the material; use these to create a photo report.
10. Draw a picture or series of pictures based on the reading.
11. Make cartoons of key episodes or turn the entire reading into a comic book.
12. Using a video camera, make a short film from the reading.
13. Put together a song medley based on themes and ideas from the reading; tape this for the class.
14. Design a poster or advertising campaign to promote the reading of this piece.
15. Design a book jacket for the reading or make a mobile.
16. Write poetry, songs, or stories about the reading in any subject area.
17. Present an oral report enlivened with illustrations, slides, photos, etc.
18. Assemble three objects important to the reading; attach a paragraph to each one describing its significance; give an oral report on the book, using these objects.
19. Make a test for the book you read. Include multiple-choice, short-answer, and essay questions. Provide answers to these questions.
20. Imagine you can turn the book into a movie. Choose actors and actresses for your film. Design a poster for the movie illustrating a key scene and write a movie review in which you try to persuade people to see the film.
21. Pretend you are a central character in your reading, real or fictional. Write a monologue in the first person telling your experiences. Tape this or perform it for the class.

- Projects. Students can be assigned to collect information about a topic under study and prepare a report of some kind about what they learned. A list for students of project alternatives, plus allowing them to use class time for visits to the library, reading, and research, can do much to ensure students' success at this task. Students learn independently through their own reading and research while the teacher acts as a facilitator, offering assistance as needed. Again, presentations and reports of all kinds for the entire class permit students to learn from each other.

     Diane Moore, a math teacher at Traverse City East Junior High School in Michigan, used two kinds of projects with her students. Her eighth-grade math students did research on biographies of famous mathematicians chosen from a list she gave them, then each wrote a "biopoem" about the mathematician. (See Chapter Nine for the biopoem format.) These were typed, bound, and published as a classroom anthology entitled "The Poetry of Mathematics." In another math class, Diane had students do research on a math concept such as infinity or zero and write a paper informing other class members about it. These were also typed and bound into a class anthology, called "Topics in Mathematics." Projects such as these encourage students to develop their own interests in a field of study and stimulate a great deal of independent, and enriching, reading beyond the textbook.
- Collaborative work. Students can work together either in pairs or small groups doing the planning, reading, and presentations for projects, reports, or research studies in any field. The combination of several young minds reading, writing, thinking, and talking about a subject can produce final products well beyond the expectations of the classroom teacher. Students will need time in class to work on such collaborative projects, but they often get so involved in the work that they meet on their own outside of class to talk and plan. Oral presentations and performances of all kinds should be the result of collaborative work.
- Reading workshop. Another method teachers may use to encourage wide reading beyond the class textbook is a weekly reading period; Friday is usually a good day for this activity. If the classroom is filled with suitable reading materials in the field and students are also permitted to bring in their own materials dealing with the subject under study, this time for independent reading can meet the needs of many students who may not have time to read outside of class or a quiet place in which to do it. The reading workshop has become an integral part of many language arts classes, but it can be equally beneficial for other subject areas. Students can keep reading logs, fill out book review file cards with recommendations for other students, write letters to each other or the teacher about what they are reading, or do a project on one of their readings.

The Content Area Teacher as Resource Person

Every teacher should have a file for collecting and keeping records of available resources in her field. We suggest an inexpensive portable plastic file box for hanging folders that can sit on a desk or on top of a file cabinet for easy access. Label each folder with a genre—fiction, videos, CD-ROMs—or a course topic—Civil War, weather, fractions—and just toss the resource information into the appropriate folder. We prefer this hanging file system because the folders can hold torn out pages, catalogues, newspaper clippings, bibliography lists, or bits of information jotted on slips of paper.

Information about potentially useful course material can come from newspaper and magazine book reviews, a trip to the local bookstore or video rental place with a note pad in hand, or the *New York Times Book Review* supplement each Sunday. *The English Journal* publishes monthly columns of teaching resources, reviews of fiction and nonfiction books, and other materials that are not just for language arts teachers. *English Journal* is especially valuable for its reviews of young adult fiction suitable for a variety of content areas. Most content areas have a journal in their field dedicated to secondary teaching; check the one in your field for its reviews of books and other useful teaching resources. Here is a list of journals for teachers in a variety of school subject areas:

Art and Music—*School Arts, Music Educators Journal, Art Education*

Business—*Balance Sheet, Journal of Education for Business, Journal of Business Education, Business Education Forum*

English—*English Journal, Journal of Reading, The Reading Teacher, Language Arts*

Foreign Language—*Foreign Language Annals*

Mathematics—*Arithmetic Teacher, School Science and Mathematics, Mathematics Teacher*

Physical Education—*Journal of Physical Education, Recreation, and Dance*

Science—*The Science Teacher, American Biology Teacher, Journal of Chemical Education, Science Education, Journal of Biological Education*

Social Studies—*Social Education, The Social Studies*

Vocational Education—*VocEd*

Just as it is important to keep abreast of research and methods in your field, it is equally important to continue to build your knowledge of commercial materials and trade books available for the classes you teach.

Using Technological Resources

No discussion of classroom materials would be complete without examining the impact of computers in the classroom and their educational potential for the future. For students in today's classrooms, computer technology is part of the world in which they grew up. The majority understand computers, VCRs, tape cassettes, electronic sound systems, calculators, and other forms of electronic equipment readily. Sometimes they have more expertise and experience than the teacher, for whom computers and other forms of technology are midlife additions. Because of this familiarity, students are comfortable with technology in the classroom and highly motivated to work with it. In addition to this, we have an ever-growing set of teaching resources ranging from word processing programs to CD-ROMs, computer-based learning programs, and worldwide information networks. All of this means we are developing numerous nonprint materials that present meaningful opportunities for teaching and learning. We don't mean to suggest that computer technology could ever replace teachers, books, and the classroom learning community, but they most definitely add another tool for teachers and students to use as part of a rich educational environment.

We think these four applications of computer technology presently offer the most useful instructional tools for the classroom teacher.

1. Word processing programs with a dictionary, spelling checker, and thesaurus help students compose, revise, and edit their work more easily in order to produce polished pieces. Desktop publishing software and graphics programs make it easy for students to "publish" their written work in a professional manner as well as learn many of the computer skills now considered necessary in the workplace. Teachers might consider such software programs as *Print Shop* (Broderbund) for making cards, posters, banners, and invitations; *Pow! Zap! Ker-Plunk!* (Queue) for making cartoons and comic books; *Story Starters: Social Studies* and *Story Starters: Science* (Pelican) to provide students with information and clip art for producing books in these fields; and *Microsoft Publisher* for producing professional-looking newsletters, flyers, and brochures using preset templates and clip art. *Adobe PageMaker* and *Quark* are professional publication software programs that would appeal to more experienced student computer users.

2. CD-ROMs support and expand students' interaction with the textbook or, in some cases, replace the text as a source of new information. This is a rapidly growing commercial industry now producing exciting materials, from atlases of the world and whole encyclopedias to informative material in all subject areas. Fred Hofstetter's *Multimedia Literacy* (1995) contains a full discussion of the many classroom uses for CD-ROMs plus descriptions of those available at the time of publication.

3. The "information superhighway " is a source of information as well as a communication network. This requires the use of a modem and specific software for electronic mail exchanges (e-mail) and for access to the Internet or its multimedia portion, the World Wide Web. E-mail enables students to communicate with others throughout the United States as well as other countries so that "pen pal" exchanges can now take place through the computer. The Internet and the World Wide Web give students access to libraries and other information sources throughout the world right on their computer screen.

4. Educational software packages designed to supplement or replace tradi-
    tional instruction. These deserve close examination before they are pur-
    chased for use in the schools. Sometimes the software package is not much
    more than a series of traditional textbook explanations and exercises trans-
    ferred to the computer. It pays to preview any piece of software to be cer-
    tain that it provides what teacher and textbook cannot.

Chapter Summary

This chapter has focused on textbooks, other reading materials, and related
classroom print and nonprint resources. Selecting and assessing classroom materials are an important first step in planning for teaching. Teachers must choose
texts that best suit their instructional goals and also meet the needs and abilities
of their students. In this chapter, we presented several ways to assess the suitability of classroom texts—quantitatively with readability formulas, qualitatively
with checklists, and through students with the cloze test plus informal observations of the text in use. We then described two procedures for introducing the
core classroom text to students, a text preview and a treasure hunt activity. The
second half of this chapter discussed materials and methods for enriching the
learning experience through the use of multiple resources beyond the primary
course textbook, including trade books, media, and technology. The purpose of
this chapter was to provide teachers with sufficient information to make appropriate selections of classroom materials and to offer alternatives in both choosing and using multiple resources as an integral part of their teaching.

Appendix A: Answers for Raygor Readability Formula Activity

1. The last word in the 100-word passage is *increasingly*.
2. The passage has *4.1 sentences*.
3. There are *36 words* containing six or more letters.
4. These two figures intersect on the Raygor graph at *college level*.

Appendix B: Answers for a Recipe for Cloze Testing

A. Constructing the Cloze Test

1. Select passage. From the content textbook, select a passage of approxi-
    mately three hundred words of continuous text. The passage should be

representative of the readability level of the entire *text*. The material must not *have* been previously read by *your* students. Complete paragraphs should *be* used.

2. Identify words to *be* deleted. Approximately 25 words *should* be left intact as *a* lead-in to the selection. *Lightly* underline every fifth word *until* 50 words have been *selected*. These words will comprise *the* missing words to be *supplied* by the students. Words *remaining* after the fiftieth deletion *should* be left intact.

3. Prepare *the* test. Type the selected *material* using double-space format, substituting *blanks* for the words previously *underlined*. Care should be taken *to* make all blanks of *equal* length.

B. Administering the Cloze Test

Duplicate the test *and* distribute one duplicated copy *to* each student. Emphasize the *following* oral directions to your *students*.

1. Supply only one word *for* each blank.
2. Encourage guessing, *as* students should attempt to *fill* all blanks.
3. Misspellings will *be* scored as correct as *long* as they are recognizable.
4. *The* cloze test will not *be* timed.
5. Before beginning, silently *read* through the entire test. *I* will then read it *aloud* to you before you *begin*.

C. Scoring the Cloze Test

Determine each student's raw *score* in the following manner:

1. *Count* only exact replacements as *correct*. Synonyms are incorrect.
2. Misspellings *are* the only exception to *the* above rule. Do not *penalize* the student for spelling *errors*.
3. Inappropriate word endings are *incorrect*.
4. The raw score will *be* the number of correct *replacements* for each student.

D. Classifying Student Performance

It *has* generally been found that *students* who score between 40 *and* 60 percent would benefit *from* use of that textbook. *Students* scoring at this level are said to be performing at their instructional reading level. The textbook might be too difficult for those students scoring below 40 percent. It may be too easy for those scoring above 60 percent.

Appendix C: Annotated Bibliography

Benedict, Susan, and Lenore Carlisle, editors. 1992. *Beyond Words: Picture Books for Older Readers and Writers*. Portsmouth, NH: Heinemann. Bibliography and classroom methods for using picture books from first grade through high school, including a chapter on picture books for learning science and doing research.

Carlsen, G. 1980. *Books and the Teenage Reader,* second revised edition. New York: Harper and Row.

Christenbury, Leila, editor. 1995. *Books for You: An Annotated Booklist for Senior High Students,* 1995 Edition. Urbana, IL: NCTE.

Dreyer, S. S. 1981. *The Bookfinder: A Guide to Children's Literature about the Needs and Problems of Youth Aged 2–15,* second edition. Circle Pines, MN.: American Guidance Service.

Gillespie, J., and C. Gilbert. 1981. *Best Books for Children: Pre-school Through Middle Grades,* second edition. New York: R. R. Bowker Company.

Irvin, J., J. Lunstrum, C. Lynch-Brown, and M. Shepard. 1995. *Enhancing Social Studies Through Literacy Strategies.* Washington, D.C.: National Council for the Social Studies. Teaching strategies for reading and writing in social studies plus annotated lists of books and materials by U.S. historical eras.

Jensen, Julie M., and Nancy L. Roser, editors. 1993. *Adventuring with Books: A Booklist for Pre-K–Grade 6,* tenth edition. Urbana, IL: NCTE.

Junior High School Library Catalog, sixth edition. New York: H. W. Wilson.

Lipson, E. 1988. *The New York Times Parent's Guide to the Best Books for Children.* New York: Times Books.

McBride, William G., editor. 1990. *High Interest—Easy Reading: A Booklist for Junior and Senior High School Students,* sixth edition. Urbana, IL: NCTE.

Webb, C. Anne, editor. 1993. *Your Reading: A Booklist for Junior High and Middle School,* ninth edition. Urbana, IL: NCTE.

Wurth, Shirley, editor. 1992. *Books for You: A Booklist for Senior High Students,* eleventh edition. Urbana, IL: NCTE

CHAPTER SIX

Assessing Students' Reading Abilities, Needs, Attitudes, and Interests in the Content Classroom

Before teachers can make appropriate decisions about instruction, it is important for them to gather information about their students: their reading abilities and needs, their attitudes toward the subject, the background of information and experiences they bring to the subject, and their interest in it. All these student-centered factors play a role in instructional planning and have a significant influence on the outcomes of instruction. Just as text assessment and selection of materials discussed in the preceding chapter are ongoing concerns when teaching, student assessment should be a continuous and multifaceted part of the classroom environment for both instructional planning and assessing students' learning.

We don't mean to propose that teachers submit students to a constant barrage of tests; in fact, we believe entirely too much testing of all kinds goes on in schools today, taking up valuable time that could be used for instruction. We are thinking about assessment in a much broader sense. We suggest that content area teachers employ a wide variety of methods to gather data about their students' reading comprehension and learning: observation, checklists, surveys, tests, conferences, written responses, interviews, formal test results, content inventories, and other appropriate measures. The idea behind this is that the more the teacher knows about her students in relation to the subject area being taught, the better she can tailor instructional strategies to meet individual as well as group needs and adjust instruction throughout the course when assessment shows it is necessary.

There are basically three purposes for assessing students: (1) program evaluation, (2) student evaluation, and (3) instructional planning. Schools and districts assess reading to evaluate their reading programs and curricula. Test results
can be used to get an overall sense of how a school's or district's reading program is functioning across the grade levels or to determine the need for program
change. Schools and teachers also gather information about their students' reading abilities in order to provide the best instruction possible for each student,
often tailoring an appropriate reading program for individual students based on
test results plus other measures of student achievement.

Appropriate assessment measures help districts, schools, and teachers
develop classroom methods and materials that address the diverse needs of their
entire student population. This chapter will discuss the wide range of reading
assessment measures now used in schools, with the intent of helping content
area teachers (1) examine the role of standardized testing in school and society,
(2) understand and use appropriate assessment measures for various kinds of
instructional decision-making, and (3) develop a set of practical assessment tools
and strategies for classroom instruction.

Types of Assessment

For program evaluation, most schools and districts give some kind of group
standardized reading test, often mandated by the district or state, to evaluate the
effectiveness of their programs on a general level and compare the test results to
other schools and districts across the state or nation. These standardized tests are
formal assessment measures and will be discussed further in this chapter.

Standardized tests don't give teachers the more specific and content-
oriented information they need to work effectively with their students, both to
understand each individual's abilities in the subject and to plan instruction. In
addition, teachers benefit from data about students' attitudes about and experiences with their subject, factors impossible to cover in a general standardized
test. *Informal assessment,* often called *naturalistic assessment,* provides the information most useful to the classroom teacher. These assessment measures are the
day-to-day evaluations teachers use to monitor student learning. They are usually teacher-created—although many informal assessment tools are available
commercially—and range from daily observations to final exams. This chapter
will present several methods for the informal assessment of reading as it applies
to subject area classes. The intent is not to hold content area teachers accountable for diagnosing and teaching reading skills, but rather to offer methods and
materials for assessing students' reading abilities, habits, attitudes, and interests as
they relate specifically to the subject. Such assessment leads to informed classroom planning that can more effectively meet the needs of the wide range of
students found in most classes.

Formal versus informal assessment is just one of the dichotomies to consider when talking about assessment. Another way of categorizing assessment

measures is to think of them as either summative or formative. *Summative assessment* is the final evaluation that shows what a student has achieved: a grade in a course or a rating on a standardized test. Summative assessment sums up achievement; it is a final score. *Formative assessment,* on the other hand, is the teacher's assessment that provides students with information about what they are doing well and what to do next to improve. It also gives teachers useful data about a student's growth and comprehension of new material. Formative assessments include responses to drafts of papers, conferences, points for daily work, quizzes, checklists, and inventories. These should be the mainstay of classroom assessment because they are so rich in feedback to students, imply ongoing improvement, and provide teachers with data useful in planning for teaching.

Finally, we talk about norm-referenced and criterion-referenced tests. A *norm-referenced* test compares students' scores to the scores of a "norming group," which represents a typical sample of students for whom the test is designed. The scores of the norming group are used to create the standards against which all others who take the test are compared. *Criterion-referenced tests,* sometimes referred to as *mastery tests* because they show the student's mastery level in a particular area, do not compare students' scores with any other group; rather, they report how the student performed based on the criteria set by the test giver. For example, the test developer may decide that the criterion for passing in a given test is 80 percent; the student who meets this criterion by getting 80 percent or more correct on the test has passed. The student's performance on the test is not evaluated by comparing it to the scores of other students, but instead by judging how well she succeeded in relation to the level of performance deemed necessary according to the criterion set by the educator using the test. Which kind of test to use depends on its purpose. According to Farr and Carey (1986), norm-referenced tests are primarily useful for comparing students to a norm group in relation to the behaviors measured by the particular test, and criterion-referenced tests are useful for determining students' accomplishments or ability to succeed on certain specific curricular objectives (174).

The remainder of this chapter will discuss the uses and limitations of both formal and informal assessment and present several methods for gathering information about students as part of instructional planning in all subject areas. It will also cover authentic assessment and portfolios for continuous assessment of content area reading and learning.

Formal Assessment: Uses and Abuses of Standardized Reading Tests in Schools

Schools and districts typically administer some form of standardized reading test on a regular basis to evaluate their programs, yearly in some cases or on a defined three- or four-year cycle throughout K–12. The standardized test may also include sections on math, science, and other content areas. Test results can identify strengths and weaknesses in the instructional program to guide future curriculum planning. For instance, if students' scores are generally satisfactory in comprehension, but are markedly lower in the test sections on vocabulary, a school can plan to focus more attention on vocabulary development. Scores can be used as a rough screening device to identify students who need more specific diagnostic testing to show where their reading problems lie. Test scores are also used to compare students' performance to that of other students at the same grade level. These comparisons are often used for accountability purposes to help a school justify its funding, request additional funding, or highlight the need for special programs. These are reasonably legitimate uses for such testing; unfortunately, their application does not stop here.

The Destructive Politics of Testing

Standardized tests have increasingly become high-stakes tests in the United States, tied to basic or special state funding in some states, used for accreditation purposes, and even linked to criteria for a state-endorsed diploma. Scores are used to place students in special programs, to determine whether or not they can move on to the next grade, and to evaluate instructional programs, student progress, and teacher effectiveness. This puts ever-increasing pressure on schools and teachers to have their students perform better and better on these tests, in whatever way this can be achieved. Schools respond with such counterproductive behavior as teaching to the test instead of creating a curriculum based on students' needs, spending an inordinate amount of time training students for the test, and even tampering with the test results by throwing out low scores or filling in correct answers in spaces students leave blank.

Accompanying this is the heightened public visibility of test scores. In many states, local newspapers publish a yearly chart of the standardized test scores in all the surrounding school districts for public comparison, usually along with a similar chart of scores for one or more previous years to show growth or change over time. The general public is given these scores with little or no explanation of the features (and problems) of the test itself, what the scores actually mean, how to interpret them, or factors that influence the scores. These scores are mistakenly reported as sort of magical numbers indicating the success of each school district relative to the others in the area. The scores have a profound effect on property values: real estate brokers have been known to carry around test scores to show prospective home buyers who have school-age children.

Schools with high scores have little reason to fear this type of public ranking, but the effect on low-scoring schools can be extremely harmful, stigmatizing students and dampening staff, parent, and student expectations. An administrator at an inner-city school that was continuously ranked among the lowest in the district on the state's standardized tests had this to say:

> Test scores may be hazardous to a school district's image. No matter how well individual students perform, we're doomed when people compare our test results with other school districts. It has reached a point where there is almost

a community paranoia about it. These scores can reinforce a community's low image of itself (Russell 1986).

Addressing the fact that there is widespread public misunderstanding about the meaning of these test scores, the administrator goes on to describe the factors that influence scores in his district: rapid turnover of students, with many at the poverty level assigned to remedial classes. "The crucial thing is where you get kids and where you take them," he says. This success factor is not recognized when standardized test scores are posted for the public.

Standardized tests have been widely criticized for perpetuating the existing socioeconomic class system in American society by unfairly penalizing non-mainstream students and the poor, who regularly score lower on the tests than middle-class white students. The tests have been accused of bias in favor of the knowledge, values, and ways of knowing associated with white middle-class American society. The two college entrance exams most widely used in the United States, the Scholastic Aptitude Test (SAT) and the American College Test (ACT), consistently show a strong correlation between family income and score levels (Zemelman, Daniels, and Hyde 1993, 186).

Standardized test scores have also been misused to place students into remedial classes without any further analysis of the student's problems or attempt to understand the factors influencing the low test scores. Students from homes where English is the second language and those with limited English proficiency often fare poorly on standardized tests written in English, and may even score low enough to be placed in classes for the mentally retarded despite their normal intelligence. Reyes (1991) demonstrates the difference in writing style and competency of a Mexican student who has been in the United States just one year when he struggles to respond to a standard writing test prompt in English and then in his native tongue, where his true linguistic competency becomes evident. Reyes concludes by observing that

> . . . an ordinarily simple task in one's native language becomes a cognitively demanding chore in the second language when it exceeds the student's current skill. Teachers may not fully realize this, however, and conclude they are dealing with a student of low intellectual capacity. (80)

Standardized reading tests make similar cognitive demands on English as a Second Language (ESL) students; using their test scores for academic placement denies them equal educational opportunity and unfairly blocks young people from developing to their fullest potential.

Many educators today are highly critical of standardized tests, arguing that they should be abolished. At the present time, however, they seem to be a permanent fixture of the American educational system, which makes it imperative that teachers understand the tests in order to explain them to parents and students, and not misinterpret or misuse the tests themselves. To this end, the next section presents an overview of standardized testing, including a discussion of problems in their design, administration, and interpretation.

A Standardized Testing Primer for Teachers

Formal, standardized, norm-referenced tests are administered and scored in a uniform way no matter where, when, or to whom they are given; all forms of the test are designed to the same standard to ensure the same results no matter which version of the test is used. Hence the term "standardized" test. This standardization permits comparisons among and between the test takers. It does not imply that the tests are judged against a certain standard of performance. Scores can only indicate how students compare to the norming group; they don't indicate whether the norming group is doing well or poorly according to any external standard of performance (Baumann 1988). Standardized tests that are criterion-referenced share the same standardization qualities as norm-referenced tests (i.e., uniformity of administration, scoring, and alternate forms), but the results depend on the test's criteria for passing.

Standardized tests are commercially prepared by educators and experts in test design and piloted and revised thoroughly before the final version or versions are produced. For norm-referencing, the test is then given to a wide variety of students across the nation from different grade levels, geographic locations, ethnic backgrounds, and socioeconomic levels. Their scores are used to create the norms against which all students who subsequently take the test are compared. The teacher's manual for a well-constructed standardized test will contain information about the norming population. Examine these data to see how the norming group compares demographically to your own students.

Reliability and Validity in Testing

Reliability refers to how well a test will produce the same results over and over again. A reliable test is consistent and can be depended upon to get roughly the same scores with a student or a group if given again within the same time period. According to Baumann, "a [reliable] test must represent consistent performance of a test taker" (24). To examine the reliability of a test, look for the number of items that test the same feature. The more test items per feature, the more opportunities a student has to show what he knows or does not know rather than chance or guessing producing the result. The teacher's test manual should give information about the reliability of the test, expressed as a numerical coefficient. Most standardized reading tests have reliabilities of .85 to .96, the higher numbers indicating greater reliability (Schell 1981, 6).

Validity is the "truthfulness" of the test. It refers to whether or not the test measures what it is designed to measure; a valid test measures what it says it does and not other extraneous factors. For example, a test purporting to measure a student's writing ability through a series of multiple-choice questions about grammar and usage is of questionable validity; a test measuring writing ability with an actual writing sample has more validity. However, if the test maker wishes to measure a student's knowledge of grammar and usage facts, the multiple-choice test would have validity. Valid tests of students' reading comprehension measure the skills used in comprehension rather than such decoding skills as phonics knowledge. Baumann claims that "validity is the single most important characteristic of a test" (27). Examine the test items and format to evaluate the correlation between what is actually tested and what the test is designed to measure.

Interpreting Standardized Norm-Referenced Test Scores

Norm-referenced tests report scores in several different ways: raw scores, percentiles, stanines, and grade equivalents. Each provides different information. It is important to understand what these scores mean and the common pitfalls of each when interpreting and reporting test results.

Raw scores are the number of correct answers on the test; sometimes the raw score is corrected for a "guessing factor." These raw scores are then compared to the scores of the norming group to convert them into percentiles, stanines, and grade equivalents.

Percentiles report the percentage of scores that are equal to or below the score a student attains in the test. They indicate the relative standing of a student at a particular age or grade level compared to the norming population. For example, if a student receives a percentile score of 85 on a standardized test, that means the student scored as well or better than 85 percent of the students at the same age or grade level in the norming population (*not* the students who took the test at this particular time), while 15 percent scored better than she did. Because percentile scores are limited to one age or grade level, the percentiles a student receives on the various sections of a test can be compared to each other, giving a rough indication of the student's stronger and weaker areas. Therefore, if Susan scored in the 85th percentile on vocabulary but only on the 45th percentile in comprehension, this wide spread makes it fair to say that Susan is weaker in comprehension than in vocabulary. But a spread of just a few percentile points may not be significant. For the classroom teacher, the percentile score is probably the more useful of the several types of scores typically reported. The percentile score should not be confused with the percent right or wrong on a test: Susan's 85th percentile score does not mean that she got 85 percent right on the standardized test.

Stanine scores are raw scores that have been converted into a *sta*ndard *nine*-point scale (hence the term *sta-nine*), which means the distribution of raw scores on the test has been divided into nine equal sections. A stanine score of 5 puts the student right in the middle of the scale, indicating average performance; scores of 6 through 9 indicate increasingly higher performance; scores of 4 through 1 represent decreasing performance. Stanines are only gross measures of a student's abilities, but teachers can use them to see how a student scores relative to the average in the norming group.

Grade equivalent scores give information on how a student's performance compares to that of other students in the norming group at various grade levels, differentiating it from percentile scores, which compare performance at the same grade level. A grade equivalency score of 10.3 means the student has performed on the test at the same level as the average student in the norming population who is in the third month of the tenth grade. The score equivalents are created by giving the test to norming groups of students at several grade levels and then calculating the average score for each grade level. For example, if the average raw score for ninth-graders was 18, the average raw score for tenth-graders was 25, and the average raw score for eleventh-graders was 30, the norms for this test then become 18 for ninth-grade equivalency, 25 for tenth-grade equivalency, and 30 for eleventh-grade equivalency. Scores in between the exact grade equivalency (in the example, scores between 18 and 25 and those between 25 and 30) are distributed equally on the basis of a ten-month school year to get the month designation.

Problematic Issues in Standardized Testing

Standardized tests are easy to use, take up a minimum of time for teachers and administrators since they are group tests, can give schools a general sense of how their students compare to other groups of students, and may be useful as the first step in understanding students' reading performance. However, they must be used and interpreted cautiously. These tests have been criticized by educators for numerous problems that include those discussed below.

Test Design and Administration

1. *Reading tests based on an inappropriate model of reading.* Goodman (1973) faults standardized reading tests for their view of reading as a series of skills to be tested individually rather than a global, meaning-making activity based on language and thinking. He argues that "a major weakness of current reading tests is a failure to articulate views of the reading process and learning to read as a basis for building tests, sub-tests, and test items. . . . In the absence of a strong base in reading theory, current reading tests substitute sophisticated test theory" (22). In other words, these reading tests are not based on our current understanding of how readers use language to make meaning as they read, but are instead a series of subtests on isolated skills that distort the reading process, with test results calculated through sophisticated statistical maneuvering.

2. *Inappropriate norms.* Tests may use norming groups that are not representative of all students taking the test or that are inappropriate for a particular school or class. This makes test scores based on these norming groups questionable.

3. *Impact of small variations in raw score.* One or two answers, especially at the upper or lower ends of the scale, may make a difference of several months or even a full year in the grade equivalency score.

4. *Use of statistical devices to produce scores.* One example of this, interpolation— the process by which scores between two adjacent grade levels are distributed equally—has been criticized for its implication that reading growth occurs at a constant rate from month to month, an erroneous notion that makes little sense to those who teach students. Extrapolation—calculating

grade level equivalents without actually giving the exam to norming groups at all grade levels but instead using statistics to calculate what the scores might be—has been equally criticized for being an estimate instead of a true measure based on norming group performances at these various levels.

5. *Ambiguous, irrelevant, poorly written, or purposely hard questions.* Many times, more than one answer might be correct, and test-taking becomes a matter of second-guessing the test writers. Irrelevant questions based on minutiae or questions so poorly written that it's impossible to figure out the right answer create problems for students who believe there really is one right answer and blame themselves for missing it. Tests are designed so that everyone but the weakest students gets some items right, everyone but the very highest scoring students gets some items wrong, and the rest fall in between. This means that some items must be purposely too difficult for most students. Sometimes, however, according to Goodman, the reasons for the difficulty have more to do with ambiguity than with content. On the other hand, sometimes the question is based on common knowledge and so easy that the student doesn't even have to read the passage to answer it.

6. *Guessing.* The multiple-choice format of most standardized tests gives students one out of four or five chances to guess the right answer—a factor that can raise test scores despite a penalty for guessing. On most standardized tests, it is possible to achieve a grade level equivalency score through random guessing. Fry (1971) labeled this the "orangutan score," urging test makers not to consider valid any scores at or below what could be attained by the kind of pure guessing an orangutan could produce by pushing levers.

7. *Test administration.* "Standardized" administration of the test no matter where or when given is a fallacy, despite the carefully designed and explained directions in the teacher's manual. In truth, many factors influence test administration, from the temperature of the classroom to the attitude of the students, including the experience of the person administering the test. One of our first-year teachers in a large urban high school tells the following story about giving a standardized test:

> The staff hadn't been given any training in test administration, but a "seasoned" teacher was assigned to work with each teacher who had never given the test before. Mine never showed up. I frantically skimmed through the direction booklet that I had just picked up at the office along with the tests and answer sheets. Timing was a problem: some of the test sections were exactly three minutes or five minutes long and the classroom clock didn't have a second hand; neither did my wristwatch. As students took the shorter timed sections, I counted slowly "one thousand and one, one thousand and two. . . ." until I figured the few minutes were up. Who knows how long my students really had to take those short portions! The longer sections, twenty minutes to one hour, were easier because exact seconds didn't matter, but during these long sections,

the kids began to talk to each other, fidget, walk around the room. Since these weren't my own students, I just couldn't control them. Large chunks of the test time were chaotic, not the tense silence I remember from my own test-taking as a student. It was clear most of these students didn't care how they did on the test, and I wonder how this attitude affected their scores.

In his *Lives on the Boundary* (1989), Mike Rose describes similar behavior by students taking a standardized test in an East Los Angeles elementary school. Another teacher describes his students this way: "What got me was that a lot of the kids were just kind of fiddling around—it just didn't mean anything to them" (quoted in Zorn 1994, p. 39). Nonstandard conditions such as those described above and students who don't take the test seriously may affect more student scores than we realize.

Misinterpretation of Scores

8. *Test scores misused as diagnostic and placement measures.* The typical standardized reading test is a survey test built upon subcategories such as word recognition, vocabulary, and literal and inferential comprehension. Because survey tests cover many reading subskills, the score for an individual category may be based on a small number of test items, sometimes as few as two or three test questions, which may not give a fair indication of a student's ability in that area. Subcategory scores are combined to yield a general reading score for each student. Low scores on a standardized reading test can indicate that a student has a reading problem, but survey tests are not appropriate as diagnostic measures. Full understanding of a student's problems for appropriate placement and instruction requires more specific, in-depth diagnostic testing. For example, a trained reading specialist might administer an individual diagnostic reading test and also gather information from teachers about the student's reading behaviors in class, then use all the available data to plan an appropriate reading program for the student.

9. *Grade-level equivalency misunderstood.* Educators and parents misinterpret grade equivalency scores as an indicator of the student's instructional reading level, but a student with a tenth-grade equivalency score on a standardized test may not be capable of reading instructional material at the tenth-grade level. The grade equivalency score reports the student's test performance compared to other test-takers in the norming group at various grade levels; it is not meant to indicate at what level the student should be placed for appropriate instruction. This is a blatant misuse of the score.

    Grade equivalency scores have also been misinterpreted as a standard of performance that all students should reach in order to get "up to grade level." By definition this is impossible because these scores are themselves an average, which means some number of the norming group scored below and some scored above to determine the grade-level equivalency. (This occurs everywhere, of course, except in Lake Wobegon, where Garrison Keillor claims that "all the children are above average.") Norm-referenced test scores are calculated in such a way that roughly half the students will fall below and half above the 50th percentile. The grade equivalency score has been so frequently misinterpreted and misused by educators that in 1981 the International Reading Association passed a resolution urging test publishers "to eliminate grade equivalents from their tests" (Baumann 1988, 41).

Student Factors

10. *Knowledge.* Reading comprehension depends to a great extent on the reader's prior knowledge of the subject; for this reason, reading tests may actually be measuring the breadth of students' prior knowledge rather than reading ability. Students who think too hard and know too much may be penalized for reading more into a question than it demands and getting wrong answers for reasons that demonstrate excellent analytical thinking abilities. Finally, there may be a mismatch between a student's thinking, reasoning, and reading skills and the skills called for in the test.

11. *Personal factors.* Individual test scores are deeply dependent on such personal factors as the amount of sleep the student had the night before; whether or not the student ate breakfast; the student's present emotional level, ability to concentrate, and interest in the test material; and the relevancy of the test to the student's personal goals (e.g., the test score will be more important to a student who plans to go to college than to one who is waiting to turn sixteen and drop out). An individual's performance may vary widely from day to day, depending on all these factors. Whether or not the student thinks and works quickly is also a contributing feature in these timed tests. Some students are just not good takers of standardized tests; their true abilities are more apparent in everyday schoolwork and classroom tests.

12. *Diverse populations.* Students whose background differs widely from that of the test makers and the norming group, English as a Second Language students, and those with minimal English proficiency are penalized when subjected to standardized tests that are designed for the mainstream population of the United States. Scores of these students require careful interpretation and caution in their use.

13. *Test-taking skills.* How testwise are the students? This is a more critical factor than test-makers care to admit. Students who have learned some tricks of standardized test-taking—e.g., skipping difficult items or reading the questions first in order to enter the reading act with a purpose—fare better than those who have not.

All of these problems concerning standardized testing strongly suggest that educators take students' scores with the proverbial grain of salt. They may not give you the information you think you are getting; the scores may be too influenced by the problematic nature of standardized testing itself to give an accurate indication of your students' abilities.

For many of the reasons listed above, the scores for an individual are far less accurate than scores for a large group, in which many of the problems balance out. Thus the scores are more useful to school districts than to teachers. Despite these problems, students in most school districts are still required to undergo some type of formal testing of reading abilities throughout their years of schooling.

Informal Assessment of Students for Instructional Purposes

Standardized test scores can give teachers a general sense of a student's reading ability and of the span of reading levels in a given classroom. However, these scores are not a good indicator of a student's reading ability in a specific content area course. Test-taking draws on different skills than those required for course-work, and too many factors not addressed in the test may influence a student's reading performance in any given class.

One factor to consider is that the passages on a standardized reading test come from many different disciplines, not necessarily yours, and they may not make the same reading demands your field does. The test results report general reading skills spread out over many reading selections. In fact, if all the passages were from your discipline, the student might receive a very different score. A standardized test score cannot predict whether a student will have success with the new technical vocabulary of a first-year chemistry course or be an active reader and interpreter of poetry.

For another, a test-taker reads very differently from a student studying for a course. Test passages are short and have no context other than the test itself. They require the test-taker to shift fairly rapidly from the content, form, and style of one passage to the content, form, and style of the next under the constraints of time, possible test anxiety, and, eventually, fatigue. Also, the purpose for reading in a test is to find the right answers to test questions. In contrast, reading for a course is focused on one subject, guided by the teacher, usually self-initiated and self-timed, and surrounded by the context of the course. Its purpose is compre-hension and learning, a more meaningful activity for the reader.

The test questions and kind of thinking they demand may also differ from the work students usually do in class. Most standardized tests are multiple-choice tests; if assessment is based on essay questions, papers, or short answers, the standardized test scores will not yield information about students' abilities to perform on these tasks. Nor do they typically draw on students' abilities to syn-thesize information from several sources or work together with others on problem-solving, lab experiments, or projects.

As we have discussed in earlier chapters, other factors such as attitudes toward reading, interest in the subject area, and prior knowledge also influence a student's reading performance in a given class. These areas are not accounted for in standardized testing.

All this underscores two points: (1) Standardized test scores should not be used to label students, since any student may do much better or worse in your class than his or her test score indicates, and (2) teachers need additional information about their students' abilities to read and comprehend the texts used in their own classes. Standardized test scores just don't give teachers enough information to make intelligent instructional decisions.

Informal Reading Assessment Measures

In most secondary content area classes, teachers hand out one or two textbooks to a class with reading abilities that may range as widely as six or more grade levels. The range grows wider as students pass into the higher grades because the effect of reading difficulties takes its toll on poor readers while good readers continue to learn more easily and become even better readers over time. This means that in an average tenth-grade class some students may be reading at the fifth-grade level while others will be able to handle college-level material.

But reading ability is only one factor that will affect students' learning in your class. Most classrooms have an equally wide spectrum of multiple intelligences, interests, background knowledge, learning styles, and personal attitudes toward your subject, especially in recent years as the population of the United States has become increasingly diverse. For these reasons, it is important for teachers to gather data early in the school year or semester as an aid to planning instructional strategies that will engage all students in successful learning. We recommend using informal group assessment measures based on the classroom reading materials, accompanied by good record-keeping procedures. The next sections describe several data-gathering tools for assessing students' interests, attitudes, and reading abilities in subject area classes.

Assessing Students' Attitudes and Interests In Your Subject

The attitudes and interests students bring to your subject greatly influence their reading and learning in your class throughout the school year. One of the best ways to find out about your students' previous experiences with your subject is to have them write a subject-specific autobiography, an informal history of their past experiences with, and feelings about, your subject.

In *Writing to Learn Mathematics* (1992) Joan Countryman discusses the benefits of this assignment and gives numerous examples of student responses from her high school math classes. Here is one student's math autobiography:

> To start off I will tell you that math is not one of my most favorite subjects. I do not yet see how some of the things we learn will help us later on in life—for example $2x^2 + 7x + 3 = (x + 3)(2x + 1)$. I do not know whether or not my feelings will change, but for now this is how I feel. One of my most favorite things to do in math is area & perimeter. Last year we did the areas and perimeters of triangles, rectangles, squares, and squares with chunks taken out. One of my most unpopular things to do in math is working with the calculator. I found

it hard to understand and therefore found it difficult to do. I found working with the compasses boring. I really liked doing percentages & decimals and working with fractions (dividing). There is one last thing I think you should know, I really do not like tests! (22–23)

As you can see from this student's writing, an autobiography gives the teacher the following:

- information about attitudes ("math is not one of my most favorite subjects")
- insight into problems individual students have had with the subject (the student's struggles with a calculator)
- things they personally like about the subject (in this case several important math concepts and calculations)
- ways the teacher might engage the student more fully (for this student, it is showing how math applies to real-life situations)

The teacher learns a lot from these informal writings, but they also give students an opportunity to share their experiences and express their feelings. For many students it can be comforting to realize they are not alone in their anxiety, frustrations, and pleasures in a specific subject area. We ask our composition students to do writing autobiographies at the start of every writing class we teach and use the writings in class to explore what it is to write. Students are relieved to hear that other students also procrastinate until the night before a paper is due, struggle to get the words and ideas just right, get writer's block, need loud music or absolute silence to write, dislike writing, love having written.

Countryman says the math autobiography "invites students to see themselves as mathematicians" (23). We believe this can be true for any subject area. This assignment asks students to look back over their lives as if they were scientists, mathematicians, writers, historians, athletes, or literary scholars, and abstract that portion of their past for consideration. It makes a superb introduction to a class, one that gives the teacher insight into students' attitudes and experiences in their subject area and at the same time sets the tone for the class as a community of learners who all have past experiences to bring to the field.

We suggest keeping the directions for an autobiography simple, perhaps four or five questions like the following for students to address in a page or so of writing:

How do you feel about _____ ?

What kinds of experiences have you had with _____ in classes before this one?

What do you like best about _____ ?

What problems do you have with _____ ?

Is there anything else you'd like me to know about you and _____ ?

Group surveys, checklists, and informal interest inventories are another approach to finding out about how students relate to your field. Rakes and Smith (1986) describe three different kinds of content interest inventories:

1. an open-ended inventory in which students are asked to complete sentences about the subject using their own language
2. a more structured, directed response survey with a combination of items such as checklists or short written responses to questions
3. a format that calls for rank-ordering their preferences from a list of titles or topics in the subject to be studied.

The following gives an example of each type of attitude and interest survey.

Three Formats for Attitude and Interest Surveys: Sample Items

I. An Open-Ended Survey for General Science

1. In the past, my science courses have been _____
2. In science classes, I enjoy learning about _____
3. In science classes, I dislike learning about _____
4. The area of science that I know most about is _____
5. The area of science that I want to know more about is _____

II. A Directed Response Survey for English

1. Put a plus (+) beside the topics in English that you most enjoy studying. Put a minus (–) beside those topics you don't enjoy studying.

__ poetry   __ biography & autobiography   __ novels
__ plays   __ writing friendly & business letters   __ writing essays
__ short stories   __ writing short stories & poems   __ grammar
__ vocabulary   __ sentence combining   __ punctuation

2. Do you read at home for pleasure, choosing material not assigned at school?
   _____ yes   _____ no

3. What kinds of reading do you prefer at home or in school? Put a plus (+) beside the material you like to read and a minus (—) beside the material you don't like to read.

__ fictional novels   __ poems   __ plays
__ short stories   __ magazines   __ comics
__ autobiography & biog-   __ romance   __ adventure
   raphy   __ westerns   __ science fiction
__ factual books with   __ historical novels   __ sports
   information   __ true accounts of histori-
__ "how to" books   cal events
__ animal stories

4. My favorite author is _____

5. The book I have most enjoyed reading is _____

III. A Rank-Ordering Survey for American History

1. Rank-order the following school subjects. Put the number 1 beside your
    favorite school subject, 2 beside your next favorite subject, and so on
    down to your least favorite subject.

    __ art   __ foreign language   __ music
    __ biology   __ English   __ math
    __ physical education   __ social studies   __ home economics
    __ American history   __ American govern-   __ chemistry
    __ physics   ment   __ typing
                            __ industrial education

2. Which of the following historical periods are you most interested in learn-
    ing more about? Rank-order them, putting the number 1 beside the one
    you are most interested in, 2 beside the one you are next interested in, and
    so on down to the period you are least interested in studying.

                    __ Colonial Era
                    __ Revolutionary War
                    __ War of 1812
                    __ Civil War
                    __ Reconstruction
                    __ World War I
                    __ The Great Depression
                    __ World War II
                    __ Korean War
                    __ Vietnam
                    __ Present world events

Keep these surveys brief, not more than a page or two, and discuss their
responses with the whole class before collecting them for your own record-
keeping. Use them early in the semester to get an idea of how your students feel
toward your subject and how much they know about it. The open-ended survey illustrated in the example just shown is the easiest to create, but will be
more difficult to assess since students are free to give their own responses. The
other two surveys limit students' answers, which makes record-keeping faster
and easier, but they take more time to create. All three formats allow the teacher
to ask students about topics, materials, and activities for the course as an aid to
instructional planning.

Assessing Students' Strengths and Weaknesses as Readers in Your Content Area

Information about your students' reading abilities in relationship to the course text is vital for appropriate course planning. This differs from the text introduction activities described in the previous chapter, the treasure hunt and the text preview, because reading assessment calls for using the course textbook diagnostically, to help you determine the range and variety of reading abilities in the classroom. Two methods provide information about how well students can read their textbook: cloze procedure and the Content Area Reading Inventory (CARI).

The cloze procedure was discussed in some detail in the previous chapter as a tool for evaluating the match between text and student. However, the same cloze procedure described earlier can also provide information about a given student's ability to cope with your course text and the range of textbook-based, subject-based reading abilities in a class. For these reasons, the cloze is an exceptionally useful classroom assessment tool with a twofold purpose: in assessing the match between text and students, you are also able to gather data about students' reading abilities with your class text to help you in course planning. The cloze can be used in conjunction with the CARI, defined below, or teachers can opt to administer only a cloze test to get a more general picture of the reading abilities in their classes.

The CARI is a teacher-made group reading assessment tool based on the core classroom text. It measures students' performance reading subject material, yielding information about students' reading abilities and specific text-related comprehension strategies or difficulties individual students may have. The CARI differs from the text preview described earlier because its purpose is to assess students' ability to comprehend the text material as well as interact with its various features.

There is no standardized way to create a Content Area Reading Inventory. Most sources recommend that it contain the following three parts: use of text components and study aids, vocabulary knowledge and strategies, and comprehension. Here is an outline of the various items one might assess:

Part I. Text Components/Study Aids

Table of contents, index, glossary

Chapter and section introductions; summaries and review questions

Graphs, charts, tables, maps, pictures, or other meaningful graphics

Practice exercises, study questions, other textbook study aids

Knowledge of external aids: encyclopedias, atlases, library reference sources, and other pertinent materials

Part II. Vocabulary Knowledge and Strategies

Defining words

Inferring meaning from context

Finding and applying definitions from dictionary or glossary

Part III. Comprehension

Finding text-explicit information (literal meaning)

Finding text-implicit information (inferential meaning)

Understanding text structure

To design a CARI, follow the steps below, using the classroom text:

1. Construct a test with twenty to thirty questions spread about equally among the three parts. Write test questions that reflect the kinds of thinking you want students to do in your class and the test formats and other skills you typically expect students to use independently.
2. For Part I, decide which parts of the text and study aids you want to be sure students understand and can use on their own. Construct questions that will show students' grasp of these items, either multiple-choice questions for ease in scoring or literal questions to be answered. Students should use their textbooks to look up the answers for this part of the test.
3. For Part II, write questions that show students' skills with several facets of vocabulary use in your classes: definitions for key words, prefixes or suffixes common to your field, use of the glossary. You might ask a question about students' word-finding skills, e.g., "List three different ways you could find the definition of a word in the textbook that you don't know." This part of the test can be designed so that students do not need to use the textbook or it can be an open book section.
4. To test comprehension, Part III, choose a selection from the textbook three to five pages long from an early section of the text but one that students have not yet read. Design questions based on this selection that involve students in the kind of thinking you want them to do as they read and study. Include some literal, fact-based questions as well as those that call on inferential and associative thinking skills. (See Chapter Seven for a more thorough discussion of levels of questioning.) Directions for Part III should tell students to read through the entire selection at their normal reading rate and then answer the questions based on their reading.

The following is a sample CARI for American history:

Section I. Parts of the Text and Study Aids

This section of the Reading Inventory shows how familiar you are with the different parts of your textbook.

1. On what pages in the text can you find information on the Magna Carta? Where did you look to find these page numbers?
2. On what pages in the text can you find a chronological list of U.S. presidents? Who was president in 1846?
3. If you wanted to know what historical events took place in 1900, where are two places in the book where you could look for this information?
4. List the pages in the text that have an historical atlas of the U.S. Using the historical atlas, find information on immigration to the U.S. During what ten-year span did the U.S. have the largest number of new immigrants?
5. What kinds of study aids do you find at the beginning and end of each chapter to help you summarize, review, and learn the material in the chapter?
6. Examine the chart on p. 87. Which of the colonies were founded for reasons of religious freedom? What other reasons are given for the formation of the colonies?
7. What does the chart on p. 536 show about the average annual wages of workers during 1898–1920?

Part II. Vocabulary Aids and Strategies

This section of the Reading Inventory will show how well you can deal with new vocabulary as you read the text.

1. Why is a word in the middle of a paragraph sometimes highlighted in dark print?
2. On p. 89, find the word "selection" in dark print. Write a definition of this word, using information from the paragraph.
3. The section surveys at the end of each chapter tell you to identify certain terms. If you can't identify a term, where do you look for information?
4. Define the term "landmark" from the way it is used in the following selection: "The Nineteenth Amendment in 1920 gave women the right to vote in national elections. This right was a U.S. *landmark* in the struggle to win equality with men."
5. What is the purpose of the superscript ° when it accompanies a word in the text?

Part III. Comprehension

This section of the Reading Inventory deals with your ability to understand what you read in this history text.

Directions: Turn to page 599 and read Section Three, "The Great Depression shatters the prosperity of the 1920s." Then answer the following questions based on this reading.

1. How is Section Three organized? (Organization)
2. How did overproduction and overspeculation lead to the stock market crash of 1929? (Inferential)
3. List the causes of the Great Depression given by President Hoover and economists. (Literal)
4. How did the Hoover administration respond to the Great Depression? (Literal)
5. Describe the effect of the Great Depression on all classes of the American people. (Literal)
6. Why were the farmers hit hardest by the Depression? (Inferential)
7. Why do you think Roosevelt won the 1932 election? (Inferential)
8. What influence did the auto license tag on p. 604 have on the 1932 election? (Inferential)

Administer the CARI to the entire class over a two- or three-day period. You might give Parts I and II at one class session and then administer Part III on another day. Be sure students understand that the CARI results will be used for their benefit—to help you plan for instruction—not recorded as a class grade in a grade book, which would be unfair since the inventory doesn't test material and skills yet covered in the course.

Observe students as they take the inventory, noting who looks stressed, who can't seem to find the answers to the questions, who breezes through the inventory, and who just gives up, scribbling answers or not working at all. Recording these observations and comparing them to the CARI scores will give additional insight into each student's inventory results and reading abilities as well as into the text's "friendliness."

Since this is not a standardized test, we recommend that classroom teachers use the same criteria for acceptable performance and same grading scale normally used in their classes. Score and record each of the three parts separately in order to have information about each student's specific strengths or weaknesses in textbook knowledge, vocabulary, and reading comprehension.

You may also find it useful to analyze students' scores in a particular reading skill important to your teaching. For example, if you often require students to find the central idea in a reading selection, do an individual calculation for questions in the test asking students to find the main idea. What percentage of students in the class gave correct answers to these questions? If, in your estimation, the percentage is low, then a lesson on extracting the central idea from a reading assignment would be vital.

Once scores are calculated, go over the CARI with the class, explaining answers and listening to students discuss where and why they had problems with individual test questions. Mini-lessons on specific text features many students missed in Parts I and II can provide just the bit of information some students need to become more successful learners. Discussion of the reasons behind the correct answers to comprehension questions can lead students to a better understanding of the very comprehension strategies the questions were designed to assess.

Scores can also be used to indicate which students will need additional help in understanding course material and which may require reading materials written at a lower reading level than the course text. The opposite is true as well: scores will indicate which students would benefit from challenging special projects and outside readings.

Finally, these scores give the teacher a starting point for instructional planning since they indicate the range of reading abilities and textbook skills in the subject area of the class, information useful for day-to-day planning, for individualizing instruction, for selecting classroom materials, and for setting long-term goals.

As with any assessment measure, the CARI should be used along with other ongoing measures of student performance, not taken as a definitive number predicting a student's success or difficulty in your class. Problems with individual items, such as an inadvertently ambiguous question, may affect scores, as can the same personal factors that affect a student's performance on a standardized test on a given day. Teachers should consider a CARI as only one small part of their instructional assessment program and plan to adjust their original assessments based on further information as the term progresses.

Now that we have discussed methods for making early evaluations of students' reading and learning in content area classes, we will turn to the final section of this chapter, which deals with recent approaches to classroom assessment of students' continuous progress throughout the school year.

Ongoing Assessment of Reading and Learning in Subject Area Classes

Current assessment literature stresses the necessity for classroom assessment to be ongoing, flexible, and varied in order to be sensitive to the individual needs of all students—a substantially different approach from the traditional practice of basing classroom assessment on homework assignments, quizzes, final exams on units of study, and paper grades. The emphasis in today's schools on the process of learning has led to a parallel focus on assessing students' learning processes as well as the final products of that learning. This means including among your assessment measures such items as paper drafts, conference notes, and observations of students as they work with others or independently.

Along with this evaluation of process, teachers are encouraged to adopt a more flexible, open-ended attitude toward assessment, to look for students' accomplishments instead of their failures and reward students for growth. Teachers have traditionally been taught to diagnose problems, correct errors, take off points for incorrect answers—a negative approach that has served to inhibit students from taking risks and to limit opportunities for the trial-and-error strategies that so often lead to authentic learning. Flexible assessment values evidence of engagement, accepts the uneven growth patterns of typical learning, and is sensitive to what students do well.

Recent assessment approaches also advocate using a wide variety of measures instead of relying mainly on tests so that all students, no matter what their backgrounds or abilities, have an opportunity to demonstrate what they are learning and have learned.

In *Best Practice* (1993), Zemelman, Daniels, and Hyde note a "clear mandate" across subject areas for assessment practices that are:

- formative, not summative (a distinction described earlier in this chapter)
- descriptive or narrative, not scored and numerical
- student-centered, involving students in record-keeping and in evaluating their own work
- approached from several angles, including observation, conversation, products, and performances
- part of everyday instruction instead of separate from it

To their list, we would like to add the features described earlier. Effective assessment practices are also:

- ongoing, flexible, and varied
- focused on building from strengths rather than pointing out deficiencies
- sensitive to processes as well as products

These assessment practices are obviously more complex than designing and grading tests, but educators moving toward more student-centered, holistic teaching find previous assessment measures inadequate for evaluating what goes on in their classrooms. The multifaceted assessment processes currently advocated provide teachers with the many kinds of information they need about students for effective curriculum planning, and also give students feedback that will help them grow as learners.

Authentic Assessment

Authentic assessment practices are based on observing, collecting, and evaluating data from the ongoing daily activities that students engage in as they learn. Instead of relying on test scores, authentic assessment measures include open-ended data such as observation, teacher journal entries, and notes from teacher-student conferences. Assessment of students' work will include evidence of work in progress as well as the final products: drafts and peer response sheets for papers; observation notes, speculations, calculations, and drafts of lab reports; written discussions of methods used for math problems; response journals for literature; research logs and learning logs in all subject areas. Authentic assessment measures may also include reports and reflections on collaborative learning, checklists recording student progress in a particular area, records of dramatic presentations such as Readers' Theater, supplementary reading reports, student-created videos, and materials or presentations from all manner of projects. Finally, authentic assessment may include examples of a student's self-evaluation and reflections on his or her work and progress in the course.

In short, the material used to assess students' performance—both for grading and for instructional planning—is the authentic work they engage in and the products they produce in the day-by-day work of the class. These measures will vary from student to student and from one class to another, but they will all reflect the actual work involved in learning the subject rather than focusing solely on final or external summative measures such as tests. Assessment, then, is not an add-on to measure what students have already learned. It is instead a natural and continuous part of instruction.

Observation Revisited

Throughout this discussion of assessment, we have repeatedly mentioned observation as a noteworthy assessment strategy. Often called "naturalistic assessment," or even "kid watching," a favorite term of ours coined by Yetta Goodman (1978), teacher observation yields daily, ongoing, personal data about students as they progress through the course. It can be as simple as observing the class and making journal-type notes about individual students or as structured as filling out a carefully designed observation chart about multiple reading and learning behaviors. But in either case it implies a conscious effort on the teacher's part to observe students at work in the classroom and learn from this observation.

Naturalistic assessment may be the most valid and reliable of all assessment measures according to Cunningham (1982). Validity depends on the match between what the test is designed to measure and what it actually does measure. It would be hard to imagine a reading and learning test more valid than observing students' reading and learning behaviors in the classroom over time.

Reliability, as explained earlier in this chapter, is based on a test's ability to produce the same results when repeated. Cunningham notes that teacher observation is also based on repeated observation and analysis of what has been observed (14–16). For example, when a teacher says that John is struggling to read the course text, this judgment may be based on repeated classroom observations of John reading and rereading the material, asking others for the answers, frowning, squirming, or showing other behaviors indicating problems in comprehending. John may also indicate he has reading problems by poorly done homework, low grades on tests, or nonparticipation in class discussions.

For these reasons, observation combined with adequate record-keeping should be an ongoing part of a teacher's classroom assessment procedures.

Using Portfolios for Assessment

In recent years, student portfolios have become the method most recommended for effective, authentic assessment. The portfolio concept originates in the artist's portfolio: the collection a professional artist puts together to present work when applying for a job or graduate school, or to show to galleries and art dealers. Artists usually select pieces representative of their best work, ones that show the range and quality of their talent as well as pieces that reflect their unique artistic vision. Typically, portfolios also include the artists' reflective personal statement about their own work, explaining what they are trying to achieve through their art. In recent years, this concept of the artist's portfolio has entered the classroom at all educational levels from elementary school through college and in many subject areas as the most promising method for developing a rich and multifaceted picture of a student's total performance over time.

For many teachers, this portfolio concept is not new; some teachers have always required students to collect their work in folders. But the present class-room work with portfolio assessment moves beyond the simple collection of learning artifacts to include many of the features found in the artist's carefully crafted portfolio collection. What makes a portfolio a portfolio and not just a folder of student work is the sense of artistic craftsmanship, purpose, organized selection and presentation, and self-reflection. The following working definition of classroom portfolios formulated by educators from the Northwest Evaluation Association illustrates these portfolio features:

> A portfolio is a purposeful collection of student work that exhibits the stu-dent's efforts, progress, and achievements in one or more areas. The collection must include student participation in selecting contents, the criteria for selec-tion, the criteria for judging merit, and evidence of student self-reflection. (Paulson, Paulson, and Meyer 1991)

The writing classroom may seem like the most logical place for portfolio assessment since so much of what goes into a portfolio is writing (and this approach has been widely accepted in writing programs), but this method also offers a variety of benefits for subject area teachers. At least two kinds of port-folios can be used in subject area classes:

- the *inclusive portfolio,* containing either the majority of the student's work or representative samples, which are sorted, organized, analyzed, and presented as representing the student's total performance in the course and growth over time.
- the *showcase portfolio,* which is prepared by selecting only those artifacts that represent the student's best work or document certain specific features or abilities. For example, in a math class, it might include samples of various types of problem-solving plus written descriptions of the processes used for each. In a writing class the showcase portfolio might include one overall best piece plus an argumentative paper, a personal experience paper, and a poem.

The type of portfolio used depends on its purpose. If a teacher wants a "thick description" of students' processes and progress over time, the inclusive portfolio will provide this information. The problem here eventually becomes the sheer volume of materials collected in the portfolio. The showcase portfo-lio, focusing on specific features and containing only "best" or most represen-tative examples, offers a way for teachers to assess learning by examining only selected pieces. Some states, notably Kentucky, now require a showcase writing portfolio for state-mandated writing assessment at grades four, seven, and ten.

Portfolios should contain examples of students' final products of all types, ranging from homemade videos to written reports. They should also contain material showing the thinking processes that went into these final products: journals and process descriptions, rough drafts, and response notes. Most importantly, they should include students' self-evaluations and final reflections on individual pieces and the portfolio as a whole. We ask students to introduce their portfolios with either a letter to the teacher or a formal introduction to their work, and we require a final reflection or summary in which students review the contents of their portfolio and discuss what they learned from this process.

Stenmark (1989) suggests the following kinds of student-produced work for portfolios in a math class:

- written descriptions of the results of practical or mathematical investigations
- pictures and dictated reports from younger students
- extended analyses of problem situations and investigations
- descriptions and diagrams of problem-solving processes
- statistical studies and graphic representations
- reports of investigations of major mathematical ideas such as the relationship between functions, coordinate graphs, arithmetic, algebra, and geometry
- responses to open-ended questions or homework problems
- group reports and photographs of student projects
- copies of awards or prizes
- video, audio, and computer-generated examples of student work
- other material based on project ideas developed with colleagues

Stan Pesick (1996), a high school history teacher who wants his students to learn to think historically, uses a showcase history portfolio instead of a final exam. Students compile a portfolio with the following writings selected from the term's work, plus a letter to the principal reflecting on their selections and their work during the term viewed in the context of a series of quotes by historians:

1. a thoughtful reaction to an individual or event that caught your attention, explaining why you would like to study this subject further.
2. one quote that you selected and wrote about that holds particular meaning and interest for you. Include the quote and your comments.
3. your best piece of writing on a particular picture or painting.
4. your choice of a piece of your writing on an issue that best illustrates your work as a historian as it is described in one of the quotes [by historians].

From these examples, you can see the breadth of authentic assessment materials that could be included in a student's portfolio to document learning. See the following list for more examples of the kinds of materials that might be included in a portfolio for any content area course that requires a lot of reading and writing.

Some Possible Elements for Reading and Writing Portfolios

- Projects, surveys, reports, and units from reading and writing
- Favorite poems, songs, letters, and comments [from course material]
- Interesting thoughts to remember [about topics studied in subject area]
- Finished samples that illustrate wide writing:
  —persuasion
  —poetry
  —stories
  —letters
  —information
- Examples of writing across the curriculum:
  —reports
  —journals
  —literature [and other subject matter] logs
- Literature [or other subject matter] extensions:
  —scripts for drama
  —written forms
  —charts
  —murals
  —visual arts
  —webs
  —time lines
- Student record of books read and attempted
- Audio tape of reading
- Writing responses to literary components:
  —plot
  —point of view
  —links to life
  —literary links and criticism
  —setting
  —character development
  —theme
- Writing that illustrates critical thinking about readings
- Notes from individual reading and writing conferences
- Writing that illustrates evidence of topic generation
- Items that are evidence of development of style:
  —organization
  —sense of audience
  —clarity
  —voice
  —choice of words
- Writing that shows growth in usage of traits:
  —growing ability in self-correction, punctuation, spelling, grammar, appropriate form, and legibility

- Samples in which ideas are modified from first draft to final product
- Unedited first draft
- Revised first draft
- Evidence of effort:
  —improvement noted on pieces
  —completed assignments
  —personal involvement noted
- Self-evaluations [and other self-reflective writing about students' work in the course]

In our experience, students are rarely asked to look back over their learning in a course and write about it. This act of metacognition is a primary benefit of the portfolio process. Students can begin to see themselves as developing learners in the field and can chart their own progress in the class. Selecting which materials to include and considering why they were chosen facilitates self-evaluation and also gives students some control over their own assessment. The review and reflection inherent in organizing a portfolio makes students active participants in the assessment process instead of passive recipients of the teacher's evaluation.

For the teacher, a portfolio collection gives insights into students' thinking and learning processes that could not easily be obtained in other ways. Change and growth over time become easier to see, too, when the materials are all there for analysis instead of relying on sometimes faulty memories and a series of numbers in a grade book. Discussions with students, administrators, and parents become more fruitful when the portfolio materials can be used for documentation. But perhaps the most important benefit of portfolios for teachers is what they can learn about their own instruction from examining a classroom of student portfolios at the end of the term or school year.

For all of the reasons discussed above, we encourage teachers to consider portfolios as a way of assessing student learning on a continuing basis. Teachers who wish to learn more about these newer assessment methods and the use of portfolios in content area classes will find a list of resources at the end of this chapter.

Portfolios Outside the Content Area Classroom

Increasingly, students are being asked to include a piece of content area writing for portfolios used to assess literacy for many different purposes. Some states, among them Kentucky, require a portfolio for statewide writing assessment that includes at least one piece of writing from a content area other than English. In Michigan, a newly instituted state writing assessment requires students to bring two pieces of classroom writing to the exam, one of which must be from a class other than English. Presently, the writings students bring with them to the exam are not assessed but are used for writing a reflection on their own writing processes; however, future plans are for these pieces to be assessed also.

Another way in which portfolios are affecting all subject area classes is the cumulative writing portfolio many schools are now requiring for all their students in order to assess literacy growth over time. These usually require writing samples from content areas other than English. In some schools and districts these pieces are collected yearly to add to each student's cumulative folder and stored in a central place until they are returned to students at graduation. They may be examined informally by teachers and administrators but are not linked to a formal evaluation process.

Other schools are using portfolio assessment on an annual or semiannual basis to evaluate the effectiveness of their writing program, monitor students' growth as writers, and encourage teachers in all subjects to use writing in their courses. Typically, students submit a portfolio of selected pieces from English and other content areas, which is then assessed by a group of teachers in the school or district who work together to create the criteria used for assessment.

A final way in which portfolios are being used is to determine placement in university freshman composition courses; the portfolio is replacing the traditional fifty-minute impromptu writing exam. The University of Michigan in Ann Arbor requires a portfolio containing a paper written in a subject area other than English (DeGroat 1994), while Miami University of Ohio asks students to submit a portfolio with one explanatory, exploratory, or persuasive essay that "may have been begun in a high school course other than English" (Black 1992).

The recent explosion of portfolio use, both for authentic assessment of learning in classrooms and for writing assessment in a variety of contexts, is part of the larger shift in education toward student-centered approaches that value the processes of learning and growth over time. For this reason, and because teachers in all content areas are often required to help students prepare pieces for their portfolios, it becomes increasingly important for teachers to understand how portfolios are assembled and evaluated in order to guide their students and become informed portfolio users in their own classrooms.

Summary

Assessment of students' reading and learning should be an ongoing and multifaceted aspect of every content area classroom as an aid to effective instructional planning and as a means of helping students evaluate their strengths and weaknesses in specific content areas. In this chapter we presented information about two broad categories of assessment: formal, standardized tests most useful for school districts in gathering data about student performance as a group; and informal assessment measures that can yield valuable information for the classroom teacher. Although we do not advocate heavy emphasis on standardized testing in the schools and find it of minimal value to the classroom teacher, we understand the pressures put on teachers to have their students perform well on these tests. With that purpose in mind, this chapter included basic information about standardized testing.

Informal assessment measures, the mainstay of the classroom teacher, should start early in the term or school year as teachers gather subject-specific data about students' attitudes, interests, prior experiences, knowledge and abilities. Attitude and interest surveys, autobiographical writings, the Content Area Reading Inventory, and cloze procedure all yield relevant information. Finally, the use of authentic assessment approaches, naturalistic observation, and portfolios is recommended for documenting and assessing students' performance and growth throughout the school year.

We find the recent approaches to assessment and grading described in this chapter promising alternatives to more traditional assessment methods that tend to penalize nonmainstream students, focus on what students can't do rather than on what they can, and rely so heavily on competitive grading. These recommended assessment practices offer positive, student-centered methods that promote learning and address the diversity of needs and abilities found in every classroom.

Additional Resources for Recent Approaches to Assessment

Belanoff, Pat, and Marcia Dickson, editors. 1991. *Portfolios: Process and Product*. Portsmouth, NH: Boynton/Cook.

Claggett, Fran. 1996. *A Measure of Success: From Assignment to Assessment in English Language Arts*. Portsmouth, NH: Boynton/Cook–Heinemann.

Educational Leadership 46 (7): focus issue on assessment.

Goodman, Ken, Yetta Goodman, and Wendy Hood, editors. 1989. *The Whole Language Evaluation Book*. Portsmouth, NH: Heinemann.

Graves, Donald, and Bonnie Sunstein, editors. 1992. *Portfolio Portraits*. Portsmouth, NH: Heinemann.

Harp, Bill, editor. 1991. *Assessment and Evaluation in Whole Language Programs*. Norwood, MA: Christopher-Gordon Publishers.

Jagger, Angela, and Trika Smith-Burke. 1985. *Observing the Language Learner*. Newark, DE: International Reading Association.

Meinback, Anita, Liz Rothlein, and Anthony Fredericks. 1995. *The Complete Guide to Thematic Units: Creating the Integrated Curriculum*, Chapter Three, pp. 63–84. Norwood, MA: Christopher-Gordon Publishers.

Phi Delta Kappan 70 (9): focus on assessment.

Routman, Regie. 1991. *Invitations: Changing as Teachers and Learners, K–12*. Portsmouth, NH: Heinemann.

Social Education 56 (February 1992): student assessment in social studies.

Valencia, Sheila, Elfrieda Heibert, and Peter Afflerback, editors. 1994. *Authentic Reading Assessment: Practices and Possibilities*. Newark, DE: International Reading Association.

CHAPTER SEVEN

Principles of Comprehension and Learning: Processes That Enable Divergent Readings in the Text

Introduction

As we discussed in Chapter Three, the act of reading necessitates a dynamic relationship between the reader and the text in which the reader makes every attempt to understand the text—that is, to make meaning out of it. In this process, the reader brings a prediction to the printed page, and the text then confirms or resists the reader's expectations. Out of this encounter, the reader shapes a "third text" by negotiating the differences between individual response and the multiplicity of connections in the text. Transactions such as these are complicated by the variety of texts that readers may encounter and the wide assortment of uses that readers make of the material. Possible responses to a given text are therefore so varied and numerous that attempts by the teacher to regulate them would be impossible and even undesirable. Many of us have experienced debates in English class where students and teacher have hotly discussed the significance of a passage or the meaning of a novel because we have read it from different perspectives. Teachers in the other content areas are surprised to discover, however, that their students also produce variant readings of a science text or a history text. Math teachers, for example, report a wide range of responses when students explain in their learning logs or journals what they read and how they understood the text. Even a reading as cut and dried as direction for factoring demonstrates how that "third text" occurs in the natural process of reading.

In this chapter, we argue that teachers can accommodate and nurture the wide assortment of perspectives and talents that they find in the classroom through an interactive model of teaching. In this model, the teacher provides the context for content area learning, which the learner in turn grasps on his or her own terms. To enable effective interactive instruction, we propose processes based on basic principles of text comprehension that encourage a student-centered classroom. Teacher guidance for learning begins with language immersion, critical thinking, problem-posing, and metacognition. Based on the whole language philosophy discussed earlier, these processes emphasize heavily the use of language to help students read their textbook assignments at their own level, formulate their own questions and hypotheses, and construct viable answers. We also examine the roles of the aesthetic response to reading. These principles of comprehension, which are extensions of critical thinking, complete the theoretical foundations that will inform Chapter Eight, on lesson and unit plan design.

Diversity and Its Role in Text Comprehension

What contributes to divergence in reading? We have indicated in earlier chapters that cultural, historical, social, ethnic, and religious differences among students shape them as readers and influence their understanding of the content. Students enter our classes from a wide variety of cultural backgrounds with distinctive linguistic patterns and ethnic traditions. Moreover, they bring with them a variety of school experiences. But even in seemingly homogeneous classrooms like those in small rural schools, teachers observe widely disparate personalities—differences in character traits, family background, economic standing in the community, and individual talents—that contribute to multiple points of view. Given the multitudinous combinations and permutations of human attitude and behavior, it is no wonder that one reader's reading is always somewhat different from another's: responses will vary as long as individuals perceive the world in unique ways. Of the myriad factors that contribute to diversity, ethnic and economic discontinuity are of the greatest concern to educators because they too often serve as predictors for school alienation and contribute to the drop-out rate. Class and racial discrimination in school lead to low school performance and, not surprisingly, account for resistance by marginalized students.

Howard Gardner's Multiple Intelligences

One more factor contributing to significant differences among students should be discussed here: the complex assortments of intelligence and talents. Unfortunately, this subject is generally taboo in teacher education courses because IQ and native talents as points of reference can potentially cause destructive labelling and other abuses. Howard Gardner, author of *The Unschooled Mind: How Children Think and How Schools Should Teach* (1991), has found a constructive approach to this issue.

Gardner addresses the potential of human variety in the classroom by identifying what he calls "multiple intelligences." By "intelligence" he means "the ability to solve problems, or to create products, that are valued within one or more cultural settings—a definition that says nothing about either the sources of these abilities or the proper means of 'testing' them" (x). Note that Gardner is not speaking in terms of ethnic groups or cultural perspectives, but of multiple competencies that can manifest themselves in multifarious ways in the school setting. Like other educational philosophers, he is concerned with diversity, but he defines human variety solely in terms of talents or "frames of mind" apart from culture or class or ethnic history. His list of intelligences includes linguistics, music, logical-mathematic ability, spatial intelligence, bodily-kinesthetic skill, and talent in personal relations. He suggests that if teachers could present content through a variety of entry points, they would help to make the material available to a wider range of individuals who will use the information differently. Multiple entries not only recognize differences among learners, but they also demonstrate that concepts can be grasped through more than one perspective. Gardner catalogues five different approaches among others that teachers might take to their subject matter:

- the narrational entry point that presents concepts through story or narrative
- the logical-quantitative entry point that calls on numerical considerations or deductive reason to explore content
- a foundational entry point that explores fundamental questions like pondering seminal words (e.g. "democracy" or "evolution vs. revolution")
- the aesthetic approach that takes an artistic perspective
- the experiential approach that deals more directly with materials using hands-on projects (244–248)

Gardner also promotes collaborative learning and a project-centered environment. At the same time, he advocates a rigorous approach to subject matter by attacking stereotype and oversimplification in the content areas. He believes that educators should challenge students to confront misconception and bias especially by closing the gap between theory and practice.

Although it is unlikely that teachers can incorporate multiple approaches into every set of lesson plans, Gardner's central point is one worth our attention: we need to be cognizant of different learning styles and plan our teaching to maximize their potentials. In that sense, multiple intelligences is one more way to consider teaching for diversity.

Addressing Diversity in the Classroom Through Inclusion

What we are finding as educators is that it is not possible or even advantageous to force uniform classroom behavior on our students through a teacher-centered curriculum because the diverse responses we observe—to reading, for example—are inevitable and the mix of viewpoints is beneficial. Because a wide variety of individual response represents in some way a microcosm of heterogeneous behaviors in the community at large, class discussions can raise awareness of perspectives that reflect the multifarious world beyond the classroom walls.

Instead of a lock-step curriculum, which has traditionally alienated marginal populations and has contributed to the drop-out rate, we urge educators to take into account culturally conditioned learning styles, multiple intelligences, and other diverse traits particular to human behavior. Rather than gloss over differences or pretend they are not significant to a core curriculum, schools should consciously design curricula that allow for differences in learning styles and language usage and encourage individuals to join the community of learning. To take a proactive attitude toward incorporating student contributions in the curriculum, teachers will have to go beyond a tokenism that defines the norm in terms of the dominant culture and all others as additives. Examples of this are our well-intentioned attempts to teach children about other cultures with a bulletin board, a multicultural center in the class, or the cross-cultural holiday celebration. The "tourist" approach reinforces ethnocentricism and continues to deny students of diverse backgrounds full membership in the dominant culture.

Accommodating individual differences should not result in accepting lower standards for learning or sanctioning poor discipline in the classroom, nor does it call for upending the hierarchy of teacher and student. Rather, it is a process of opening up new ideas and concepts, a process that is often demanding of both student and teacher, because the instruction will often follow in the direction of the class's line of inquiry. We also suggest plenty of lessons that offer opportunities for critical thinking, exploration, and independent learning through problem-solving, as well as varied activities that create a climate for individual pursuits.

The Transactional Model and the Role of Language in Text Comprehension

Using the transactional model of teaching we propose that control over the subject matter be shared between teacher and student, a process in which teachers guide students toward independent learning and thinking through language immersion. The founding principle of such a program assumes that thinking and inquiry require intensive use of language and active problem posing. The concept behind natural language activities is that students internalize the subject matter through risk-free (i.e., without being graded at the exploratory level) opportunities to open up key concepts on their own terms. Learners clarify information by asking their own questions, finding their own answers, and translating knowledge into their own words. Students construct knowledge for themselves, transforming what they have heard or read to fit their own schemata; in turn, they may contribute their own insights to the community of learning. Collaborative learning, group work, interactive strategies, and hands-on interest centers shape much of the classroom structure. To foster a classroom of reciprocal teaching and learning we suggest the following tenets:

- emphasis on challenging the facts and setting problems based on those facts
- conscious integration of language use and development into all curricular content, through tasks that focus on meaningful exploration of the subject matter
- focus on developing higher-level cognitive skills rather than factual recall
- genuine dialogue between student and teacher on all levels using written and oral language
- encouragement of student–student talk
- encouragement of meaning-making language use by students rather than an emphasis on correctness of surface forms

In short, we are advocating methods that develop a stronger sense of self and inner direction, and we believe that developing an understanding of how to ask meaningful questions and a strong emphasis on reading, writing, and social interaction are the best means to those ends. Content may be introduced by the text and the reading of the text may be guided by the teacher, but the final understanding of the content must be achieved through the student's reflective experience; that is, in the reconsideration and questioning of that experience through the use of language.

Vocabulary Building and Its Role in Text Comprehension

Because language is what mediates between the students' thoughts and the learning community, most educators consider word knowledge crucial to effective reading comprehension and communication. Certainly the extent of our vocabulary reflects much about our reading habits—the kinds of materials we read, their content and depth—as well as the amount of reading we do. And a good case could be made that the broader our students' vocabulary, the more comfortably they read across the curriculum.

Standard classroom procedure for building vocabulary has either advocated looking up lists of words in the dictionary and putting them into sentences, or memorizing words and their definitions for a quiz. Some English classes teach ten words a week regardless of the class's other activities. Although these methods have been effective for learning some new vocabulary, they account for relatively few words compared to the thousands of words learned in daily activity. To construct an effective method for teaching new vocabulary, we need only think about where we learned most of our words. Linguists speculate that the average adult increases his or her vocabulary by a third after leaving school. This estimate is credible if we think about the new words that we have suddenly begun to use in the wake of computer technology. Since the advent of the personal computer, for example, most Americans have started using words like "input," "fax," "software," and "interface" without taking home a single list of definitions to memorize. Recognizing that we learn most of our vocabulary in context lends credence to the natural process of acquiring new vocabulary through whole language activity, particularly immersion in meaningful activity.

Ignoring the traditional method of memorizing lists of strange words and their definitions, many content area teachers quite successfully introduce unfamiliar words through activities that emphasize using new vocabulary in the context of explaining new ideas or using them in exploratory exercises. Information about the substance of the course not only encourages interest in the material, but builds a repertoire of word meanings, and an increased vocabulary furthers an interest in the content. Actually, very little of the new vocabulary has to be taught directly because students want to use the most useful words they can collect to connect with their world, in and out of school. They readily adopt the vocabulary they need to know to function in class. If they are given a purpose for the new language and recognize its relevance, they respond by quickly reaching out for the most useful tools, including vocabulary. If a student is measuring the density of concentrates in chemistry class, he will wrestle with problems using words like "mole" (an arbitrary measurement) and "molar" until he makes sense of his experiment and the concepts behind his vocabulary. Especially when asked to write and speak about his solutions, he naturally absorbs and digests both the concepts and the language. He remembers the concepts because of the new words he has digested, and he learns the vocabulary because he has employed the language of the discipline to explain the concepts to himself. In this way, the student works from making meaning out of a whole idea to a refinement of its parts. Once students have adopted the vocabulary for their own use, they learn it for life because there is an inseparable relationship between the word and its social and conceptual context, between the word and the behavior that required it.

The potential that language has for making personal connection is precisely what makes language immersion an effective method for teaching vocabulary. Words have the power to express our thoughts and manipulate our ideas. Schema theory tells us that words serve as labels for a cluster of concepts that we attach to the concrete particulars of our outer lives and the abstracts of our inner lives. The exciting feature of this mental filing system is its flexibility. We may establish categories by initially assigning distinctive features to each grouping and hold the members of the category in temporary assignment until they are joined by others or manipulated to a different grouping. Then the categories are likely to shift. The flexibility of language allows ongoing shifts of meaning and association. Words may shift slightly with each new social and cognitive context. In this sense, language is a somewhat private system operating through internalized concepts that are linked in our minds in ways that are unique to each of us. The word "run," for example, might simultaneously be stored in our memory as (1) a jogging competition, (2) a series of printing jobs, (3) a hole in nylon stockings, or (4) a political campaign. Not only can the headings adjust to new situations, but the subordinate terms in each category can shift as well. Under the label "run" we may list all the candidates of a certain political campaign—and amend this list at any time—or we might restrict the category to include only those who have formally announced. Categories and connections for a given vocabulary inventory are specific to the individual, dependent on personal experience, cultural assumptions, and reading history.

Thus, conceptualizing with language is an ongoing process of grouping ideas, experiences, and objects, and then regrouping them with each new addition of information. One might even argue that learning takes place only when there is a change in the categorical list or in its properties. Students with a wide exposure to people, places, and events and students who read broadly will inevitably develop a richer vocabulary because they have at their command more labels and a denser network of relationships. Not only do they have more words to manipulate, but they can also be more flexible in their word associations. The result is that the more students know about, the more new vocabulary they can adopt, and vice versa. Immersion in meaningful activity that uses language allows them to exercise their new vocabulary and test the ways in which they can use those class relations and set new criterial features for each cluster. Increase in a student's vocabulary awakens her to the ideas of others.

List-Group-Label

One reading strategy that can encourage the process of classification and help students realize new concepts when they discover new relationships is *List-Group-Label* (see Taba 1967). In this strategy, the teacher selects a few key words, all of which point to an important concept, for students to brainstorm. A list of words is constructed from their responses until it contains about twenty-five items. For an example, students might list all the characters of a novel or all the features of a living organism. Then they are asked to group the words that have something in common. They need at least three words for each category. They can use the teacher's original word list, selecting a term more than once, and they can add words if they need them to form a minimal grouping. They must label each category with a heading that accounts for most of the items. In the case of the novel, students might use labels such as "antagonists," "protagonists," and "static characters." In the case of the living organism, they might use categories such as "locomotion," "respiration," and "reproduction."

Students then write their groupings on the board stating how they have formed their categories. The teacher can reinforce the idea of multiple categories by asking for and praising alternative ways to group the words, and she should take some time to investigate the words that defy categorization. One final step is also important: students should take the time to write out an overview of the principles they used for setting their categories. List-Group-Label is a particularly good follow-up exercise to reading about a well-explored topic because it allows both a review of the key vocabulary and an opportunity to assess the students' comprehension of the topic at the essential core of its language.

Naming things and enumerating their parts—the process of classification—is one of the most valuable functions of the intellect. Other cognitive functions exist as well, such as oppositional relationships (such as compare/contrast) and metaphorical relationships (such as similes, metaphors, and analogies). Working comfortably with relationships in which one object may have an affect on another—such as cause-and-effect or comparative relationships—is important to critical thinking. We should also include the ability to address our own thoughts metacognitively and the emotive use of language that enables self-

expression. Metacognition uses language to examine our own thinking processes ("I can solve that problem if I first understand . . .") and makes manifest
the workings of our knowledge or feelings ("The reason I believe the music is
unusual is that . . ."). The point here is the importance of consciously examining one's own thought processes. Analogy, comparison and contrast, cause and
effect, and metacognition are only a few of the ways of knowing that we call
"critical thinking," a term that will be discussed at greater length in the
next section.

Critical Thinking and Its Role in Text Comprehension

While reading the textbook's new chapter, students ideally find themselves in
situations where they become increasingly engaged in thinking and reasoning
and meaning-making of their own and thereby discover how to think deeply
about the material from their own perspective. Unfortunately, this ideal is rarer
than we would like to admit. To encourage students to reach beyond the
single-answer approach to education, our lesson plans should include strategies
that prod students into taking a critical stance toward the subject matter. Activities that promote questioning and decision-making are usually called a "higher-
order literacy" or "critical reading/thinking." Too often, "critical thinking" has
come to mean whatever educators want it to mean. Often it is used to lend
legitimacy to a curriculum without an earnest effort to incorporate valid critical-
thinking activities. We believe that critical-thinking exercises require problem-
solving and/or decision-making in one form or another. The goal of critical
thinking is the students' awareness of their own world and a conscious critical
understanding of the problems that need solving. The goal is critical thinking
and action through problem-posing dialogue.

　　Problem-solving skills begin with reading and research. At the beginning
comes simple comprehension of the text. One example of a comprehension
exercise is a simple summary that helps students to see the whole picture in a
chapter. To write a good summary, students must select only the main points
and employ language that reflects the emphasis and intent of the original material. All of these steps require decision-making and authorial judgment. Other
examples of critical thinking may be found in math "story problems" and in
science classes where students must apply the principles of science to "real-life"
or theoretical situations.

Benjamin Bloom's Taxonomy as a Basis to Critical Thinking

Critical thinking is often identified with Benjamin Bloom's taxonomy of educational objectives (1956), in which he lists six levels of thinking beginning with
the one that is intellectually least demanding of the student and ending with a

level of critical thinking that is most difficult for students to carry out. The taxonomy is useful for laying out a full range of questions or for providing a checklist for teachers who want to make certain they cover a range of activities that challenge student thinking. Tasks at every level of critical thinking find a rightful place in the classroom. Starting from the least difficult end of the taxonomy, Bloom's objectives for cognition are as follows:

1. *Knowledge:* This probes the specifics of any reading and those that are explicitly stated in the text. Here are definitions, facts, symbols, dates, principles, theorems, stated sequences, classification schemes, etc.
2. *Comprehension:* This builds on the literal message of the text. In this category are tasks that require translation, interpretation on the simplest level, and extrapolation. One must read between the lines to infer meaning, but need not to create new ideas. Students need only paraphrase what they read or otherwise demonstrate that they understand the relationships of the parts to each other.
3. *Application:* At this level, one usually applies abstract idea, precept, theorem, or principle to a problem.
4. *Analysis:* Here one works from the whole to its parts. This usually entails identifying the constituent parts, determining relationships among them, and/or recognizing the structural relationships that lend significance to the whole. In this category Bloom also includes tasks that require recognition of bias, value statements, and distinguishing fact from opinion.
5. *Synthesis:* This is a difficult task that asks students to put two or more elements together to form a new whole—that is, to perceive a new pattern, a new idea, or an original invention. The final product is usually an amalgam of parts drawn from several different sources. A research paper is one of the most common examples.
6. *Evaluation:* This skill requires making decisions to judge or evaluate. It normally involves setting criteria or understanding externally imposed standards. Critiquing then is largely a matter of weighing the logic of the criteria, judging how well they are carried out, and considering alternatives.

When we use "critical thinking" or "critical reading" in this book, we are referring to the cognitive activities at the most challenging levels of Bloom's chart—breaking out an idea from its whole into parts (analysis), fusing the parts into a whole (synthesis), and making judgments about material (evaluation)—as well as the ability to compare, contrast, and classify. All these tasks at the higher end of the taxonomy require manipulation of information, some problem-solving, and decision-making. Although higher-order thinking is a desirable goal, teachers often initiate the most fruitful explorations by setting up activities at the comprehension level and shift to the higher-order questions and back again. Questions should not be restricted to one type of thinking, nor should teachers feel that they must proceed mechanically through the steps beginning at the bottom and working to the top.

A compound task that requires more than one step to complete, is vocabulary building, which often takes students through the processes of application, analysis, synthesis and/or evaluation before the word(s) are fully digested.

Cubing

Cubing, an activity developed by Elizabeth Cowan Neeld (1990), parallels Bloom's taxonomy. Often used as a heuristic device for brainstorming a composition topic, cubing asks students to define an object or concept using multiple perspectives. Students view a subject from a number of approaches and thereby develop a more complex understanding of it. It is not an exercise in definition, but a technique that lets students look at one aspect of an object for three to five minutes and then move on to another line of thinking. A physics teacher, for example, might get students to consider a "light wave" using each of the following steps (Neeld 1990, 314–418):

1. Describe it.
2. Compare it.
3. Associate it.
4. Analyze it.
5. Apply it.
6. Argue for or against it.

Teachers using the cubing model need not slavishly walk through all of the steps to be effective. Some of the steps can even be consolidated. Take the city of Flint, Michigan, as a subject that could be explored at all levels. In a social studies class on their own state history, a teacher might tell students who live in the Flint area, "Try to capture Flint in a one-sentence statement." That is a question on the most simple level of knowledge. After students share their responses, the teacher could then say, "Write a one-sentence statement about some aspect of Flint that was different when you were younger and compare it to what it is like today." Their answer requires a comprehension level statement. This should draw a variety of responses, which students could also share in a discussion. The teacher might continue, "Now describe in two or three sentences what you think needs changing in your neighborhood." The goal is to elicit an analysis of city life that should draw many different responses. These the class could then sort into categories (synthesis). Following the classification of problems the teacher could ask, "What are the most fundamental problems here?" and "What could be done to address them?" Finally he or she might ask, "Would our plan work?" Starting with the most basic level of Bloom's taxonomy and using inquiry that touches on every level through the most complex thinking activities enables a class to think critically about the city. It deepens the students' understanding of central vocabulary with analysis, synthesis, evaluation, and a problem-solving approach.

Teachers who find cubing a useful strategy might turn it into a game by covering a tissue box with construction paper and labeling it with the six instructions. During their turn in the game, students can toss the die and apply the instruction (e.g., "argue for or against it") to their word. Another idea is to construct a circle with six segments, which can be used with a spinner. For older students, these props might be eliminated in favor of an informal journal assignment.

Drawbacks to Bloom's Taxonomy

As a framework for critical-thinking exercises, Bloom's taxonomy offers excellent opportunities for questions that invite open curiosity and inquiry from a variety of perspectives. Students and teachers need to remember, however, that taxonomically framed questions are only one avenue to higher-order thinking. As useful as Bloom's taxonomy is, it overlooks equally rich possibilities for exploring an affective response. This need is most acutely felt in literature classes, but an overly analytical approach can turn the thrill of an "aha" in the science lab into a dry experience. A biology teacher can rob students of their awe of emerging life, for instance, with too many analytical questions. Although various taxonomies provide a useful catalogue for questions, they will never press as far into the imagination as the free-ranging mind of the adventurous student. While we recognize the value of analytical thinking, we also want to stress the importance of the affective response that occurs most often in a pre-analytical experience when a student asks, "How do I feel about this?" or "What does this remind me of?" or "What have I noticed?" or "What do I question?" All of these questions bring personal insights that last longer in the student's mind than most of what the teacher might say. Indeed, teachers sometimes need to choose whether to risk squelching an emotional response by paying deliberate attention to prereading questions and guided response or to provide little or no guidance, which fosters free play of the imagination and an unencumbered affective response, but potentially sacrifices a clear understanding of the material.

Although clarity is crucial, teachers should avoid oversubscription to Bloom's taxonomy and other such questioning systems and their hierarchical approach to ways of knowing. These taxonomies provide a place to begin thinking about effective questions and establishing schemas for higher reader comprehension. They are by no means reading teachers' only tools.

The Role of Question-Asking in Text Comprehension

What we learn from Bloom's taxonomy and other taxonomies is that the range of questions one might ask is far wider than the simple knowledge-level question that abounds in most classrooms today. Other kinds of questions are invaluable for expanding the horizons of students. From elementary to high school, from special education to gifted, all students need plenty of practice answering and posing questions in every category both because this encourages whole language activity and offers occasions for divergent thinking. We need not wait till high school to ask higher-order questions. Elementary school children are capable of working with higher-level questions too and thrive on them. Gifted students or original thinkers enjoy experimenting with challenging ideas, but ordinary students also surprise themselves during the rich question-asking process, both in the questions they are asked and in the questions they learn to pose on their own.

Three Levels of Questions

Educators Harold Herber (1978) and his student Richard L. Vacca (1981) have collapsed Bloom's six categories to produce their own system, which has three levels. Their variation on Bloom's taxonomy challenges students to explore material at its literal level, for the author's implied meaning and for its implications in their own lives. As long as a fair number of questions in all three levels are raised, critical thinking will surface in one form or another to foster more active participation in learning. These three levels of questions are as follows:

Literal Level
At the *literal* (or *factual*) level students are asked to recognize and paraphrase stated information in the text. Sometimes called "reading the lines," these statements need not duplicate the original text word for word, but they should reproduce the text fairly closely so that students do not have to use much judgment in deciding if their information matches the original. At this level, students are called upon to recognize main ideas that are made explicit, as well as to be able to identify stated sequences, stated instructions, and any stated fact that appears in the original text. Corresponding to the knowledge level in Bloom's taxonomy, this level also emphasizes a close and accurate reading and establishes a common understanding of the most basic aspects of the text that can be useful for setting up subsequent understanding. Since these are the easiest questions to ask, teachers usually rely on them for instruction. They tend not to demand much of the student, however, and so they should be used less in the classroom than they are now.

Interpretive Level
At the *interpretive* (or *comprehension*) level, the reader is determining what the author intended to say. To read on this level, students must combine two or more explicit statements to make generalized statements about the relationships between the facts. They must read between or against the lines of the text. They must also be able to recognize and understand organizing structures, like cause-effect and comparison-contrast. They must also be able to form values and make judgments, and they must be able to look ahead to predict outcomes based on the reading. To accomplish these tasks, they must draw on their reading experiences

as well as their own beliefs and prior knowledge. Questions at this level ask, "What does the author mean by . . . ?" or "Would the author object to . . . ?" or "Do these facts imply . . . ?" The interpretive level of reading corresponds to Bloom's comprehension level of cognition. Most of the questions in a teacher's lesson should come out of this level of cognition.

Applied Level

At the *applied* (or *evaluative*) level, students discover connections beyond the lines of the text. Linking what they read in the text to their own experiences and ideas, students form concepts new to them and make broad generalizations. Operating at the level of application, analysis, synthesis, and evaluation, students are performing at the highest order of critical thinking. Here, they are asked to be creative, curious, and rational. Students at this level are usually applying what they have learned to the "real" world and finding evidence in their own lives of what they have read. Perhaps they are testing the author's assertions, separating fact from opinion, and recognizing bias by asking "What does the author assume when . . . ?" or "Are there flaws in the author's position on . . . ?" or "Do I agree with the author when . . . ?" The value of such questions lies in their ability to encourage students to acknowledge at least two points of view, theirs and the author's, even though it is not possible to know what the author is thinking and the views of the respondents will be culturally conditioned. Other questions at this level may expand the math lessons to simple engineering problems or to writing research papers. Since the applied question is the most difficult for teacher or student to pose and takes the longest to answer, fewer questions come out of this category.

The Role of Student Generated Questions in Text Comprehension

In the classes of our dreams, students' hands are up in eager anticipation to ask more about the material. Unfortunately, this rarely happens in our secondary classes. Without students raising questions, the teacher is left in full charge, orchestrating the class without being in close touch with students' thinking. Even worse, a teacher's questions often become an attempt to manipulate the class's thinking and to control what is learned. When the teacher does most of the thinking, only the most willing learners buy into the process because just about everyone recognizes it as either a game of "I'll reward you if you can guess what's in my head" or "I'll pose a question that one of you will answer and then I'll pose another question." A better version of this game is one in which there is a give-and-take with many of the questions coming from the students.

Students do not ask the questions they need to ask. There are several reasons for this. Adolescents too often feel intimidated—sometimes by the teacher but mostly by peers—to raise their hands and ask about what they don't know. Afraid of seeming stupid or too intellectual, they hold back. Once in a while the few who want to show off. They ask questions to trip up the teacher or to take the class off track as a cover for not having done their homework. In the largest category are reticent students who want to ask questions, but either are uncertain about what they don't understand or don't have the vocabulary to frame their questions intelligibly.

Getting students to ask their own questions is crucial to developing a critical consciousness and to reducing resistance. It is the primary goal of a classroom that prizes independent thinking. For one, it immerses students in language-making activity. Once students take charge through their own questions, teachers can set lessons to accommodate more fully the students' interests and abilities. Being more focused, students can also set their own purpose in reading by predicting and clarifying techniques. Furthermore, they learn to anticipate their teachers' testing processes by learning better the basis on which most questions are set—explicitly stated knowledge, inferential knowledge, or knowledge beyond the text. Modeling effective strategies for asking questions in all the content areas, teachers reinforce this behavior and make it more common in the classroom. Secondary school students can easily be taught the three levels of questions, for example, and can be encouraged to try their own hand at asking questions in these three categories.

Study Guides

Understanding the differences among the three levels takes a certain amount of modeling and practice, but students quickly catch on and are grateful for the study tip. Students may find study formulas like SQ3R useful in approaching new material:

- Survey the material before reading.
- Ask Questions based on the headings and subheadings, and about what is already known regarding the subject.
- Read the material to answer the questions.
- Recite a short summary of what was read.
- Review the ideas by periodically returning to the material.

A similar study formula is PORPE:

- Predict potential questions.
- Organize the information.
- Rehearse through recitation and self-testing.
- Practice through writing.
- Evaluate for accuracy.

There are a number of other study formulas that follow roughly a similar pattern: to ask questions about the text prior to reading, to raise questions about the text during reading, to paraphrase the material following reading, and to note more questions if necessary. The point of these study formulas is to encourage prediction and review, but students equipped with sound questioning techniques of their own can accomplish much the same goals without the mechanical step-by-step process of reviewing every section.

Encouraging Students to Ask Questions

The best strategy for promoting question-asking is to put the student at the center of the discussion. One method is to ask the class frequently, "Can anyone ask another question like that one?" or "Can anyone phrase that question another way?" Another procedure is to get everyone to write a question on a sheet of paper without using their names and pass them in. The questions are then answered by the class, not the teacher. As soon as an answer is given, teachers can encourage discussion by asking, "Does anyone have another answer?" The journal is another place to encourage questions, and many teachers have asked the class to construct upcoming tests. The ultimate goal of all of these tactics is to turn the classroom over to the students by making them the agents of inquiry. To remove themselves from the center of the discussion, teachers also use a variety of models for classroom interaction such as the following:

- whole-class discussion
- pooling of information by small groups before beginning whole-class discussion
- "think-pair-share," which is a few minutes' discussion (nothing more) with a partner
- individual journal writing before discussion is opened up to the whole class
- conferences with one or two students while others work alone
- student projects where students ask their own research questions, participate in class-wide problem-solving activity, or follow a line of inquiry that they set
- student-run debate

Whatever the model used, it is best to be clear about what one is trying to accomplish. So that everyone is operating with a common set of expectations, students working in groups should know what they need to do and how to do it. Often this requires selecting a leader for the discussion and assigning other roles like recorder, skeptic, and leader. After a few closely monitored sessions, however, students will quickly set to work without guidance.

Tips for Asking Questions

Content area teachers ask questions not only to stimulate cognitive thinking, but also to assess what the students have learned and to assign grades. Indeed, questions have been called the teacher's stock in trade because they are the best tool we have for finding out how we all are doing. To get a handle on the process of questioning, educators over the decades have discovered some home-tested principles about asking questions.

1. Pause at least ten seconds after asking a question before calling on any one person. Surprisingly, many teachers wait only three seconds after asking a question before they answer it themselves. The average teacher might wait as long as four seconds. And yet students will wait around fourteen seconds before answering questions. Many studies tell us that silence is the single most important technique for involving a number of participants (see, for instance, articles by J.T. Dillon (1979 and 1981) on the duration of student and teacher response).

2. Understand your instructional purpose(s) for asking the questions. Most questions can be divided into open and closed questions—questions that elicit an assortment of answers and those that elicit only one or two. They can be further subdivided into those that feed the discussion and those that are best for short-answer homework. Or they can be subdivided into probes for exploration, which emphasize trial and error, and for assessment, which demand precision and care. All have their place in classroom practice.

3. Avoid asking questions for which you do not know roughly the answer you are seeking.

4. Try some alternatives to asking questions, especially when your purpose is to transmit information or to determine the extent of student comprehension. If you want to explore material openly, announce that as your purpose and invite multiple, risk-free responses.

5. Call on students at random, ask students to call on other students, or ask directly for more volunteers. As soon as one student is selected, most of the others will sit back and allow the appointee to do the work, so selection should vary. To pull answers from a wider variety of students, you might try the following:

   - Withhold judgment of the student responses.
   - Use reflective statements that attempt to paraphrase students' answers: "What I'm hearing you say is . . ."
   - Invite the respondent to elaborate. You can also ask the student, "Do you mean . . . ?" or "Can you say that another way?" or "Can you say more about that?"
   - Ask for alternative answers from classmates or ask someone else to paraphrase the first student's answer.
   - Play devil's advocate.
   - Build the questions around one or a cluster of topics.

6. Avoid the scattershot approach, which asks several questions that paraphrase the same question. Students are often confused when they don't know which question to answer. When the question seems confusing, you can ask a student to reformulate it or you can "slice" a question by taking a simpler form of it and asking that one first. Once an answer to that question is established, then you can use it as a building block.

Correcting Student Responses Tactfully

To correct student answers in recitation, try some of the following options suggested by Cathy Collins (1987, 816–818).

1. *Think again.* If you think [students] who gave an incorrect answer [have] the background to answer correctly, ask them to think again: "I'm sure you'll think of it if you just give yourself a little more time."
2. *Give a prompt.* When students give a partial answer, or need you to provide more structure, offer a small piece of information.
3. *Differential reinforcement.* Tell the part of the answer that was correct: "You're right, bears are mammals. Do you recall whether mammals are warm-blooded? Are human beings warm-blooded?"
4. *Paraphrasing the question.* If it appears no one knows the answer, yet you judge that they learned the information, rephrase the question.
5. *Expanding the answer.* Ask [students] to tell why they answered the way they did or why they believe their answer to be correct.
6. *Making students accountable.* If a student gives two incorrect answers to the same question, or if two students answer incorrectly, give the answer and tell them they will need to remember it. (This gives them incentive to remember the question and the answer.) Return to the student(s) again before the period is over and ask the same question.
7. *Asking for clues.* Ask fellow students to give clues, or ask the student who missed the question to call upon a classmate to help by giving either a clue or the answer.
8. *Incorrect "if" statements.* If you recognize why the answer was wrong, supply the question for which the answer would have been correct. For example, if you asked, "What is the capital of New Zealand?" and the student answered "Canberra," you could respond, "Canberra would be the answer if someone asked about the capital of Australia. How about the capital of New Zealand?"
9. *Examples of possibilities.* Use oral multiple choices at the close of a lesson or unit or as a review. "Who was the first European to see the Pacific Ocean? Balboa, Cortez, or Cabeza de Vaca?"
10. *Nonexamples or opposites.* If students don't raise their hands to answer a question, tell them what the answer is *not*.
11. *One thing I learned today.* Toward the end of class, students are called upon to tell one thing that they learned that day without repeating any item previously stated by another student.
12. *Expand for clarity.* Ask students to explain the rationale behind their answers.

If we as teachers want to facilitate student learning by acting as catalysts for problem-solving and by creating the environmental conditions that support active learning, then we must begin by asking questions that help students to realize what they know and to recognize the significance of that knowledge. More than that, we want to model meaning-making strategies so that students will eventually become responsible for coordinating and applying these strategies to their own personal quests for knowledge. Critical thinking is but one avenue to an educational process that enables learning for life.

The Aesthetic Response and Its Role in Textbook Comprehension

Over the last fifty years, many educators have reacted against Bloom's taxonomy and zealous question-asking because they potentially restrict student response to a narrowly defined behavior. Because critical thinking is not the only response to literature and the fine arts, educators have longed for a more aesthetic approach to these fields.

Roman Ingarden has explored the conditions most conducive to the aesthetic response in *The Cognition of the Literary Work of Art* (1973). He believes that an aesthetic response is more likely to occur in the first unguarded moments of perception, and that it can be forestalled or attenuated if the perceiver's primary goal is to analyze the reading. If a reader of a Robert Frost poem is allowed to react first to the humor and beauty of the lines, Frost's images could make a powerful aesthetic impact. If, however, the teacher asks students to scour the poem for explanations of irony or its rhyme scheme, then the aesthetic experience can be smothered. Although Ingarden was speaking about readers' responses to literary texts, he could be describing a perceptual experience of works of art and ordinary phenomena as well. Since aesthetic response is almost always directed by the intentions of the perceiver, some readings of the text are best left up to the whims and inclinations of the student.

Sometimes the best teaching is no teaching at all, but mere observation to witness the learning process in action. In his book *How We Understand Art* (1987), Michael Parsons presents a taxonomy that describes five stages of aesthetic development. Parsons applies these maturational stages to works of art, but he could just as well be describing aesthetic responses to the enjoyment of music, dance, drama or some form of literature. These stages roughly follow the direction of development from the individualistic and unaware response of an inexperienced audience to the sophisticated, considered response that is weighed after analytically examining the opinions of others. Although they often correspond to the stages of the maturing process, these progressive levels of aesthetic response are not fixed to specific age groups. The first stage describes the delight that a young child might take in surface features. In this stage, she forms strong preferences for favorites, often for their sensual pleasure but also for their associational value. The young appreciator might prefer a picture because it has a dog like his in it or a book because it mentions his teddy bear. Whether the child is attracted to yellow toys or wants certain books to be read aloud again and again, at this stage she knows what she likes and she defines her preferences by her own personal reactions regardless of what anyone else says.

In the second stage, children are drawn to artworks mainly for their realistic representation, their resemblance to familiar sights and sounds. In the third stage, older children—often in their teens, but not necessarily—are able to judge artworks for their ability to "express aspects of experience, states of mind, meanings, [and] emotions" (70). As young adults, they no longer need a work of art to represent their world with pictorial accuracy, but the artwork still has to make sense emotionally. Although they are beginning to realize that the artist has a purpose that deserves recognition, viewers at this stage demand that the work correspond in some degree to their own subjective experience so they can relate to it on some plane. By this point in their maturity, they can grasp the fact that different people will have different responses and they can validate divergent opinion, but they still trust their own gut responses above all else.

Students at stage four, however, realizing their opinion is just one among many, begin to compare their interpretations with others. They can appreciate technique and form, respond to mastery of certain effects, and display a knowledge of styles. Gradually they are becoming aware of the social character of art. They are realizing that there is a community of viewers and trends and schools of art as well as a whole history of preferences and modes of representation. Exploring art at this stage of maturity, they are realizing how tastes are socially mediated.

It is only in the most mature stages of aesthetic development that any appreciator of art can judge and think about judgments in the arts with some sort of autonomous perspective. In the fifth stage evaluations are based on set criteria, independent of or contiguous to those of tradition. The critic may be drawn to the Impressionist painters or medieval literature or Spike Lee films, but not because he has accepted wholesale the judgment of others about these works; rather he articulates his own reasons for valuing them, and many times he sees in them something more than the strengths and weaknesses of execution or style. He responds because a particular work points to a meaning beyond the artifact itself. The choices are still personal, just as they were at stage one, but it is a choice based not only on an awareness of the opinions of others, but also on the person one imagines becoming. Parsons explains that at this level, aesthetic response is "a constant exploration of our experience, a trying-out of the self that we might be, and a continuing conversation with others about both" (152).

The value of Parsons' taxonomy for the content areas is that it reaffirms the place of the aesthetic response in some forms of learning. Parsons also helps us understand that reading analysis has little or no meaning for children in the earliest stages of appreciation. Whether they are looking at a poem by Robert Louis Stevenson or a novel by Henry James, readers are not going to enjoy critical interpretation until they are maturationally ready. At the early stages—whether the students are five or fifteen—it is better for the teacher to sit back and allow them to set their own modes of responses. At the more sophisticated levels of appreciation, reading teachers can begin to help students articulate multiple sets of standards: those for their own personal use and those for measuring responses in the community of readers. Only at the highest level can we expect students of any age to appreciate and apply literary history, tradition, and the theories of criticism to justify or explain the artistic nature of the texts. English teachers should therefore be wary of killing a young person's appreciation for reading by asking analytical questions too soon or by measuring a text for its conformity to certain rules of the genre, such as looking for the rising action, the falling action and the climax of a short story. After they have beat poetry to death with scansion rules or some other dissecting tool, many freshmen and sophomores never want to read it again. Whether the poem is a sestet in rhyming iambic pentameter means very little to unsophisticated readers. Literary analysis gives the teacher plenty to talk about, but means very little in appreciation of the works until students are intellectually prepared for it, and so it should be undertaken with caution. Language immersion is the best approach at the less sophisticated levels. Plenty of reading, writing, speaking, and listening with an emphasis on what the texts mean and what they signify on a personal level not only fosters a love of the works, but also enables students to supply a rationale for their preferences and communicate their choices. Once they can articulate what they like and why, students have moved to the most sophisticated stage, a step that will serve them in lifelong appreciation of the arts, whether it's reading a novel, listening to music, or enjoying the more untraditional arts.

Metacognition and Its Role in Text Comprehension

One of the most potent ways we can groom students to become independent learners is to show them ways to monitor their own learning processes and recognize trouble. The experienced reader usually can tell when the material becomes too dense to penetrate; she then takes steps to remedy the situation. Many young, unaggressive readers, however, get lost in the text and imagine they are comprehending the material when they are not. Other students blame themselves or the teacher and quit reading in disgust or frustration. Metacognition strategies, which build a self-conscious awareness of one's thinking processes, can be key to helping young students mimic mature reading behavior. Metacognition comes in various forms, but it often falls in three stages: task, strategy, and performance awareness.

Task Awareness

The framework and many of the ideas for this section were based on "Developing Metacognitive Awareness," by Wade and Reynolds (1989). The first step in metacognition is task awareness. Students should first understand that reading requirements vary from text to text. Demands placed on a student by a math text, for example, are far different from those imposed by a set of basketball regulations in a physical education class. It is often up to teachers to help students find ways to cope with the texts in their classes. In one of the most extensive discussions of metacognition anywhere, *Teaching Reading Comprehension* (1986), Thomas Devine says that the most important step is the setting of a purpose for the reading by teacher or student, preferably the student.

Teachers should discuss the nature of the reading with the students as they encounter trouble. In these lessons on metacognition, students should be taught ways to confront difficult passages by changing their rate of reading, rereading if necessary, or going to another source for help. They might learn how to pay attention to the topic sentences, the openings and closings, the questions at the end of the chapter, the boldface type, or the repetitions in images. Students may also be encouraged to ask themselves repeatedly what they understand and where the difficulty lies. More frequently than not, the trouble spots occur where students lack background in the subject matter. Students need to understand this. They would become more confident readers if they were told how to deal with an obstacle that confronts all readers at one time or another: a lack of information. Competent readers deal with this problem often without conscious awareness of what they are doing.

Some study skills—such as SQ3R, discussed above—help students learn to rehearse what they've read. Study skills are often designed to foster sound prereading metacognitive techniques like making educated guesses about the content of the piece based on its subject headings, illustrations, and other textual cues. Paraphrase and summary at frequent intervals are outstanding self-monitoring devices.

Strategy Awareness

Once the student understands the task at hand, she needs to outline, mentally or otherwise, what should be done to meet the task. Whether the assignment calls for skimming, a close reading, analysis of its parts, or looking for a statement of the problem, the student needs to know metacognitively how to approach the text. So the second step in metacognition is strategy awareness.

At this point the students are ready to develop a list of coping strategies to read successfully. The best approach is to make students aware of the kinds of strategies they already use. The class may want to make a comprehensive list of their strategies. These may include physical actions like outlining, making out charts, and consulting a dictionary, or mental ones like visualizing, rereading slowly, or using mnemonic devices to sort out names. Wade and Reynolds (1989, 10) suggest these possible strategies:

1. Observable study methods

Highlight or underline

Copy the information exactly as it is written in the text

Write down information in your own words

Outline to show main ideas and supporting ideas or examples

Draw a diagram to organize information

2. In-the-head study methods

Look over before reading (skimming)

Read at your usual rate

Read slowly

Go back and read again

Review or memorize

Put together ideas in your head

Relate ideas to what you already know

Make a picture in your mind

Question or test yourself

Guess what will happen

Process journals describing what it was like to tackle various specific tasks help students discover their points of difficulty.

Depending on the material, students should be encouraged to make educated guesses about the author's purpose and to move on when the material becomes dense. This is especially important when reading a chapter with new vocabulary. As long as the unfamiliar words are not carrying the content, students can usually supply provisional synonyms with reliable success. They can make these guesses using prior knowledge of the content, free association, and the structure of the text. If the chapter is organized around a cause-and-effect pattern, for example, students can make intelligent guesses about the two parts of the discussion, the cause and the effect. Tentative hypotheses (sometimes called heuristics) may help bridge impenetrable or poorly written material until the reader is back on familiar ground. Relating the material to what students already know and focusing on the important parts of the text are also sound practices.

Performance Awareness

The third step in the metacognitive process is performance awareness, in which the student looks back at the first two steps and asks, "How did I do?" He examines his fix-up strategies to evaluate which ones were effective. A teacher who frequently models these techniques may periodically solicit student advice by getting them to "say back" their experiences—to describe their reactions to the strategies for coping with hard-to-read material. To do so, she may ask these questions: "How well did you cope?" "Did the strategy help you learn the material?" "How do you know when you have learned something?" The optimum time for students to monitor their own comprehension is after the lesson, once mastery of the reading is assured, and at a time when metacognitive evaluation is not competing with the students' attempt to grasp the content.

Think-Alouds

B. Davey (1983) has devised a quick checklist for judging one's self-correction strategies. Although it is by no means a complete list, it serves as a model for poor readers, which a teacher might rewrite to meet his own assignment (Figure 7–1). As this Read Aloud Chart indicates, the procedure encourages readers to think about what they do by thinking out loud while asking themselves questions. The teacher can orally model thinking aloud before the class. The advantage to the Read Aloud procedure is that it provides a list of strategies needed to complete the task. A variation on this assignment may use a more student-based approach, in which groups design their own list from scratch or make additions to the teacher's list.

During the discussion on metacognition, the teacher could also describe her own rules for developing questions and strategies that students might use for answering them. From time to time, she should call attention metacognitively to strategies for asking and answering three levels of questions and encourage students to formulate their own questions. The point is not to teach about the arcane aspects of cognition, but to encourage students to think about their own thinking processes.

Metacognition is one of the most powerful and yet least explored tools of learning. It remains unexplored largely because teachers seem reluctant to take time away from the content for talking about reading, thinking about thinking, and explaining the learning process. And yet, if they took time out to talk about the techniques of metacognitive thinking, teachers would be doing more to encourage independent learners in their field than any other single effort they could make.

While I Was Reading, How Did I Do?
(Put an X in the appropriate column)

	Not Very Much	A Little Bit	Much of the Time	All of the Time
Predicting				
Picturing				
"Like-a"				
Identifying Problems				
Using fix-ups				

FIGURE 7–1. A Read Aloud Chart

Summary

In this chapter we discussed several principles vital to textbook comprehension. We have argued that the best approach to diversity is the transactional model of classroom interaction, which little by little shifts the burden of solving these reading problems to the student. We have also endorsed the critical thinking tasks of problem solving, asking questions on three levels of cognition, making vocabulary an integral part of learning, evoking the aesthetic response, and thinking metacognitively. At the center of each principle is an emphasis on making meaning, in which students grasp meaning while attaching meaning to what they read and establish a critical stance toward their own learning and toward their culture. Meaning is what the reader supplies and learns to question. In the intersection between text and reader, the student *makes* meaning by lending significance to the information and concepts on the printed page. Since meaning is what the reader makes of the material, reading is interactive and intensional. What the reader gleans from the text depends to a large extent on what he decides to attend to and what he expects to see. A holistic concept guides the learning. Add to these lessons incisive questions that focus and embrace multiple perspectives, and they take on a larger meaning for the reader. In the classroom that immerses the student in language activity, questions are asked by student and teacher as a way of establishing and reinforcing an atmosphere of open investigation, in which the teacher prods the attention of students toward activities that make sense of the whole. In the principles for comprehension lie the basis for lesson planning discussed in the next chapter.

CHAPTER EIGHT

Lesson Designs for Text Comprehension

Comprehension

Although most of the basic principles governing the reading process are understood, many of the issues surrounding comprehension have yet to be settled.
The intricacies of comprehension are only now being fully appreciated. Why so
many children have trouble reading for pleasure, for instance, is not well understood, and how much comprehension depends on the social negotiation of
knowledge is still up for debate. The influence of television and other popular
media on our nation of readers is another chapter yet to be written.

Given the complexity of the reading process and the factors that point to
the priority of individual interpretation, how do we teachers know when a text
is comprehended? Frank Smith (1975) says about reader comprehension that
"what matters is meaningfulness" (*Comprehension and Learning,* 121). In other
words, if readers can make sense of the reading, relate it to the world they
already know, the text is comprehended. In *Understanding Reading* (1978), he
writes, "As we read, as we listen to a speaker, as we go through life, we are
constantly asking questions; and as long as these questions are answered, and our
uncertainty is reduced, then we comprehend" (66). David E. Rumelhart (1984)
agrees with Smith and explains comprehension in more technical terms:
"Readers are said to have understood the text when they are able to find a
configuration of hypotheses (schemata) which offer a coherent account for the
various aspects of the text" (3). Note how both Smith and Rumelhart leave the
final determination of comprehension up to the reader. How then will the
teacher know if the student has comprehended the text to her satisfaction? She
will never be certain about the level of her students' understanding. Because
comprehension depends on how well the text fits the reader's schemata, it is
relative. Neither the testing process nor classroom discussion can control or
standardize the way a text is understood. And so the autonomous nature of
reading both protects the private satisfaction of the student and confounds the
teacher who would like more public ownership of the ideas and assurance of
some shared understanding.

What then is the teacher's role in ensuring comprehension? The teacher must attempt to structure classroom activities to that end. She must also monitor the basic concepts that underpin a text—those that, to the best of her knowledge, were intended by the author—and guard against student misconception. According to Rumelhart there are at least three reasons that a reader may fail to understand a passage:

- Readers may not have the appropriate schemata. In this case they simply cannot understand the concept being communicated.
- Readers may have the appropriate schemata, but the clues provided by the author may be insufficient to suggest them. Here again readers will not understand the text, but with appropriate additional clues they may come to understand it.
- Readers may find a consistent interpretation of the text, but may not find the one intended by the author. In this case, readers will understand the text, but will misunderstand the author. (18)

Although misconception is not easy to monitor, the teacher may reduce the possibility of confusion or misunderstanding by providing classroom reading lessons that suggest avenues to comprehension. This process is not easy to monitor, however, since at the same time she is monitoring for misconception, the teacher has to allow freedom for individual interpretation.

To turn more responsibility for learning over to the student, the teacher often uses strategy lessons, which are coordinated activities that guide and monitor understanding. These lessons are different from asking direct questions, even though both help to manage the internal and external consistency of the various readings and both serve as a corrective when students need clarification. The difference is that the best strategy lessons are more leading than questioning and they defer conclusive answers, leaving the ultimate conclusions up to the student. When done correctly, strategy lessons for reading can help students think broadly and steer them toward independent thinking. They ask students to respond to and find support for information rather than pressure them to articulate larger implications and pinpoint complex connections before they are ready to do so. As soon as students are more conversant with the material, they will be ready to respond to questions that either demand a firm right or wrong answer or require multiple factors for a complete answer.

Planning for Instruction: A Comprehension-Centered Design for Lessons

Traditionally, reading assignments have consisted of assigning a section of the text to be read, plus an activity based on the reading such as answering questions in the text or working text-based problems. The reading was generally followed by a checkup on the assigned work, a question-and-answer session, or a lecture.

Essentially, all work with the text occurred *after* students had read it on their own. Instruction was relegated to follow-up and review.

Reading theory now tells us that what happens *before* students sit down with a book can have a profound effect on comprehension by awakening background knowledge and setting purposes for the reading. During and post-reading, too, teachers can help students deal more effectively with the text material. Therefore, we recommend instructional planning for all units of instruction, from daily lessons and short blocks of instruction to comprehensive thematic units, which includes strategy lessons for all phases: prereading, during-reading, and post-reading.

Most lessons are prepared in units that cover a particular topic in depth and last from one to several days. For the sake of coherence, the lesson is usually organized around a central concept (e.g., Reconstruction after the American Civil War was painful for the North and the South), a critical-thinking skill (ie. measurement or genetics), a structure (e.g., circles), or a genre (e.g., travel stories). There are many versions of lesson plans and each discipline has its own favorite format. Typically lesson plans contain the following items:

1. Title(s) of the reading materials and other resources. Material selection is fully discussed in Chapter Five.
2. A clearly articulated central concept that sets the framework for the lesson. This is also called the "main idea." The main idea is discussed later in this chapter.
3. The goals of the unit—often called "objectives"—for both the learning skills and the content matter. These goals are tied to the central concept, but are generally more specific and detailed than the main idea.
4. A list of the key vocabulary needed to grasp the central concepts. We explored the principles of vocabulary for text comprehension in Chapter Seven, and we will offer more suggestions for reinforcing vocabulary in this chapter.
5. A sequencing of assignments or activities that allows for guided practice and independent work in the pre-reading, during-reading, and postreading phases.
6. Critical thinking and/or problem-solving that involves reading, writing, thinking, and speaking. Many practical ideas for guiding critical thinking appear in this chapter.
7. Some means of evaluating students and a plan for assessing anticipated outcome(s) of the lesson for future planning. We discussed this fully in Chapter Six.

The object of a good plan is to help students explore the ideas of the lesson. Good lesson plans therefore include a variety of activities at all cognitive levels of performance using both group work and individual investigation. A multidisciplinary approach and the contribution of ideas and skills gathered beyond the classroom walls also enrich the subject matter of the course.

Guidelines for Successful Lesson Plans

Above all, when making out lesson plans there is no substitute for sound teacher preparation. The more teachers know about their subject matter, the better their plans will be. In most disciplines, this means that we as teachers need to read widely and deeply in our fields and in any adjacent fields. To begin a lesson, we need to study the texts at hand and be certain we really know and understand the points well. This may seem self-evident, except that we can never study at the university long enough to become the teachers we want to be. For extensive units, therefore, extra library work and other kinds of research may be necessary.

Then we need to decide how to relate this information to our students' lives. What devices, questions, and associations can we use to engage students personally with the material? In what ways does it relate to their own experiences? Once the overall course of action is worked out with a list of activities and assignments, we need to remember to find ways to help students make a community of meaning. To do this, teachers ask for student contributions. Rather than tell students what to think, they offer plenty of opportunity for class discussion and they affirm student responses. Once a common context for the unit is understood by the class, the teacher should confirm it by setting a main idea, a one-sentence concept that will serve as the guideline for the lesson. This concept lends coherence to the lesson by informing all the activities that drive it home.

The Main Idea or Central Concept

Because most textbooks are not fully clear, may often contain extraneous material, and are never completely tailored to local need, the teacher must decide where to focus student attention and how to activate relevant schemata. For some students the experience of reading some of these textbooks may be like reading the following passage:

> Hocked gems financed our hero. Scornful laughter had tried to prevent his scheme. Bravely he persisted. An egg, not a table, typifies this unexplored planet, he said. Now three sturdy sisters sought proof. They forged along turbulent peaks and valleys. Days became weeks as doubters spread fearful rumors about the edge. At last welcome winged creatures appeared. Momentous success was at hand.

Many of us find this information difficult to absorb until we learn that it is about Christopher Columbus. Once the schema is suggested to us and we grasp the whole, then the details of the passage make sense. The world being shaped like an "egg not a table" is understood as a metaphor for Columbus's argument, for example. And we instantly identify the three sisters. Our difficulty in negotiating the above passage without the schema, the main idea, gives us some insight into the difficulties that students face when a history text, for example, contains fact after fact without making a central point. Until a central idea is suggested and the details take on relevance in relation to that idea, often the textbook chapter reads like an endless stream of loosely organized facts. It is up to the teacher to suggest a main idea that will help students understand the principles or core concepts that lend the material relevance and meaning.

Before suggesting a main idea, the teacher must first decide how much the students already know and can understand of the text's content. Once she can identify the extent of student knowledge, she looks for an overarching concept central to the unit's subject matter. Through the concept, she can see how the parts of the unit fit together. Choosing a main idea requires some winnowing, ignoring some of the text's subject matter in order to concentrate on the seminal ideas. A good main idea should be focused, yet productive for suggesting other lines of thinking. While teaching a chapter on Thomas Jefferson's administration, for example, one may have to forgo a discussion of the Burr–Hamilton duel to emphasize the larger ideas of expanding the territory through the policy of "continental destiny" and the Louisiana Purchase.

After determining one central idea that embraces others, the teacher should cast it in the form of an argument, a law of science, a geometric theorem, or perhaps even a cognitive skill like map reading. To present a unit on weather forecasting, for example, a teacher might put forth this main idea: "To forecast the weather, one must understand the interactions of solar energy with the cooling of land, air, and water." Or to open a unit on F. Scott Fitzgerald's *The Great Gatsby*, a teacher might contrast the irrational dreams of the characters against the reality they must live. The point is that the main idea of any body of writing should provide a way into the material, an avenue that helps the student bring the myriad of detail into focus, organize it, and see its relevance to other information. There are additional reasons for establishing a main point:

- to set a purpose for the reading based on an idea or practice
- to help students make meaning by focusing on content
- to lend a focus to "unfriendly" texts that teach skills, vocabulary, and facts without clear connections
- to link the lessons to particular student needs and interests
- to take advantage of the teacher's enthusiasms and interests
- to compensate for material that glosses over the contributions of ethnic groups or undervalues multicultural perspectives
- to provide a context for details, subskills, and formulas, which are easily forgotten by students once they have taken the test
- to suggest schemas that can continue to generate a rich network of ideas that further learning

A Caveat When Formulating the Main Idea

Despite the numerous payoffs for setting a main idea, some lessons are best left open to exploration. Particularly in a literature, social studies, or history class, but also in the sciences, a restrictive main idea may turn out to be too prescriptive, and thereby squelch individual interpretation. Premature closure may be especially confining or deadening in a multicultural classroom. For example, facts about the arrival of Columbus or the American Civil War may evoke strongly differing responses among class members. In these disciplines, the most workable main ideas are those that challenge students from a variety of backgrounds to generate fresh ideas. In short, the best sort of main idea introduces a network of concepts that stimulate an even wider constellation of associations. Above all, the most effective main idea is not stated simply as a topic or unanswered question, or as a didactic and overly simplistic message that shuts out alternative responses. Instead it teases out a dense web of possibilities that leaves plenty of room for creativity, change, and individual responsibility.

If the English teacher were doing a unit on John Knowles' popular novel *A Separate Peace,* for example, he might choose as a main idea "the boys' uncertainty about how to respond to World War II is reflected in their inability to resolve personal conflict." This controlling concept helps students solve the problems of the book but in a way that suggests a wide assortment of personal applications. A more strangling form of the main idea might be a rigid statement like "Knowles condemns war and fighting in *A Separate Peace.*" This statement not only codifies a position that Knowles has not made explicit, but it also preempts students' responses.

This top-down approach to reading—beginning with a main idea or a set of objectives—should be considered only one approach to teaching a short story or novel. One reason is that mature readers often want to establish their own purposes for reading. A fiction reader, having decided that she wants quick pleasure from her book, might skim for its plot and skip the dull parts, or a researcher might scan an article for ideas that may or may not be of primary importance to the author. Also, young readers resist this top-down approach, and rightfully so, because they like to remain open to the surprises of the text. If it is too controlling, the top-down approach can rob students of that open road of discovery and aesthetic experience. The best way to assign some kinds of reading, therefore, is simply to announce the assignment without preparation or directives based on a main idea. The choice is up to the teacher's discretion.

Sensitivity toward these issues, particularly in English class, is important nurturing an aesthetic response to literature, but it applies to other disciplines as well. Bringing premature closure to an experiment in science class by supplying students with ironclad fact can easily kill the excitement of inductive discovery. In a biology lab, for example, students might first try to guess what causes sour milk and then attempt to design their own experiments to confirm their hypotheses. The teacher can ruin the thrill of the search by explaining too soon about milk-spoiling bacteria in the air. If allowed to pursue all "silly" ideas, students might discover the principles of sound hypothesis formation and research design and develop an understanding about air-borne bacteria. Furthermore, self-discovery encourages the gifted who need opportunities to exercise their creative energies through divergent activity.

How the Main Idea Is Determined

Having acknowledged these disadvantages, we still believe that setting a main idea is a useful tactic to establish a central focus when complex texts demand too much of their readers. Take, for instance, the following passage, which presents both facts about the animals that migrate and the scientists who have attempted to understand them:

> Some animals travel over very long distances in the course of their lives. Salmon in the Pacific, for example, hatch eggs laid at the headwaters of mountain streams, some of them hundreds of miles from the ocean, and they return each year at mating season to spawn in the waters of the same stream. But there are other examples of migration as well. Eels—both European and American —swim out of freshwater streams to return each year to the Sargasso Sea, and the giant leathery turtles from the South China Sea make their annual visit to the beaches of the East Coast of the Malay Peninsula. Scientists have long studied this phenomenon without understanding it fully, because the animal's navigational strategy may depend on the animal identifying landmarks through sun cues, smell, or some other body chemistry.

Like so many textbook passages, this one connects many facts with thin threads. The main idea is difficult to identify because it has not been stated directly and the focus is divided among migration, reproduction, and navigation. Knowing the priorities of the class, the teacher can identify the main idea at some level of generalization, thereby bringing coherence to the reading and a focus to the class activities.

One of the most useful formats for formulating a main idea statement is the principle, rule, theorem, or precept that supplies a "hook" on which to hang most of the material in the unit. In the sample passage, this might be "Animals migrate, often using unknown navigational methods, to the spawning grounds where they originated." We believe that the best means of expressing this main idea combines all the key words with a verb that indicates their concrete relationships, (e.g., "Scientists are still trying to understand the methods that animals use to return to the same spawning grounds every year.") If the teacher were to name simply the gist of the passage, "animal migration" or "scientific mysteries" for example, some of its valuable dynamics of the passage would unfortunately be omitted. Based on their compilation of references in leading journals of the 1920s and 1940s, Moore and Cunningham (1986) have posed the following questions to establish a common framework for identifying the main idea in a teaching unit or lesson:

- What is the unit mostly about?
- What concept(s) are most important to teach for future lessons?
- What is the book trying to show us?
- How directive should the teaching unit be? Will the main idea overdetermine the way the student reads this teaching unit?
- How challenging should the unit be?

- How many other topics should the unit include? Should the scope be broad or narrow?
- Is the generalization accurate? (3)

The operative strategy here is not only to include all the main points of a given piece of material, but also to reveal how they connect to one another. Is the connection one of cause and effect? comparison/contrast? chronological? whole to parts? The main idea should clarify relationships, suggest a schema for storing and retrieving the data, and draw connections to allied material.

Examples of the Main Idea in Each Content Area

In the sciences and mathematics, the main idea is easy to identify because their textbooks are already organized around theorems or principles. An example of a main idea in math might therefore be "To establish congruency, one needs at least two sides and an angle."

In social studies and history, the main idea may be a generalization that illustrates historical trends that effected change, like "Railroads brought industrialization to many parts of the United States." The best of these main ideas draw together the key concepts of an era in relationship to one another. The main idea then may be an overarching statement that helps to put many of the details of the period in perspective. Another form of the main idea should prod students into thinking like historians, perhaps by asking them to compare different versions of the main event.

In foreign languages, unlike other disciplines, the main idea is often just the topic that carries the most content vocabulary for that chapter: "travel in Senegal," "school in Mexico," "the department store in France." Since a good deal of time in foreign-language study concentrates on grammar, which usually is not related to the content of the unit, it is difficult to include all the content of a chapter under the umbrella of its theme. The main idea, even if simply stated as a topic that disregards the grammatical aspects, still may serve to remind student and teacher that meaning-making with the new vocabulary and grammar should be the primary task at hand, rather than mechanical work with empty exercises that disregard the ability of those words to communicate.

In the arts, the main idea may point to a principle of criticism like "Art need not be realistic to be 'good'" or a process for producing an artistic work, like "Animated cartoons grow out of a series of pictures." The main idea in art history might appear in the form of applied lessons: "Just as Picasso borrowed the shapes and expressiveness of African masks to articulate emotion, we too can construct African-like masks to express our feelings."

Once the main idea is spelled out, the teacher can select vocabulary that is key to it, and she can select the most salient facts with some confidence that they will be remembered because they support a unified whole. It also helps to lay a foundation for the unit's discussions, exercises, and tests. Even the subordinate ideas become clearer because they are given a context that illuminates their significance and sets them in a relationship to one another.

Daily Content Objectives

After choosing the main idea for the lesson and selecting the supporting text(s), teachers usually define the daily content objectives. We recommend daily objectives that support the main idea. For example, the main idea might be that "The Age of Exploration, in which Christopher Columbus, Vasco da Gama, and Ferdinand Magellan sailed the seas, might never have occurred without certain technology in navigation." A daily lesson might be to understand how to use an astrolabe. In one or two sentences, teachers state what they want their students to learn, discuss, or think about during this lesson. They define these objectives in terms of the more specific ideas or concepts they want to focus on. Examples might be "Because of lower air pressure, water takes longer to boil at higher altitudes" or "To solve for two unknowns, we must first eliminate one of the unknowns" or "Daisy rejected Jay Gatsby because she was conscious of their class differences." Often it is helpful to ask students to add to the list of daily learning objectives, both for the value of their contribution and for the class's use.

Sample Lesson Plan

The actual lesson plan that appears in teachers' logs usually includes an objective, a list of activities for the class, and a homework assignment. Each teacher has to work out how detailed this lesson plan will be (e.g., whether or not to include questions and details of an experiment). Most teachers keep the plans simple like this:

> Objective: To examine the functions of a nervous system of vertebrates
> In-class activity: Experiment that contrasts motor and sensory neurons using a frog.
> Question: Looking at the book's diagrams, try to guess the sequence of a nerve impulse in vertebrates.
> Question: What is the major difference between a frog's system and a human's?
> Question: Where do humans experience involuntary reflexes?
> Question: Do frogs feel more or fewer sensations than humans?
> *Homework assignment*: Read Chapter 13 on Nervous Coordination. Write a short paragraph contrasting sympathetic and parasympathetic nervous systems.

The Prereading, During-reading, and Postreading Framework

Prereading Comprehension

After the teacher sets the main idea, she will design some activities that introduce the lesson in a framework that includes prereading, during-reading, and postreading activities as part of a larger lesson plan or unit. Prereading exercises are in-class activities conducted over one or more lessons before students begin reading the new chapter. Knowing what she wants students to understand immediately or by the end of the chapter, the teacher asks herself the following questions:

- What do students need to know before they read?
- How can I get them involved in the ideas?
- How can I prepare them to read and learn this material successfully?

As Frank Smith might remind us, the most compelling reason for introducing a chapter with prereading exercises is to reduce uncertainty, since comprehension takes place in the absence of uncertainty. If the text suggests too many possibilities for interpretation, perhaps because the text is vague or the vocabulary unfamiliar, and there are too many alternatives for the reader to eliminate some outcomes, confusion sets in. The young reader is likely to give up the reading altogether. Since newly assigned material is bound to lead to some uncertainty, especially in science and math courses where entirely new concepts are being explored every week in the texts, serious preparation for the upcoming material is important. To tackle this potentially unfamiliar material, students need either a rich background in related subject matter or lessons in the prereading phase that fill in needed information with a conceptual overview.

How successful students are at tackling unknown material depends on the purposes that are set either by their own initiative or by their teacher's. Here are some possible prereading approaches to dull or unfamiliar material:

1. Teachers may allay anxiety and forestall frustration by offering exercises that link students' prior knowledge and the new material. To make material more accessible, the best strategy is to build on the reader's existing schemas. Without links to the reader's framework of ideas, that "worldview in the head," reading is just a matter of pronouncing words and processing surface features on the page. Prereading activities are used to remind students of related information from earlier chapters, to draw analogies to student experience, or to connect the information to practical problems that the students might eventually confront.

    One additional use for a prereading activity, especially for teachers new to a school system or new to teaching, is to find out what students already know about the material and what interests they have that may help them connect with the lessons. A quick questionnaire or journal writing can tell the teacher a great deal and raise interest in the material. The following sample questions could be used to arouse interest in Arthurian tales before students read them and test their familiarity with the material: Describe the most perfect place anyone could live; how would conflict be settled in such a place? Name three things that come to mind about King Arthur. What do you know about Merlin? Such a list can trigger prior knowledge and create student interest as well as provide a quick assessment.

2. Teachers may stress the importance of specific key passages in the new text (see also Selective Reading Guides below).

3. Teachers may help readers decide whether to skim or to read slowly and deliberately.

4. Teachers may draw attention to particular information, recognize new relationships, and set aside less important material—all before the assignment of especially difficult chapters. For material that appears to be very foreign to the students, these prereading tactics are helpful:
   - Explain key concepts.
   - Discuss key vocabulary.
   - Demystify the subject matter.
   - Dispel myths or misconceptions about the subject.

5. Teachers may even shape the students' stance or attitude toward their reading. For example, students could conceivably read any Richard Selzer article by scientifically examining its description of the human anatomy with objective criteria and dissecting it in a cold, analytical way, or they could read the same piece for its emotional content and the pleasures it imparts in language and passion. They could also read mathematic information—Euclid's fifth postulate, for example—as a descriptive and practical mathematical formula or as a piece of elegant prose, or both, but the aesthetic reading must precede the efferent reading..

6. Teachers may reduce ambiguity in a text. Take the newspaper headline "Tourists Drink in the Bottle House"—it's a double entendre, to be sure. Some discussion before reading can help students appreciate these games that writers play—irony, puns, tropes, and metaphors—to understand their purpose and to work out strategies for reading them.

7. Teachers and students may point out the features drawn from a list of the most common structures in prose: definition, enumeration, inductive or deductive argument, comparison/contrast, cause/effect, whole to part, chronology, and narrative.

8. Teachers can encourage risk-taking with difficult material. As we know, in the reading process the effective reader makes educated guesses about the material and predicts what's ahead.

When designed carefully, prereading preparation sets the tone for the day's lesson or the whole unit, both in terms of what is learned and how the information is regarded. Comprehension thus occurs in terms of what students are looking for as guided by the teacher. Since the purposes for prereading—to set a focus, to tap prior knowledge, to arouse interest and curiosity, to lessen anxiety, to make the content more accessible—are too varied to accomplish with one exercise, teachers usually choose to tackle only one of these purposes before making the first reading assignment of the lesson.

The Prereading Assessment

Teachers often check to see what their students remember from prior lessons about the topic. The most common method for doing this is the pretest, usually a small quiz that poses a few questions about material from past chapters that will be needed for the upcoming reading. For example, French students may have to review the verb *être* before studying the perfect form that uses *être* with the participle. The pretest or any other quick assessment helps the teacher and student evaluate the need for further review. Its disadvantage is that students who don't know the material can feel defeated and negative about the content before the lesson begins. Other assessment tools are the Anticipation Guide, KWL, and semantic maps.

The Anticipation Guide

A less intimidating version of the pretest is the Anticipation Guide first introduced by Readence, Bean, and Baldwin in 1981. This is a one-of-a-kind prereading exercise that contains a series of about ten to fifteen statements that reflect one narrow aspect of the material. The students must usually make binary choices to respond to the statements: yes/no, likely/unlikely, then/now, agree/disagree. Two examples of Anticipation Guides are Figures 8–1 and 8–2. The Anticipation Guide is rarely graded and in many classes it is used to generate discussion as a stimulus to reading:

The best feature of an Anticipation Guide is that it taps into the store of students' prior experiences and asks for responses based on their prior knowledge. Often these statements challenge commonly held beliefs or draw analogies

---

Fats in Foods

Rank the following foods for the amount of fat they contain based on your "gut-level" common sense.

 1 = least amount of fat
10 = the most amount of fat

____ Two scoops of vanilla ice cream in a cup from your local convenience store.
____ One large, green apple
____ A Big Mac
____ A small order of fries from Wendy's
____ A regular-sized bowl of Cheerios with whole milk
____ One serving of Kraft macaroni and cheese
____ One pork chop
____ A small bag of Fritos
____ A serving of broccoli with a pat of butter

FIGURE 8–1. Anticipation Guide (Health)

Congruent Angles

Directions: Before we discuss the next chapter on congruency angles, try to think back on what you have learned earlier about congruency and the functions of angles. If you agree with the statement, mark a plus (+); if you disagree, mark a minus (-).

_____ 1. If two angles are complements of congruent angles (or the same angle), then the two angles are congruent.

_____ 2. Vertical angles are not congruent.

_____ 3. We can determine congruence by laying one triangle on top of the other.

_____ 4. If two angles are supplementary, the sum of their measures is 360°.

_____ 5. If two lines are perpendicular, they meet at right angles.

_____ 6. If two lines do not intersect, they are parallel.

_____ 7. We can tell an isosceles triangle by the sum of its angles.

_____ 8. An equilateral triangle has two congruent sides and a right angle.

_____ 9. The sum of the measures of the interior angles of a triangle is 360°.

FIGURE 8–2. Anticipation Guide (Math)

between the assigned reading and a familiar event. Alternatively, they can quiz students on already learned material. Here are the steps for constructing an Anticipation Guide:

- Identify the major concept in an upcoming text selection, lecture, or film;
- OR identify the students' beliefs that will be challenged or the experience that will be evoked, or the review material that needs to be pretested;
- THEN, create statements reflecting, in part, your students' prereading beliefs or experiences. Some of these may be mistaken notions, and some should be

consistent with both your students' experiential background and the concepts presented in the material or lesson.

While writing Anticipation Guides, make certain to consider the following features:

- clear instructions
- short, simple-to-read statements
- single coherent focus to all the statements
- statements that contain few (if any) extreme qualifiers like "never," "always," "all," or "every."
- a balance of true and false statements—not too many trues or falses
- items worded in a parallel format

The Anticipation Guide has several advantages over other prereading lessons: it can accomplish one or more of the above purposes as well as provide a quick way to open up discussion. Especially when it touches on familiar ideas it becomes a nonthreatening tool, since it is usually not graded by the teacher. Moreover, it may be used as a starter for group work or journal writing.

K-W-L

Still another way of assessing the students' prior knowledge and piquing interest in the material is the K-W-L, an exercise devised by Donna Ogle (1986). K-W-L stands for *K*now, *W*ant to know, and *L*earned. The teacher asks students to brainstorm what they know about a given topic and writes their ideas on the board or on an overhead transparency that can be saved. The point of the exercise is to generate curiosity, so it helps to list as many ideas as time allows; pausing to encourage the more reticent students to contribute involves as many as possible. Then the teacher asks, "What do you want to know?" Students then suggest a new list for the board, this time with question marks. The goal of this step is to demonstrate to students the importance of asking questions of the material before reading. These lists become a reference for the last question which comes up later: "What have you learned that is new and what do you still want to learn?" Ogle also adds these questions:

1. "What categories of information do we expect to use in looking for this information?"
2. "What information do we predict the text to contain?"
3. "What answers have you found in the text to the self-initiated questions we had about the topic?"

Ogle is asking students to recognize certain signals, such as subject headings, that are commonly used by content area authors to convey their information.

The point of this exercise is to help students anticipate the organizational devices used in expository texts and help them see the overall pattern of informational structures. The exercise also helps students understand the kinds of information that a text might provide and the sorts of questions that will be left unanswered. K–W–L not only helps the teacher assess the student level of understanding, but also models the learning process and activates thinking on the topic. This activity is quite popular among middle school students, especially when linked with other sources for satisfying their curiosity. The following table shows an eighth-grader's K–W–L worksheet about "Japan and the Japanese."

K (Know)	W (Want to Know)	L (Learned)
The Japanese look Asian.	What do they wear every day?	Japan is a series of Islands near China.
They play baseball.	Will they ever be in the World Series?	The Japanese eat raw fish and rice.
They make Toyotas, Hondas, and VCRs.	What do they eat?	Japan is a rich country because of its exports.
Their writing is different.	How do they do math with their numbers?	Japanese children go to school long hours, even after school.
		They learn the Latin alphabet and Arabic numerals in addition to three kinds of Japanese characters.

Other Prereading Suggestions

In addition to K–W–L, teachers may choose among numerous other possibilities for prereading activities. Final selection rests on the nature of the ideas to be taught, the difficulty of the reading, available resources, and student need. Other activities are the following:

- Reading aloud the text's prepared preview questions.
- Drawing up a classification system of ideas in a taxonomy or jot chart. Some of this chart may be left blank for the students to fill in as they read.
- Making a text preview, list, or outline of the new material using the chapter headings and other quick sources of information.
- Outlining the key vocabulary in a hierarchical relationship with a semantic map that illustrates the relationships among the content words.

- Working with key vocabulary using a maze or a cloze passage. (See Chapter 5 for further discussion.)
- Laying out a problem to be solved. The problem may be situational, using something topical out of the newspaper or a school event that can be used to exemplify the issues raised in the text.
- Discussing related concepts in small or whole-class groups.
- Playing a relevant game.
- Showing a film.
- Preparing students for the chapter's layout, which may be in the form of a laundry list (enumeration), a comparison/contrast, or a historical narrative. Other rhetorical forms are cause and effect, problem-solving, analogy, and chronological order.
- Setting up situations that require ethical choices. This is a particularly effective method for activating high school students' interest in the material.

During-Reading Comprehension Activities

Since editors set the lengths of their chapters to be covered in about a week, teachers usually plan a few days' activities to help guide thinking while students are completing the chapter and to assist in focusing on what is important. They may also be concerned with maintaining the level of interest, checking the level of student understanding, and continuing to monitor vocabulary and organization of the passages. At this point the teacher wants to help students with difficult concepts by asking questions and setting tasks that draw on all three levels of comprehension and encourage multiple responses. Often in this phase, she has an opportunity to extend comprehension by exploring the implications of the main idea with the students. She may also extend usage of the vocabulary and aim for full understanding through immersion. Depending on the amount of material and the teacher's own background and understanding, the during-reading period can last one day or several weeks. During this time she is asking the following: What concepts do I want students to understand? What facts, skills, and terms do I want them to learn? How can I guide them toward comprehension?

Most during-reading exercises are used when students are working their way through a long chapter or a book and need time to finish the reading on their own. Of course lectures, discussions, exercises, and films may enrich this phase of the reading process as well, but the focus is on informally assessing what the students still need to know, creating opportunities for students to interact with each other, selecting new lessons to guide their discovery, and asking well-placed questions to monitor the comprehension process. Below are some activities that effectively shepherd students through their reading.

Directed Reading-Thinking Activity

Directed Reading-Thinking Activity (DR-TA) is a stop-and-start technique, developed by Russell Stauffer, that is used in class to help students read through a particularly difficult text. DR-TA is also one of the best exercises around for guiding interpretation, fostering prediction, and teaching students how to break material into chunks. Because each part of the passage is read aloud and discussed thoroughly, it is especially useful for drawing attention to passages and parts of chapters that are crucial to an understanding of key concepts.

To execute DR-TA, the teacher divides the passage into meaningful segments and thinks about how these parts fit into the whole. She asks students to predict upcoming passages and to comment on the whole reading afterwards. A DR-TA typically proceeds like this:

1. Discuss author's background, if appropriate and necessary.
2. Ask about title and subheadings to glean what information they suggest.
3. Ask students to predict what might lie in the first segment of material. Or ask them what purposes they set for themselves in this reading. Be careful not to dismiss any of the predictions or goals.
4. Read the preselected segment aloud or silently.
5. Ask students one or two questions about what they just read. Discuss any knotty concepts or difficult vocabulary.
6. Ask students to predict the next section. The suspense can be heightened with a little debate or even a poll. Be careful not to allow a protracted discussion between points of reading because it will fragment the ideas.
7. Repeat steps 3–6 until the reading is completed.

At most of the stopping points the teacher is asking the student first to review the material just read and second to make a prediction about what's ahead. A typical lesson plan for DR-TA looks like this sample based on a chapter on acids and bases in a chemistry text:

- Questions on title: What sorts of acids can you think of? What do they have in common? How are they used? Can anyone think of a base? Read to the end of the paragraph on page 51.
- Questions for reading up to page 51. What is the definition of an acid? What part of the definition probably points to the liquid that burns your skin? What will the chapter discuss next? How do you know?

The point of this line of questioning is to help students make connections among the parts of their reading and to make predictions. Furthermore, they need to justify their answers using their prior knowledge and any data they have collected from the text. Questions like these should be asked at all the logical stopping points. For very difficult material, the stops may be numerous.

The DR-TA can be adapted to all sorts of uses, not only to help students unpack difficult reading, but also to teach them how to monitor their own reading techniques. DR-TA affords opportunities to observe the reading behaviors, guide reader-text interactions, and extend learning.

Selective Reading Guides

This is another activity that walks students through difficult text. The main difference is that it applies to reading at home alone. The instructions direct students to the most important information and ask questions about it. In addition to guiding student reading, the questions effectively model the kinds of behaviors that we want students to adopt for reading textbooks. The following steps for the Selective Reading Guide were taken from a list drawn up by Cunningham and Shablik (1975):

1. Based on the main idea for the lesson, the teacher determines the goal(s) for the reading assignment as a whole.
2. The teacher selects key passages that will be emphasized to exemplify and clarify the main idea. Most often these instructions are followed with questions about the content that will direct the students' attention toward the implications of the main ideas.
3. The teacher decides on directions for the students, based on reading strategies she would use if she were reading the assignment.

The following piece provides an example of a Selective Reading Guide for a textbook section on forecasting weather.

Weather Forecasting

This exercise should enable you to understand how the circulation of air is created by heat transfers among land, water, and air. You should also begin to think about the basic processes and dynamics of atmospheric circulation.

Directions: Read ONLY the parts of Chapter 8 indicated here and answer the questions based on your reading.
1. Skip over sections 8:1–8:2. We will pick up some of these sections in later lessons.
2. Read Section 8:3. In your own words, explain IN GENERAL what is being measured in atmospheric pressure.
3. What changes the gauge, pushing the needle toward a higher or lower point?
4. After reading Section 8:4, explain how the earth is heated or cooled and what conditions help the earth hold both hot and cold temperatures.
5. Read about Heat Transfer in Sections 8:5 and 8:6. Explain how heat and cold move around either by explaining conduction or convection (p.154).
6. What do conduction and convection have in common?
7. In paragraph one on Heat Transfer (p.153), there is an example of radiant heat. Can you think of another one?

Text Pattern Guide

The Text Pattern Guide also is a set of questions that will guide students through a reading, except in this case the questions closely reflect the text's organizational pattern. The questions may form a pattern that leads students to recognize the text's structure, which may be one of the rhetorical structures listed above. For example, take this chronological sequence from a biology text:

"Explain the steps that cells undergo in their transformation to permanent tissue." Or consider this example of comparison/contrast: "Compare the Phylum Arthropoda to the Phylum Mollusca using the following systems—respiratory, reproduction, circulatory, and nervous." Or this cause/effect from biology: "Because ecology deals with mutual relations of organisms and environment, it is concerned with adaptation or fitness. List all the types of adaptation discussed in this chapter." In each case, the students are being asked to look beyond the details to recognize a larger pattern.

One of the architects of the Text Pattern Guide, Richard Vacca (1975), suggests the following steps:

1. Determine the predominant pattern of the reading. Consider standard rhetorical structures when trying to make this determination.
2. Discuss this organizing pattern with your students. Recognizing these structures is very difficult for the uninitiated and so pointing them out at every opportunity is instructive for most of them.
3. Show students how to spot the transitional words and other linguistic signposts that point to the pattern. This part of the lesson may be followed by small-group or whole-class discussion.
4. Help students see how the pattern supports the chapter's lesson.

One way to reinforce the uses of these rhetorical structures for both reader and author is to follow up this exercise with a writing assignment that will encourage them to employ the structure. A very effective assignment is the abstract or summary that forces the student to articulate the whole idea in terms of the rhetorical structure. Examples of text pattern guides that demonstrate three different rhetorical patterns appear in Figures 8–3, 8–4, and 8–5.

The Summary Writing Assignment

Also called a précis or abstract, the summary is a condensation of a longer piece of writing for easier and faster reading. The summary is frequently used in academe, especially in the sciences and social sciences, to provide quick access to technical information. It is used in business to circulate information within the company, and it provides a shortcut for the reader who may want to follow up the original piece in greater detail. Because it is one of the best assignments for both analysis and synthesis, it is one of the most common exercises in European school systems.

The summary is one of those time-honored assignments that has dozens of variations. Here are the steps for writing an abstract or summary:

1. Read the material thoroughly to find the main theme.
2. Jot down notes or underline the most salient points.
3. Write your paragraph connecting all the points with transition words like "nevertheless," "however," and "yet," so that you have a smoothly flowing product.
4. Proofread for errors made in haste.

Separation of Powers Between National and State Governments

One of the on-going tensions in American History is the give-and-
take between the powers assigned to the federal and state
governments and those reserved for the people. Your task is to
identify the powers of each branch.

Directions:

1. Use your text to identify the seat of power for performing
each of the following functions. You may check more than one
column.

2. On the bottom of this page, write a paragraph that the authors
of your text should have included to explain what characterizes
each of the powers.

NATIONAL   STATE   PEOPLE

_____   _____   _____   1. Raise taxes

_____   _____   _____   2. Perform marriage

_____   _____   _____   3. Levy duties on imports & exports

_____   _____   _____   4. Determine matters of free speech

_____   _____   _____   5. Create a public school system

_____   _____   _____   6. Regulate commerce

_____   _____   _____   7. Discipline children

_____   _____   _____   8. Wage war

_____   _____   _____   9. Mint money

_____   _____   _____   10. Build roads

FIGURE 8–3. Text Pattern Guide (Comparison/Contrast)

It sounds simple enough, but a good summary follows some fairly strict guidelines:

1. It covers only the main points, so it indicates only main themes, generali-
    zations, and conclusions.
2. It does not include examples, specifics, or arguments.
3. It does not use any direct quotations from the original, except for an irre-
    placeable phrase like "Riders of the Sea."
4. It uses a structure parallel to that of the original. If the original, for exam-
    ple, is written in an inductive argument, the summary should be shaped as
    an inductive argumentative statement.
5. It does not allot undue space to a minor point or, conversely, slight a
    major point. The spread of topics should be roughly proportionate to that
    of the original article.

German Pronouns for the Direct and Indirect Object

Examine each of the following series and fill in the blanks below with the appropriate pronouns:

Wem bringen Sie das Heft?
Ich bringe es dem Vater.
Ich bringe ihm das Heft.

Für wen kaufen Sie die Kuche?
Ich kaufe sie der Mutter.
Ich kaufe ihr die Kuche.

Wem geben Sie den Messer?
Ich gebe ihn dem Mädchen.
Ich gebe ihm den Messer.

1. Ich zeige dem Schüler das Buch.
   Ich zeige _____ das Buch.
   Ich zeige _____ dem Schüler.

2. Ich spiele der Freundin die Musik.
   Ich spiele _____ die Musik.
   Ich spiele _____ der Freundin.

3. _____ liest er den Roman?
   Er liest _____ der Gäste.
   Er liest _____ den Roman.

4. Der Grossmama hat die Freundin gefallen.
   _____ hat die Freundin gefallen.
   Ihr hat _____ gefallen?

5. Wem zeigen sie die Gitarre?
   Sie zeigen _____ dem Schilehrer.
   Sie zeigen _____ die Gitarre.

FIGURE 8–4. Text Pattern Guide (Model with Variations)

6. It adds no material to the original and never contains the opinion of the summarizer.

7. It is concise. It rarely runs more than a page, regardless of the length of the original material. Most abstracts are only one paragraph long.

The Three-Level Statement Guide

Another exercise for extending the lesson is the Three-Level Statement Guide. Built on the taxonomy of three levels of questions discussed in the last chapter, it serves much the same purpose. Instead of questions, however, the three levels in this case are cast in statement form, so the students are asked to draw on different skills to complete it. It offers a fresh approach and exposes students to new complexities in the material. Providing students with a variety of activities helps to prepare them for standardized exams that might otherwise be unfamilar.

The Three-Level Statement Guide usually consists of three tiers of statements that reflect increasingly complex relationships in the material.

1. In the first tier students are asked to put a check next to the statements that are *found in the text* or to check the statements that are true according to the text.

```
            U.S. Reconstruction 1865-1877
Following the Civil War a number of events led to events which
influence conditions we live with today.  Given the following
causes, name at least one result:
1. Cause: Lincoln is assassinated.
   Result:
2. Cause: Congress seeks to punish the South.
   Result:
3. Cause: Congress determines to aid the former slaves.
   Result:
4. Cause: President Andrew Johnson vetoes the Civil Rights Act.
   Result:
5. Cause: Congress passes laws to limit the powers of the
      presidency.
   Result:
6. Cause: White Southerners turn to violence.
   Result:
7. Cause: Blacks seek a better life economically.
   Result:
8. Cause: The South begins to build a new economy.
   Result:
```

Figure 8–5. Text Pattern Guide (Cause and Effect)

2. In the second tier, students are asked to check statements that are *implied by the text*.
3. In the third tier, students are asked to check statements that appear to be true *based on knowledge or beliefs drawn beyond the text*.

Figure 8–6 and Figure 8–7 are examples of Three-Level Statement Guides.

Harold Herber (1978), author of the exercise, gives the best advice for constructing the Three-Level Statement Guide, which is paraphrased here:

1. Begin with an understanding of the author's organizing concept (rhetorical structure of the text) and write the statements for the interpretive level first. The key to a good Three-Level Statement Guide is taking a deep look at the author's ideas and knowing what you want students to discover in the reading. The author's ideas are best brought out at the interpretive (second) level.
2. Then write statements for the other two levels. Work at finding links among the levels so that statements at the first two levels prepare students for responses in the applied level. Add some distractors to each level, not to lead the students astray so much as to second-guess what mistaken notions they are harboring. The applied (third) level of statements affords an ideal chance to raise misconceptions and talk about them.

PROBLEM: Ben has $24 in his savings account. He plans to add $2 every week. How much will he have in his account after "x" number of weeks?

I. Directions: Given the equation $y = 2x + 24$, check those statements that form true solutions to the equation.

_____ 1. After 2 weeks Ben has $28 in his account.

_____ 2. After 5 weeks Ben has $70 in his account.

_____ 3. After 8 weeks Ben has $40 in his account.

II. Directions: Given the table and the graph, check those statements that form true conclusions from the data.

$y = 2x + 24$

X	Y
0	24
1	26
2	28
3	30
4	32

_____ 4. The slope of the equation is 1/2 .

_____ 5. The slope of the equation is ?.

_____ 6. The point (0,24) indicates that Ben began it $24 in his account.

_____ 7. Using the graph, you can predict that after 10 weeks he will have $50 in his account.

_____ 8. Extending the table indicates that after 8 weeks he will have $40 in his account.

_____ 9. The *constant* rate of increase indicates that this is a **linear equation**.

III. Suppose that you have been charting IBM stocks for six weeks. If the stock goes up for three weeks and falls for a week, then continues to rise, imagine how the graph might look. Compare this imaginary graph with the one that charts Ben's savings. Are they both linear equations? Be prepared to defend your answer.

FIGURE 8–6. Three-Level Statement Guide (Math)

LITERAL LEVEL- Check the items that clearly represent what you have
read so far.

1._____ People living in the Secret Annexe have to live by strict
rules to prevent discovery.

2._____ Anne feels very sure of who she is and sees herself as a
strong person.

3._____ Anne's most outstanding traits are that she is rebellious,
optimistic and brave.

4._____ Anne believes in the good of man despite Hitler's mission
to destroy and exterminate.

5._____ The Franks knew the Germans were good people and planned to
return home after the war.

6._____ When Anne began her diary she didn't think her interest
would last for long.

7._____ When the Allies started bombing Amsterdam, the Franks knew
the end was in sight.

8._____ Winston Churchill's voice on the radio represented the Franks
greatest hope for survival.

9._____ The Franks were wanted because they left Germany.

10._____ The Franks didn't want to listen to the radio because all
they heard was bad news.

II. INFERENTIAL LEVEL: In the statements listed select the ones that
Anne really believes and put a check mark on the line provided.
You may have to support your answers.

1._____ Anne wants to run away from everyone because she is used to
being spoiled and pampered.

2._____ Anne loves reading and writing and uses these tools to
creatively fill her time.

3._____ The reason Anne is rarely silent is because she feels she
has important things to say.

4._____ The Franks believed they had done something wrong and would
be punished for it.

5._____ As evil as Hitler's plan is, Anne never loses hope in the
goodness of man.

6._____ While this group of people hid from the Nazis, you never had
the feeling they would be caught.

III. APPLIED LEVEL While reading these statements try to fully
understand what they mean and apply the information to what you
already know. If you think these statements are supported by
Anne's beliefs place a check in the space provided.

1._____ No matter what evil you know is going on around you, you must
try and keep your belief that man is really good at heart.

2._____ Not standing up for yourself and what you believe in, will
severely handicap your sense of identity.

3._____ The more suffering you endure the more empathy you will
have for others' suffering.

4._____ A person without hope is like being in a boat without oars
in the middle of the lake.

5._____ Human dignity is the birthright of all people.

6._____ The history of a people's suffering can be read in the
story of a young girl.

FIGURE 8–7. Three–Level Statement Guide (English)

3. Typically, the Three-Level Statement Guide contains 5–6 statements at the literal (first) level, 5–6 statements at the interpretive (second) level, but fewer statements at the applied (third) level since these statements take more thought to formulate and more time for response. Generally, directions at the applied level ask students merely to think about their responses and to be prepared to defend them.

When done well, statements at this level will elicit a wide variety of commentary. Of the three sets, the third-level statements are also best for prompting discussion in whole-class or small-group work because they tend to be more open-ended and complex.

As with all these reading activities, the Three-Level Statement Guide runs the risk of rigidly structuring the class. Although it is effective in helping students through the reading, it should be used judiciously. Overreliance on it as a reading exercise can be deadening in a class that doesn't need the guidance, boring to classes that have been over exposed to it, and fragmenting to a lesson that may need to be discussed in broader strokes. The Three-Level Statement Guide can be, moreover, difficult to construct. The best guides take some teacher perspicacity and ingenuity to make them effective. Despite these caveats, we heartily endorse the Three-Level Statement Guide as one of the best tools around for exposing students to all levels of thinking and for setting up thought-provoking discussions and excellent writing possibilities.

Postreading Comprehension

Because there is such a rich assortment of activities that a teacher may use to follow up a lesson, it hardly seems necessary to discuss them in great detail. Postreading events are limited only by the time and resources available to the teacher and by the students' level of interest. They can range from tests to films to field trips, or time spent developing major projects. Teachers might also consider metacognitive exercises that look back on "the lesson that was" and examine how students negotiated its hazards. Many times there is a fine line between study strategies and postreading exercises. The biggest difference is one of emphasis: study strategies aim more to clarify any confusion about the reading, and postreading exercises to enrich, refine, and heighten interest in the topic of the lesson, as well as to give students occasion for expressing themselves and for rehearsing the ideas aloud. Here are some ideas for postreading activities that help students reinforce the content of the chapter:

- Students talk about what they read. Class discussion is usually fun and effective if participation is good, but a more structured format for oral reporting of information is also powerful. One exercise may be to present a "story" to the audience as a mock television presentation or news item through interview and narrative. Students should be allotted only two or three minutes for their oral report. Another possibility is to select five or so key concepts, or the idea that is primary to the reading. A third activity may be to debate a central issue. This activity takes careful planning with firm ground rules to keep it from degenerating into a shouting argument. A fourth option is that students may teach other students what they know.

- Students write about what they read. Again, the possibilities are endless. Students may write paraphrases of the text, or try writing summaries and abstracts. Other concise forms of writing are the piece for a time capsule or a news story with the who, what, when, where, why, and how facts and a headline, or telegrams. Personal reactions are best recorded in journal entries, summary/response papers, or essays. Report writing can appear as rewrites of the chapter for other students, persuasive essays, dialogues between well-known figures in history, how-to manuals, or book reviews of the text. All of these ideas are more effective and less cumbersome than the formal research paper for producing lively writing that enlists students' imaginations.
- Students read other books and articles on the subject.
- Students play games, see films, and explore the community around them for applications of the information.
- Students discriminate between biased opinion and more objective judgments.
- Students discover the significance of a concept through cognitive conflict.
- Students make charts about what they read. Among the most obvious of these are jot charts and criterial matrices. But there are also graphs, pie charts, outlines, and maps. List–Group–Label (discussed in Chapter Seven) provides another study tool.
- Students take tests on what they read. The most common use for postreading is evaluation for comprehension. Quizzes, informal questioning, and discussion of the assignment are all time-tested methods for evaluation, but new methods should be investigated as well. A more extensive discussion of assessment for reading comprehension appears in Chapter Five.

The Goals of Postreading Instruction

Whatever the teacher chooses to do as a postreading follow-up, he should strive to reinforce learning by encouraging a summary and review of the key concepts in the lesson. He can do this by stressing synthesis, argumentation, and reorganization of the ideas. He can also reinforce vocabulary and use this time for assessment. At this point he reminds himself once again about the main idea and how he can extend the students' learning beyond the initially proposed main idea and beyond the text. More often than not, this period of learning is critical for turning much of the lesson over to the students. This is a time for them to share what they have learned with each other, to argue controversial questions, to do independent projects and writing assignments. It is also a time for the teacher to evaluate what students have learned. Teachers should continue to ask themselves what key points raised in the text selection should be reviewed and reinforced. What postreading activities will synthesize ideas and leave students with a coherent sense of the material? How can I extend the students' learning beyond the text and link it to the course material that will follow? How will I know whether students have comprehended the material and are ready to move on?

Developing Lessons into Larger Units

Lessons that begin with comprehensive main ideas can be developed into extensive units covering lessons that last three to six weeks or longer. If instruction is approached with the three-phase process described below and attention is paid to developing lessons at each phase, students will receive the scaffolding that leads to more purposeful interaction with the reading materials. These units have the added advantage of placing control of the content into the hands of teachers and students who shape it for their own uses. Because textbooks are being used selectively, teachers who design their own units with multiple resources can bypass mistakes and avoid the canned material found in many textbooks. Furthermore, they can focus the lessons according to their own strengths and their students' interest. They may also tailor the lessons to a particular school's needs and the problems that students pose. Each time that the unit is pulled out of the cupboard for a new class, the teacher may add to it and change it accordingly. Students too may be encouraged to supplement the reading with materials of their own, and even parental expertise may be considered a supplementary resource. In the end, variety and choice help students understand the implication of the main idea in terms of their own "worldview in the head."

The Thematic Unit

Meinbach, Rothlein, and Fredericks define a thematic unit as "the epitome of whole language teaching." The thematic unit, a collage of materials and a blend of ideas from a variety of disciplines and media, offers exciting possibilities for the language arts. Its purpose is to arouse the natural curiosity of students and to engage them in their own learning through continuous reading and writing. Originally the thematic unit took a multidisciplinary approach to a theme, but it works equally well when built around a concept, principle, or theorem. The point is to offer a series of lessons that present a coherent unfolding of ideas largely through the use of problem-solving and discovery activities. The thematic unit integrates the language arts—reading, writing, speaking, and listening—focusing on a main idea. It offers a foundation of meaningful, coherent material that students can question in terms of their own experiences. In elementary schools, such a unit might be taught for an entire day or longer. In the secondary schools, it might last three to six weeks.

The best thematic units combine all the features we have been advocating in this text:

1. lessons that focus on the relationship between the text and the "real world"
2. questions that evoke students' prior knowledge, relating the information to what they are learning and prodding them to pose questions or problemetize the lessons on their own
3. activities that reinforce reading and writing skills in meaningful and holistic ways by allowing for question-asking activity
4. assignments that enable students to discover solutions with guidance

Assignments in a thematic unit are carefully selected to introduce, reinforce, and extend concepts that the teacher has identified in the planning.

Like lesson plans, thematic units vary from elementary to high school and from discipline to discipline; nevertheless, they tend to share many elements with the lesson plan. They both take careful preparation in the pre-, during-, and postreading stages, and they both stress activities that clarify the reading. The primary difference is that the thematic unit addresses a larger range of ideas and covers a longer period of time. Like the lesson plan, the thematic unit may include the following components:

- a main idea that informs all the daily activities
- a map that visually represents connections among key parts of the main idea
- a list of sources that, in this case, includes print materials as well as multimedia and community resources
- a bibliography of books written at the various levels of students in the class.
- a list of key vocabulary, both new words to be learned in this unit and vocabulary to be reviewed from prior work
- questions posed at all three levels of cognition
- lessons for the pre-, during-, and postreading stages. These should afford plenty of choices that appeal to students from all corners of the school. Included should be work choices that consider the multicultural community as well as children with multiple intelligences and other special populations.
- an instructional framework—that is, a series of well-considered lesson plans that fit together in a coherent whole
- metacognitive activities (see Chapter Seven)
- assessment that is ongoing and authentic

The best of thematic units also incorporate self-initiated activities and plenty of time for discussing and sharing. Coherence is achieved through a steady focus on the main ideas of the discipline. Without a central concept, the lesson plan and thematic unit are likely to disintegrate into weeks of busywork rather than meaningful activity. After identifying the main objectives, the teacher may then draw up a map to assist in visualizing the connections among the subtopics.

Mapping the Key Terms or Key Concepts as Prereading, During-Reading, and Postreading Activities

A handy format for laying out the main idea in their relational parts is the Graphic Organizer, also called a Structured Overview or Idea Map, which spatially represents the relationships among the most important ideas of a text. In each case, teacher or student can build a coherent and concise model for representing the ideas of a reading in a concise yet visible form. They can be used to develop students' conceptual knowledge about a topic, open up expository (rhetorical) structures, and force decisions about relevant and irrelevant information. Commonly used structures are cause/effect, comparison/contrast, cycles, general to specific, large to small, and temporal sequence. Maps can take many shapes: algorithmic trees with forking paths, nesting squares, circles with rays, flow charts, contrasting pairs in columns, triangles, hierarchical pyramids, netting, and even the old-fashioned outlines laid out in an informal pattern.

The Graphic Organizer is instrumental for establishing the primacy of ideas and for setting the secondary order of topics. By illustrating the conceptual arrangement among ideas, it establishes priorities for lesson plans, serves as an outline for quick reference, and provides a needed plan for action in the prereading stage. Used as a guide for reading, it is called an Advanced Organizer: An example is given in Figure 8–8.

In the during-reading stage, the teacher may hand a simplified version of her map to students for use as a study guide for particularly dense material. The map helps students recognize new relationships, organize additional information, or develop a synthesis. It can remind them of what they know or it can alert them to new information and thus be an especially effective tool for organizing their thoughts. In postreading assignments, students may be asked to develop their own maps from scratch or they may be given a partially completed map with blanks. The blanks may omit specifics like the subheadings or headings. Each part of a map affords different challenges for critical thinking. As a postreading device, it can act as a summary or review and it may even be used diagnostically.

Constructing a Map

The steps for constructing a map are simple. Maps may be constructed from the top down or from the bottom up. The top-down approach begins with a large concept, so the task is to lay out its parts. The bottom-up approach—also called "clustering" or "webbing"—begins by brainstorming many possibilities; the task then is to discover a connection among the parts. This connector becomes the overarching principle that outlines the relationship among the parts.

Here are steps for the top-down approach:

1. List the central concepts or key terms.
2. Arrange them to establish interrelationships. The most frequently diagrammed relational structures are whole to parts or general to specific, cause/effect, cycles, analogy, and comparison/contrast.

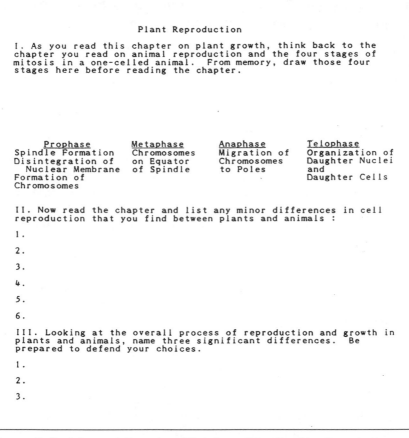

FIGURE 8–8. Advanced Organizer (Variation of the Graphics Organizer)

3. Add secondary and tertiary ideas or terms or subject heading. Label the connectors. Draw single lines between the most important relationships and double lines between the secondary relationships.
4. Check to see if the terms on each level are parallel, that is, if they share the same degree of importance, similar categories, or common themes.
5. Use cross-links if additional relationships are suggested.
6. Check to see if the most general ideas are emphasized and eliminate unnecessary detail. The point is to keep the map easy to read and follow, without too much detail.

Despite the simplicity of these directions, teachers will be amazed by the variety of maps students may produce if asked to lay out the concepts from a given body of material. The maps they produce will reflect the diversity of interpretations in the classroom and underscore the validity of divergent viewpoints. The generic map, or graphic organizer, has many offspring. A variety of mapping configurations are shown in Figure 8–9. Variations on the map adopt this simple verbal picture for other uses as well:

- Story mapping: the main features of a narrative (setting, plot, characters, motivation) arranged to illustrate the theme or some other set of relationships
- Listing: laundry lists, word sorts, outline
- Semantic maps: key terms arranged in a hierarchical relationship. These are also called word maps. They provide a framework for students to add new word to as the lesson progresses. Semantic maps are used specifically to illustrate superordinate, ordinate, and subordinate aspects. They also emphasize the characteristics that the terms hold in common.

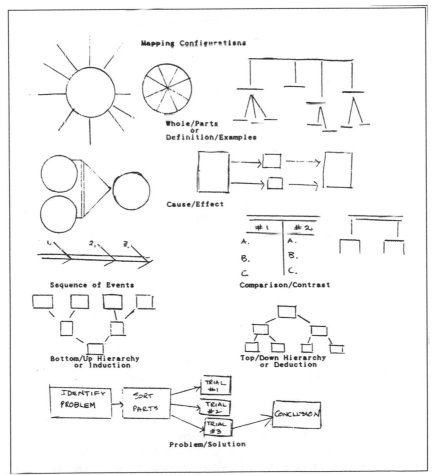

FIGURE 8–9. Mapping Configurations

Vocabulary in Prereading, During-Reading, or Postreading Lessons

Although some textbooks will provide a list of critical vocabulary at the beginning of the chapter, and sometimes the vocabulary appears in the form of a graphic organizer at the beginning of the chapter, very few of these lists make sense until the reader has digested the chapter's main points. Sometimes, however, it is necessary to teach a few key words—the ones that carry the main idea—before reading the chapter. This is particularly important in the sciences. If the chapter is about osmosis, the teacher should make certain that her students understand such words as "cell," "cell wall," "permeable," "membrane," and that they understand the general concept that pressure on one side of the cell wall will allow certain solvents to pass through it. In short, the prereading vocabulary words are taught in conjunction with the concept that they articulate. Words taught in the prereading stage serve to prepare the way for the reading ahead and to lessen the density of new vocabulary that students have to confront in many science texts.

The most useful stage for vocabulary instruction is in the during-reading stage and at a point when the lesson moves from a general grasp of the material to a more refined understanding. The postreading stage is also opportune for reinforcing vocabulary that has only been vaguely understood. Vocabulary learned strictly in the context of the reading may often be insufficiently delineated, especially in disciplines such as math and chemistry where exact definitions are crucial to comprehension. Although a context cue often hints at a word's meaning, it alone cannot always provide enough information about unknown words. In fact, context is most useful when the reader already knows something about what the word means and has confronted it in other settings. The reason is that the solitary definition suggested by a singular context is not adequate to full understanding of a word's possibilities. Unidimensional definitions offer only superficial introductions to the word. Students know a word best by trying it out for themselves, explaining its meaning in their own words, experimenting with synonyms and antonyms, and connecting it to their own storehouse of knowledge in a variety of ways, including writing and speaking. That's why language immersion is important to the process of assimilating new words.

The question then becomes how best to supplement the natural uses of language in our daily lives in and out of the academic setting. The following are suggestions for activities that encourage students both to understand the word's technical meanings and to use it in reference to larger ideas.

Semantic Feature Analysis or Concept Charts

Semantic feature analysis, also called feature analysis or criterial analysis organizes new vocabulary in a matrix by its properties. First suggested by Johnson and Pearson (1984), the charts supply a framework for the information and establish a focused set of relationships for the new words. Moreover, they improve skills for categorization. In Figure 8–10, students are asked to evaluate similarities and differences among types of African topographies.

Types of African Regions and Their Products

Evaluate the following areas for their ability to yield food. Use a "+" if the food will grow there and a "-" if it will not.

	Savannas	Rain Forest	Veld	Mangrove Swamps
wheat				
palm oil				
bananas				
rice				
citrus fruit				
cattle grazing				

FIGURE 8–10. Semantic Feature Analysis or Critical Analysis

Other matrices use the similar strategy of placing two sets of material in relation to each other. Also called *jot charts,* these information maps provide handy cross-references for study and review. The task of working with criterial features can be assigned again and again at increasing levels of difficulty. Possible variations are as follows:

- Teachers can list the vertical and horizontal terms in the grid for students simply to fill in
- Teachers can supply words for students to arrange in charts for themselves.
- Students set up their own charts from their reading materials, searching also for categories to use in meaningful relationships with the new terminology.

The disadvantage to such matrices, especially the feature analyses, is that they sometimes create an artificial system of binary choices when the relationships are often more complex. Teachers should be aware of choices that are not so clear-cut and use them as opportunities for discussion and the development of a more sophisticated set of relationships.

Scavenger Hunts

Like the old parlor game, this is a fun and instructive activity used when the vocabulary is primarily a list of nouns (see Vaughn, Crawley, and Mountain 1979). Student groups can be handed the same lists or similar lists of items to search out. On the lists can be invisible processes (such as direct electrical current, and alternating current, for which they find examples in electrical systems in their surroundings) as well as visible items (such as transformers). The words may be categorized already, or one of the requirements may be to arrange the words in categories. The teacher usually sets a fairly short time limit of a day or two and awards points for each found item. Depending on the list, students may have to bring back reports of where these items can be found, or cut pictures out of magazines and newspapers, or bring in samples or tracings, or use a combination of these methods.

Scavenger hunts have the added advantage of attaching words to the physical-sensory as well as the cognitive domains of learning. All of us can think of situations in which we have learned words and then link the words to the sensory experience. Psychologists have long observed the effectiveness of visual and auditory stimuli as reinforcements to cognition, so the physicality of searching out examples of words will long stick in students' memories.

Vocabulary Journals

Vocabulary journals also encourage students to connect words to their physical surroundings. In this case, however, they select their own words. Teachers can assign journals in various ways, but one suggestion is that students keep personal lists of unfamiliar vocabulary in a permanent notebook. They should record where the words were found, the sentence or situation in which they were heard or read. They should also date their entries and attach to them a definition that they either surmise from the context or rephrase from a dictionary. This activity is especially effective in second- and third-year language classes in which students read a variety of texts to improve their vocabulary base. Justifying their choices may also be instructive. Of course, the best vocabulary instruction happens in "teachable moments," during discussions that introduce the terminology in point of fact. Since most new vocabulary is learned through experience and everyday contexts, the value of many formal exercises may be rightfully questioned. Below is a quick list of vocabulary applications—some familiar, some experimental:

1. Fill-in-the blank or cloze exercises are more effective than the word drill if the sentences are cognitively linked around a given topic and are not isolated, meaningless units. The sentences must form a coherent thought and form a reading long enough to establish a context for the words.
2. Teaching students Greek and Latin roots, prefixes, and suffixes is also useful if the vocabulary list is connected to the lesson in some meaningful way.
3. Asking students to write sentences or paragraphs with vocabulary words is likewise effective if they form a constellation around a given topic or unit.
4. Paraphrasing a paragraph or two from the book is another tried-and-true method of improving comprehension when the book depends too heavily on technical terms.
5. Some schools have adopted a list of thirty to fifty words that every teacher, regardless of discipline, tries to use daily so that they come up again and again in appropriate contexts, in class discussion and in student writing. The program is fun for teachers and students who look for occasions to use these words. Another variation on this approach is the new-word-a-day, in which each teacher, regardless of discipline, draws attention to a new vocabulary word that is featured again and again throughout that day's

lesson. These schoolwide programs create a both playful and serious atmosphere for vocabulary enrichment and build respect for learning.

There is certainly no dearth of possibilities for effective vocabulary assignments, so these suggestions are just a starting point. These exercises share the goal of linking the content of the lesson to the new words. Most offer more than one perspective on the new words either by setting the terms in relation to other terms or by asking students to supply multiple definitions. A necessary complement to all these exercises are periodic metacognitive discussions about how to handle "big" words in context, about when it is useful to stop one's reading and look up words in the dictionary, and about how to identify key terminology using heuristic methods.

Among the least effective methods of vocabulary instruction is asking students to memorize lists and lists of isolated words with their definitions. Even worse, however, are the word search puzzles, crossword puzzles, and similarly superficial assignments. Students will find it difficult to link most of these words cognitively to their own schemas, so they will be quickly forgotten. The act of looking up dozens of strange, meaningless words in the dictionary is tedious and time-consuming; it often teaches students the frustration of vocabulary enrichment and little else. Instead, they should be learning strategies for adding personal words to their vocabulary, because these are pathways to larger ideas. The dictionary is valuable for precise definitions and provides a reliable reference, but it is not the only source.

Chapter Summary

We have suggested here a brief lesson-planning format that is goal-oriented, comprehension-centered, and considers all phases of the reading process—prereading, during-reading, and postreading. We begin first with the content objectives, which should state what ideas or concepts you want to focus on during this unit of instruction. The activities that teachers select should guide students before they read, as they read, and after they have completed the assignment. At least one activity should support each difficult concept in the reading. If students are doing the reading assignment in class, the plan may divide itself roughly into the beginning, middle, and end of a class period. More often than not, however, the reading is assigned as homework between two class periods, with class time on the first day spent in prereading activities to prepare students for the reading they will then do at home accompanied by some during-reading support. Class time the following day may focus on a postreading activity, which expands and reinforces students' learning, plus preparation for the next reading assignment. The postreading period must often be used to evaluate whether or not students have understood the assignment. Not every teacher feels the need for a written daily lesson plan when she enters the class-room. But we still find a measure of security in a briefly written plan for each class session since it forces us to think more carefully about what we are trying to achieve in each lesson.

CHAPTER NINE

Using Writing as a Tool to Improve Reading, Thinking, and Learning

Writing represents a unique mode of learning—not merely valuable, not merely special, but unique . . .

—Janet Emig

. . . writing is more than a frozen record of thinking. It is an action and a way of knowing.

—William Irmscher

. . . writing can become a deeper kind of thinking than is otherwise possible.

—R. D. Walshe

We do not write to be understood; we write in order to understand.

—C. Day Lewis

For the writer, writing is a process, a way of seeing, of hearing what he has to say to himself, a means of discovering meaning.

—Donald Murray

When you sit down and write your thoughts, they are reinforced, and you actually think harder than just by reading and thinking without writing.

—A college sophomore

These comments, from writers as diverse as composition theorists, a Pulitzer Prize–winning author, and a college student, testify to the power of writing as a tool for learning. In using their own language to write about new information, students not only learn the material better, they also discover what they do and do not know about the subject and come to a much clearer understanding of it than they get from reading alone. They not only discover meaning; they create it for themselves. Writing is a meaning-making activity. Yet recent studies of writing in the schools show that teachers fail to make use of writing in ways that support this process of thinking, discovering, and learning.

A study of writing in the British schools (Britton et al. 1975) showed that only 5.5 percent of the student writing the researchers collected was informal writing, the "thinking on paper" that supports learning. The majority of school-based writing by British eleven- to eighteen-year-olds was written to the teacher, particularly for the teacher as examiner, and was informative or persuasive writing to communicate what the student had already learned (63.4 percent).

We see a similar absence in Applebee's study of writing in various content areas in two midwestern high schools (1981). He found that although writing made up 44 percent of the observed class activities, this writing was dominated by informational uses of writing (20 percent), predominantly note-taking, and what the researchers termed "writing without composing" (24 percent). This included such mechanical uses of writing as multiple-choice exercises, fill-in-the-blank or short-answer exercises requiring phrases or brief answers, math calculations, copying from text or dictation, and translations. Students were asked to compose at least a paragraph only 3 percent of the observed classroom time. Imaginative and personal uses of writing were limited mainly to English classes, and even there only half the students reported these types of assignments, which occupied merely .8 percent of the total class time observed in all the disciplines studied (30–31). As in the British study, teachers used writing primarily to see what students knew rather than in ways that encouraged critical or analytical engagement with the material. Teacher response to the writing they assigned centered heavily on identifying and correcting errors rather than on responding to students' ideas, yet another indication that teachers were not encouraging the thinking processes inherent in writing but instead were using writing as if each assignment were a test of what the student knew and how adequately he or she could communicate that information on paper.

Not surprisingly, the 1986 National Assessment of Educational Progress report on writing (Applebee, Langer, and Mullis 1986) shows that "students have difficulty performing adequately on analytic writing tasks, as well as on persuasive tasks that ask them to defend and support their opinions" (11). The majority of students were able to respond on at least a minimal level to simple writing tasks appropriate to their grade level, such as descriptive writing that drew on their own experiences. However, when they were asked to perform more complex writing tasks that required reasoning skills, only a small percentage of students could perform adequately. For example, when asked to write a letter persuading the school principal to drop a school rule, only 22 percent of the eleventh-graders, 15 percent of the eighth-graders, and 4 percent of the fourth-graders produced an acceptable piece of writing. The researchers were especially concerned that eleventh-graders don't have adequate literacy skills for the writing demands of the workplace or college. The report concludes by suggesting:

> Because writing and thinking are so deeply intertwined, appropriate writing assignments provide an ideal way to increase student experiences with such types of thinking. . . . Students need broad-based experiences in which reading and writing tasks are integrated with their work throughout the curriculum. (11)

Despite this dismal national picture of writing, in many classrooms informed and innovative teachers are having much success in using writing to enhance their students' learning, giving them the kinds of writing experiences that improve critical thinking as they increase knowledge. In *Roots in the Sawdust* (Gere 1985) we see teachers of art, German, social studies, special education, science, math, philosophy, and history using a broad variety of writing activities and forms in their classrooms, aimed at providing students with "a way of thinking, not a set of facts" (3). In her introduction, Anne Gere explains that adopting writing-to-learn strategies does not necessarily mean changing what is taught; rather, teachers are incorporating writing into already existing course content, replacing or augmenting methods previously used to teach the course. From "descriptive listing" of visual elements in a work of art, to "biopoems" and journals in a science class, we find students in these classes using writing in ways that make the learning meaningful to themselves while stimulating critical interaction with texts. The teachers in Fulwiler's *The Journal Book* (1987) and Atwell's *Coming to Know* (1990) also demonstrate many ways in which teachers in all disciplines at all educational levels have developed courses in which writing is central to students' learning.

Using writing as a tool for learning is part of the larger shift in education away from the transmission model of passive, teacher-centered learning dominated by lectures, workbooks, and memorization, toward the active, inquiry-centered paradigm of the transactional classroom. In this model, the teacher's role is no longer primarily to transmit knowledge to the student. Instead, the classroom teacher creates an environment and structures activities that involve students in their own processes of learning. Writing is a primary activity in these classes.

The use of writing in this movement was illustrated by Elaine Porter, a high school English teacher in Linden, Michigan. She said,

> "I used to give my senior students lectures on symbolism in a piece of literature. Now I'm more likely to ask them to write in their journals about any symbolism they see as they read. I have them share these journal-writes with each other in class; then together we build an understanding of the way symbolism is used in whatever text we are reading."

It is important to establish the difference here between *teaching writing* and *using writing as a tool for learning* in content area classes. When writing is advocated as a learning strategy, the intent is not to turn math and social studies teachers into English teachers, adding on to the already considerable content of their courses. However, writing about course material is an important way to learn and understand it better. A quite natural outcome of all this writing in content areas beyond English is that students become better writers, but this results primarily from constant practice with a wide variety of writing forms, topics, and audiences rather than from increased direct instruction in writing skills. We are also suggesting that some of the writing strategies routinely employed by good writing teachers can achieve more satisfying results, and more permanent learning, than merely giving a writing assignment and expecting students to produce a finished piece on their own.

The purpose of this chapter, then, is twofold:

1. To present the rationale and specific teaching strategies for using writing to enhance reading comprehension and learning
2. To describe ways content area teachers can help students achieve polished pieces of writing that are the products of personal exploration, thinking, and knowing.

Why Write?

The Writing-Thinking Relationship

Writing, composing in language, is a thinking process as well as a process of using language. The writer must select and organize ideas in his mind, turn them into language, and turn this language into the written symbols representing these ideas. This is a remarkably complex process often marked by extreme concentration. Students have described this as "getting lost in the writing," an experience of such intense thinking that their surroundings disappear. The writer recedes into her own mind only to come out of this process moments or even hours later as if surfacing from underwater with a sense of "where am I? what time is it? what's been going on?"

A teacher need only watch a class of students writing to observe thinking taking place. A student writes intently for a few moments, stares off into space for a while, then bends down toward the paper once again with renewed intensity. Another student doodles spirals on paper with eyes half closed and then starts, hesitantly at first but then picking up speed, to fill a page with writing. Another writes, rereads it, scratches out some words, stares off to the left, squinting a bit, bites the top of his pen, and plunges in once more. If minds were wired for sound, a writing classroom would be unbearably noisy with audible thinking.

To better understand this thinking/writing relationship, try the following exercise (adapted from a workshop by Toby Fulwiler and Randall Freisinger, Michigan Council of Teachers of English, 1980).

Part I. Write informally for about five minutes on each of the topics below. Do these as free writings, without any planning or attention to grammar and mechanics. Just jot your ideas down on paper.

1. What do you already know about writing to learn?
2. Make a list of the different kinds of writing you do both in your personal life and as a teacher. When do you put pen or pencil (or computer) to paper?
3. Arrange the items in #2 into two lists: the writing you do for yourself, and the writing you do for a reader or readers.

4. Examine your two lists. Do any patterns emerge? Can you make any generalizations? Write about what you see.
5. Describe either a very fine writing experience you have had or a very bad one.

Part II. Re-examine these jottings in terms of the cognitive activities involved in each one. What kinds of thinking did you have to do in order to accomplish each writing task? Here are some of the responses you might have:

Jotting #1. Draw on prior knowledge.
   interpret the phrase "writing to learn"
   remember
   select
   organize ideas

Jotting #2. Make a list.
   visualize
   remember
   select

Jotting #3. Arrange list.
   categorize
   evaluate
   reorganize

Jotting #4. Examine lists.
   analyze
   generalize
   evaluate

Jotting #5. Write about a past experience with writing.
   remember
   select
   organize chronologically
   decide where to begin
   engage emotionally

By examining these responses, and those you made yourself, we can see that a given writing assignment induces a particular set of cognitive behaviors. For example, jotting #4, in which you were asked to search for patterns in your two lists of writings, drew on more complex thinking skills than jotting #2, when you had to do little more than recall the numerous ways you used writing throughout your life. Also, the cognitive behaviors necessary to organize the material in each of these jottings varied widely: random listing for #2, categorization in #3, and chronological order in #5—all different ways of thinking about information. Finally, some of these tasks were more personal (#2 and #5), involving the affective domain, while others (#1 and #4) asked for a more objective response to the topic.

This exercise was designed to help you better understand that writing *is* thinking. Every time you give students a writing assignment, you give them a thinking assignment. Well-designed writing assignments can offer students an opportunity to think about a subject in ways they would not ordinarily if left on their own. According to Walshe (1987), "writing can become *a deeper kind of thinking than is otherwise possible*" (23). Students can be asked to write in response to questions as described in the previous chapter. Writing can also be planned to develop students' critical-thinking skills and creativity as well as to encourage them to interact with course material in ways that are both personal and analytical.

Writing and Learning

In her seminal essay "Writing as a Mode of Learning" (1977), Janet Emig makes a case for writing as a uniquely effective learning strategy by showing correspondences between writing and certain powerful learning strategies. The first of these correspondences draws on Bruner's categories of ways we learn:

1. *enactive*—by doing
2. *iconic*—by portraying in an image
3. *symbolic*—by turning ideas into language.

The act of writing incorporates all three modes of learning simultaneously as we use the hand to produce marks on the page, the eye to see these written symbols, and the brain to turn thought into language and language into its representational symbol system. Thus, writing involves all three ways we make new information part of our existing knowledge base. Emig also argues that writing makes the fullest use of both spheres of the brain. The left side of the brain is engaged in the linear processes of producing language and representing it on the page, while the right side of the brain contributes a holistic sense of the piece plus creative and intuitive insights. This hypothesis accounts for the flashes of insight that occur as one writes, the digressions that appear as one follows what seems like a logical path in a written piece, or the sudden discoveries that practicing writers so often refer to when discussing their writing processes. This concept of writing as bispheral also helps explain the concentration of a writer at work: both hemispheres of the brain are deeply involved in the task at hand.

Reinforcement, another factor necessary for successful learning, is immediate for the writer as he scans the written symbols even as they appear, able to reread, to review, to reflect immediately on both the thinking process that just took place and on the effectiveness of the verbal symbols that represent it. In addition, Emig reminds us that "successful learning is . . . engaged, committed, personal learning" (127) and is "self-rhythmed," proceeding at the pace best suited for the learner. Writing shares these attributes. The writer commits her own ideas, perceptions, and language to the page, producing a uniquely personal written product that did not previously exist, proceeding at a self-controlled rhythm and pace.

In large measure, the power of writing as a learning tool can be attributed to the multifaceted learning strategies it draws upon. It is active learning in the best sense of the word, engaging multiple parts of brain and body in the complex process of turning invisible thoughts into visible symbols.

James Britton (1970) points out that writing also shapes and forms our ideas, bringing amorphous, undefined thoughts into focus. When we write about something, we are forced to come to grips with our vague and general ideas on the topic, to give those formless concepts a shape and clarify our thinking about them. Britton describes this as "shaping at the point of utterance" (33). Oral language has this shaping function, but writing, because it allows time for premeditation and can be revised, provides for an even sharper shaping process (30). One of our college students was aware of exactly this phenomenon when she wrote in her final reflection from a college writing course that "sometimes you have so much mulling around in your mind, when you get the jumbled mess on paper, you can formulate ideas."

Another way in which writing reinforces learning is through reprocessing ideas and information—using them again by writing about them. The more often one revisits material, manipulating it with language, the more likely it is to be understood and remembered. Writing about the information one is learning is a simple and effective way to ensure that students process it again after reading or hearing about it. If students share these writings with each other, they are given still another opportunity to reprocess the material.

Britton tells about a piece of research in the British schools that further demonstrates the importance of writing as a means of learning. In a large lecture class, the students were divided in half. One group was permitted to take notes during the lecture while the other group was not. At the end of the lecture, the notes were collected from the first group. When the students returned to class, they were told to prepare for a quiz on the material. Those who had taken notes were given back their own notes from which to study; the other group was given the lecturer's notes to study from. The students who studied from their own notes did significantly better on the test than those who studied from the lecturer's notes. A follow-up test given at a later date showed that those who studied from their own notes also retained the material better than the other group.

Britton's story illustrates the value of turning someone else's ideas into one's own language so that new material makes personal sense and is couched in vocabulary and syntax familiar to the learner. Instead of memorizing some-one else's ideas, students make new material their own by writing about it. In this process, students are forced to organize and clarify their thinking. They can also see what they don't understand if they are unable to articulate its meaning for themselves through writing.

Writing and Language Development

Understanding and using new vocabulary is an important part of learning in any discipline. Often it is the specific vocabulary of the discipline that carries key concepts students need in order to understand new material. Traditionally, we have taught vocabulary through word lists, drill, and quizzes. Writing, however, encourages students to learn vocabulary holistically by using the words of the discipline when writing, thus increasing their "productive" vocabulary—their ability to communicate about the discipline in the language of the discipline. Through frequent writing in a given content area, students cannot help but use the vocabulary they are reading and hearing as they articulate their own mean-ings on paper. Reading these pieces aloud to other students or sharing them in whole-class discussions gives students yet another chance to use vocabulary for authentic purposes, thus making it their own.

In addition to specific vocabulary, each discipline has its own ways of using language, shaping prose, and organizing material for readers. For example, in the sciences students write lab reports, in history courses they may report on historical events or periods, and in English classes they write essays of literary analysis—all very different forms of writing. One way we make students "insid-ers" in our discipline is to teach them its writing conventions, formats, and vocabulary by asking them to write within the discipline. By asking them to do such writing, we also help them become better readers of material in that con-tent area because they develop an insider's understanding of how the discipline's discourse is constructed.

Writing also fosters language fluency, syntactic development, and the abil-ity to communicate more effectively with others. If you want your students to feel more comfortable with the subject matter you teach, writing encourages them to talk, think, and communicate with more sophistication and confidence about what they are learning in your class.

Cultural, Social, and Personal Benefits of Writing to Learn

The diverse populations of today's classrooms are well served in a writing-supported learning environment. By inviting them to write frequently about material as they learn it, you offer students opportunities to express their own unique ways of knowing and understanding. Instead of ignoring the differences in prior knowledge and individual schemas, writing can validate them by encouraging students to put their own thoughts and responses down on paper. In this way, writing can be used to connect the subject matter to whatever background knowledge students bring with them to the material. When students share these writings, they can learn from and with each other, filling in knowledge gaps, questioning each other's ideas or seeing how they complement their own, recognizing and learning to accept diverse opinions and ideas. Writing and sharing do much to build a learning community in the classroom, one in which students and teacher become co-contributors to the learning process.

Writing also encourages personal learning and deeper involvement with course material because it permits students to approach knowledge from their own perspective, applying their own language skills and background knowledge to whatever they are learning. A writer putting his own ideas down on paper makes a commitment to these ideas, and in doing so, he develops a more personal stake in learning than he has when memorizing material from a text or lecture. Writing also fosters independent thinking and supports students' self-confidence as learners.

Classroom Factors

One of the most important benefits of writing in the content area classroom is that it produces 100 percent involvement in the task at hand. When we ask a question in class in order to invite discussion, only a handful of students respond—usually the same ones each time. When we ask students to write, we are involving every student in thinking about and responding to the topic. We find, too, that students are more willing to engage in a discussion after they have written about the subject. They have had a few minutes to reflect about the topic instead of the few seconds an oral response allows, and their ideas are already down on paper, which offers a measure of security for entering the discussion.

From the teacher's point of view, examining students' written responses can quickly pinpoint gaps in understanding by the whole class or by individual students. This can be an enormous help in planning lessons and understanding what needs to be reviewed before moving on to new material. Quizzes may show who did or did not read the material, but writing is more likely to reveal whether students understood what the material meant. The teacher can also target students who need special help.

In most classrooms, teacher-talk dominates, a fact well documented by research into classroom language use (see, for example, Barnes, Britton, and Rosen 1969; Cuban 1993). Writing gives student voices a chance to be heard, not the parroting back of answers to questions or the echoing of text information, but the authentic sound of students at work using written language to think, explore, and respond in personal terms as they learn.

Finally, writing is active learning at its best: committed, involved, personal knowing. The passive classroom dominated by lectures and workbook exercises can be energized by involving students in writing, sharing, and talking about the subject. In *Smart Schools* (1992), David Perkins advocates "thoughtful learning. . . . schools that are full of thought . . . that focus not just on schooling memories but on schooling minds" (7). When students write often and thoughtfully about the material they are reading and learning, we are providing the "thinking-centered" environment that leads to successful teaching and learning.

Written and Oral Language Relationships

A central theme running through the previous discussion of writing is its link to oral language. This linkage occurs in two ways in a language-oriented classroom. When students write as they learn, they draw on their oral language base to support literacy growth. But the oral skills involved in sharing these writings, either by reading them aloud or by talking about them, also provides an even greater opportunity to develop literacy. Both the process of writing and the act of sharing encourage a strong level of involvement with the material at hand and reinforce the students' command of the unique discourse of the discipline. More passive learning permits detachment from the material even while it is being studied. The interplay of talk and writing fosters deeper involvement with text and subject. To quote Britton once again, classrooms should be "afloat on a sea of talk" (quoted in Judy 1974, 187); we add that they should be anchored in pages of writing.

The Functions of Writing

As the research cited earlier in this chapter shows, in schools we are most likely to use writing to discover what students already know through essay tests, research papers, and book reports—writing in which the primary purpose is communicating knowledge. The important purpose writing can serve as a support system for learning—writing in which thinking is the primary purpose—is rarely drawn upon in a school setting. James Britton's division of writing into three purposes or functions explores this differentiation. See Figure 9–1.

Britton states that all writing stems from the *expressive,* the informal, personal writing that is basically thinking on paper. Through this medium we explore ideas, discover what we do and do not know well enough to verbalize, and make vague thoughts concrete so we can learn from them. Expressive writing is writing to learn. It is writing as a way of thinking. It is usually what we mean when we talk about writing as a tool for learning. Unstructured expressive writing, often just jottings or lists or half-formulated ideas, causes the writer to interact with ideas in order to shape them into language on the page. The end product is what Flower (1979) terms "writer-based prose,"—writing not shaped for a reader but rather used to explore and make visible the thought processes of the composer. Expressive writing is the primary mode in journals and jottings, notes and lists, observation notes and reading notes, early drafts and planning notes.

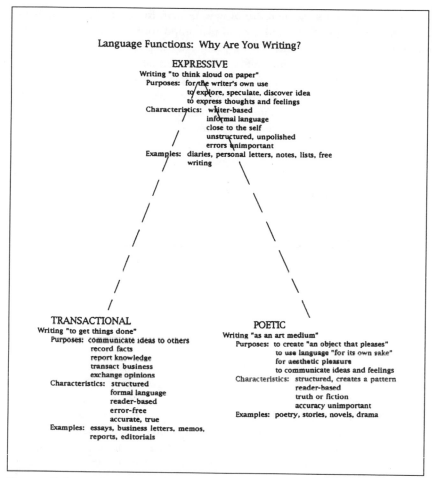

Language Functions: Why Are You Writing?

EXPRESSIVE
Writing "to think aloud on paper"
Purposes: for the writer's own use
to explore, speculate, discover idea
to express thoughts and feelings
Characteristics: writer-based
informal language
close to the self
unstructured, unpolished
errors unimportant
Examples: diaries, personal letters, notes, lists, free writing

TRANSACTIONAL
Writing "to get things done"
Purposes: communicate ideas to others
record facts
report knowledge
transact business
exchange opinions
Characteristics: structured
formal language
reader-based
error-free
accurate, true
Examples: essays, business letters, memos, reports, editorials

POETIC
Writing "as an art medium"
Purposes: to create "an object that pleases"
to use language "for its own sake"
for aesthetic pleasure
to communicate ideas and feelings
Characteristics: structured, creates a pattern
reader-based
truth or fiction
accuracy unimportant
Examples: poetry, stories, novels, drama

FIGURE 9–1.

From this base of writing as exploration, as thinking on paper, the writer can move into more formal modes, producing pieces whose purpose is more communicative in nature, shaped for a reader. Britton divides this more structured writing into two types: *poetic* and *transactional*. Poetic writing is writing as a work of art, what we usually call "creative writing" in this country. The primary purpose here is an aesthetic one: to please the reader. The term itself is misleading as it may include poetry, fiction, drama, and even personal memoir. The other outgrowth of expressive writing is transactional writing, writing to get the world's work done. This is "expository writing," the shaped and formed "reader-based" (Flower 1979) pieces most often assigned in schools and those that most populate the public world beyond school in the workplace, political arena, information media, and advertising. The primary purpose here is the communication of information to an audience. While all three types of writing overlap, it is the primary purpose of each that separates them into these categories.

According to Britton, all forms of writing stem from the expressive. Writers of all types begin their thinking and planning process with such expressive forms as notes, jottings, observations, journal writing, and free writing. From this they begin the shaping and crafting of more formal pieces. This mechanism offers insight into ways we as teachers can help our students become more effective writers. However, before we explore these uses of writing that are audience-centered, let us examine the ways in which classrooms can make full use of the expressive mode to enhance learning.

Writing to Learn

The Class Journal or Learning Log

Informal journal writing is one of the most effective ways to involve students in making the writing-thinking connection that lies at the heart of writing to learn in the classroom. The classroom journal is not a personal diary, nor is it a set of lecture and reading notes. It is a collection of short, informal, expressive writings that can constitute a central learning strategy for a course. Some teachers prefer to call these "learning logs." These writings may be collected and responded to by the teacher, but they do not have to be; their value lies in the writing itself and the way in which it is used in class. In most cases, teachers have students keep these writings together in a journal that is collected and evaluated periodically. Students may do this writing right along with their class lecture and reading notes or on individual sheets that are collected after they are used in class. There are advantages, however, to having students keep them together as a record of their learning in the class. Fulwiler (1982) credits the success of the class journal to the fact that "every time a person writes an entry, instruction is individualized; the act of silent writing, even for five minutes, generates ideas, observations, emotions," making it "harder for students to remain passive" (16).

Journal-writes can be used in many ways. During class time or as homework students can be asked to engage in three to five minutes of writing in response to a question or a task. The brief jottings you were asked to do earlier in this chapter to illustrate the writing-thinking connection are examples of journal-writes. If students have never done this type of writing before, it can be helpful to instruct them to do these as nonstop "free writing" focused on the topic or question. In free writing, the emphasis is on jotting ideas down as they occur without much attention to organization or preplanning. Peter Elbow (1973) points out that "many people are constantly thinking about spelling and grammar as they try to write" and worrying about getting it right (5). Informal nonstop writing frees writers to concentrate on their ideas. Free writings focusing on the topic at hand may be exploratory, speculative, even messy. But the act of writing itself often leads to unexpected connections or expression of ideas previously unrealized.

If students have never been asked to write expressively before, they may feel insecure and worry about whether they are doing it "right" or "wrong." It helps to explain the purpose for this type of writing in class—that it is "thinking on paper" to encourage them to express and clarify their ideas—and to assure them that your primary purpose here is to give them a chance to voice their own thoughts and opinions. Teachers' directions may sound something like this:

> I'd like you to write for about five minutes now on _____ . Do this as a free writing focusing on this topic. Just get your ideas down on paper and don't worry too much about spelling or punctuation. Be sure you can read your own writing, though, because I'll be asking you to share your responses in a small group.

A supportive environment for writing to learn can be further reinforced when serious attention is paid to students' ideas as they read their writing aloud to the class. Praise for good thinking or creative insights and the teacher's commitment to treating students' ideas with respect go a long way toward creating an atmosphere of trust. The way teachers handle students' journal writings in class also models ways students should respond to one another's work in pairs and small groups.

When teachers plan writing-to-learn activities, Zemelman and Daniels (1988) suggest they consider the following questions:

1. What specifically is the *content?* What are the key concepts for students to engage with?
2. What kind of *thinking* might students do in relation to this particular content?
3. What kind of *writing-to-learn activities* will help kids think about the content in those ways? (105)

Here are some ideas for informal writing-to-learn assignments that can be adapted for use in almost any subject.

1. To start a class, a lesson, or a unit. Writing can be used at the beginning of a class to focus students on the day's work or help them recall what they read for homework. When starting a new topic or unit of study, students can be asked to spend a few minutes writing down everything they already know about the topic. These writings can then be shared in a discussion that leads to building the fullest possible student-generated background to the subject of the day's lesson or the unit of study. At the completion of the day's lesson or unit, students can refer back to this piece of introductory writing and compare it to what they now know about the topic.
2. During a class, a lesson, or a unit. Students can be asked to respond to a discussion question in writing before a whole-class discussion begins. If a discussion seems to be rambling or moving off the intended focus, writing for a few minutes in response to such questions as "What are the main

points of the argument set out so far?" or "What conclusions have you come to about this topic?" can give students time to reflect and refocus their ideas. A lecture can be broken up into shorter chunks of passive listening by asking students to write about preplanned questions as part of the lecture. This, too, gives students a chance to pause for reflection instead of just collecting pages of lecture notes for a full class period (Fulwiler 1982). At any time in a lesson, unit, or reading assignment, students can be asked to make lists of new information, jot responses to ideas, and generate hypotheses or questions.

3. To conclude a class, a lesson, or a unit. A good way to wrap up a class or unit is by asking students to write responses to such questions as "What was the most interesting or important thing you learned today?" "What still confuses you about this material?" "What more would you like to learn about this topic?" Teachers sometimes call this an "exit slip." Students can leave these with the teacher at the end of the period, but this writing can also be shared with a partner or just kept in the journal notebook.

To reinforce new information, these concluding writings can ask students to summarize the key points in a lesson, describe in their own words a concept just presented, define a term, write an explanation of the lesson for an absent classmate, or write a brief note to a parent in response to the question, "What did you learn in chemistry/math/history/English today?"

A concluding writing can also be used to motivate students to do the reading assigned for homework by asking students to preview the reading assignment, then write in their journals about what they think they'll learn as they read. In a literature class, students can be asked to predict what a poem or story will be about, judging from the title. One of our student teachers once shared the following experience with us after using such a journal-write:

> I finished the lesson I'd prepared and we still had ten minutes to go until the period ended. I didn't want the class to waste ten minutes, so I asked them to take out their literature anthology and turn to the story assigned for homework. I had everyone read the title and the opening paragraph and look at the pictures. Then they each wrote what they thought the story would be about. They grumbled a bit, but they did it. The next day, everybody had read the story—the first time this ever happened with this class! They told me they wanted to see if they had been right in their guesses. Since everyone had read the story, we had the best class discussion we'd ever had, including some lively sharing of everyone's predictions and what cues had led to them.

Thus, these informal writings can be useful pre-, during-, and postreading strategies: to access prior knowledge, make predictions, and motivate students for prereading; to focus and involve students in the material being read or presented; and to review information and reinforce learning for postreading.

4. Informal writing can be used to connect classroom learning to students' experiences. Students can be asked to write in response to "How do we use this information?" or "Where do you see this in your own life?" For example, in math, students can be instructed to "write about all the ways you and your family use percentages." In English, students can be asked to "write about a time you had an experience similar to the one described in the story."

5. Writing can be used to elicit students' responses and reactions to course material: "How did you feel about _____?" "What did you like best or find most interesting about _____?"

6. Students can do informal writings from texts to encourage active reading and guide them toward more analytical and critical involvement with the material: take notes, write a short paraphrase of a text in their own words, create a statement of the central idea in a reading, select a key quote and interpret its meaning, list main ideas, discuss in the student's own language how a proof is constructed or a problem in the text is solved.

7. Students can also be led toward more complex thinking about text and course material through writings that encourage them to engage analytically. They can take positions on an issue, write debates, discuss societal or mathematical problems and possible solutions, explain how they would go about solving a problem in math or write math story problems based on real-life situations. They can write definitions of a concept and then apply it to real life with examples and illustrations.

8. Moral issues can be addressed in the journal, giving students an opportunity to grapple with issues that often do not have a right or wrong answer: "In the novel we just read, did _____ to the right thing when he _____ ? Would you have behaved the same way or not? Why?" "Was the United States justified in dropping the bomb on Hiroshima?" "Should we use the knowledge we have of genetic programming to clone special human beings?"

The NCTE Guidelines for Using Journals in School Settings, approved by the NCTE Commision on Composition, November 28, 1986, gives suggestions for using journals successfully across the curriculum.

Guidelines for Assigning Journals

1. Explain that journals are neither "diaries" nor "class notebooks," but borrow features from each : like the diary, journals are written in the first person about issues the writer cares about; like the class notebook, journals are concerned with the content of a particular course.

2. Ask students to buy looseleaf notebooks. This way students can hand in to you only that which pertains directly to your class, keeping more intimate entries private.

3. Suggest that students divide their journals in several sections, one for your course, one for another course, another for private entries. When you collect the journal, you need only collect that which pertains to your own course.

4. Ask students to do short journal writes in class; write with them; and share your writing with the class. Since you don't grade journals, the fact that you write too gives the assignment more value.

5. Every time you ask students to write in class, do something active and deliberate with what they have written: have volunteers read whole entries aloud; have everyone read one sentence to the whole class; have neighbors share one passage with each other, etc. (In each case, students who do not like what they have written should have the right to pass.) Sharing the writing like this also gives credibility to a non-graded assignment.

6. Count but do not grade student journals. While it's important not to qualitatively evaluate specific journal entries—for here students must be allowed to take risks—good journals should count in some quantitative way: a certain number of points, a *plus* added to a grade, as an in-class resource for taking tests.

7. Do not write back to every entry; it will burn you out. Instead, skim-read journals and write responses to entries that especially concern you.

8. At the end of the term ask students to put in (a) page numbers, (b) a title for each entry, (c) a table of contents, and (d) an evaluative conclusion. This synthesizing activity asks journal writers to treat these documents seriously and to review what they have written over a whole term of study.

Of all writing assignments, journals may be the most idiosyncratic and variable. Consequently, good reasons exist to ignore any of these suggestions, depending on teacher purpose, subject area, grade level, or classroom context. However, these suggestions will help many teachers use journals positively and efficiently in most school settings.

Other Types of Journals/Learning Logs

The course journal or learning log described above has the widest application to learning in all disciplines, but there are other types of journals that can be used with more specific purposes in mind.

• Personal journal. Closest in format to a daily diary, this is a record of students' activities, reflections, and feelings, used in English or composition classes to give students practice in writing, to increase writing fluency and comfort, and for personal growth. Teachers find it gives students a way to express the mixed emotions of adolescence, in a sense ridding themselves of these troubles by writing about them so they can then get down to the work at hand in the classroom. A teacher in the Flint, Michigan, schools explained it this way: "Sometimes they have no place else to say it, so they put it down on paper here."

• Writer's notebook. A collection of writing ideas, observations, resources for future writing, unfinished pieces, drafts, jottings. A writing resource for the developing writer, the writer's notebook is a collection strategy commonly used by the professional writer as well. Closest in purpose to the artist's sketchbook, this is the type of journal frequently used in composition classes at all levels. Dorothy Lambert (1967) describes this type of journal as "a treasury, a jewelry box, a storehouse, a collector's cabinet, a snapshot album, a laboratory, a wardrobe, a drafting board, a psychoanalyst's couch, a tape recorder, a history, a travelogue, a mystical exercise, a letter to oneself" (286).

- Reading response journal. The purpose for this type of journal is to record responses, questions, reflections, interpretations, and emotional reactions as one reads. Used most often in literature courses to capture students' thinking during the reading process, it is equally effective with reading assignments in any discipline. The assignment can be as general as saying, "As you read or immediately afterward, write your responses to the reading: What do you think it meant? What do you consider the most important point in the reading? Why? What questions do you have?"

- Dialogue journal or dialectical notebook. For this journal format, students are told to divide each page of the journal in half with a line directly down the center, creating two columns. Label the left column "What the Book Says"; label the right column "What I Say." Students copy key quotes or ideas directly from the text in the left column and write their responses to these quotes in the right column. In some classes, additional columns are added, stretching the entries across an open two-page spread, so that a column can be added for a peer to write a response to the student's entry and another column for the teacher's response. An alternative to the reading response journal, the dialogue journal opens up avenues for multiple dialogues among texts, readers, and the teacher.

- Project or research log. When students work independently or in small groups on individual projects or research reports, it is useful to have them keep an ongoing record of work as it is accomplished, including plans for what else must be done, reflections on the work, questions that must be answered, and discoveries as they occur. It is not only a valuable work record; it can also be an excellent resource when writing a paper or planning a presentation. The log captures ideas and language that can be used when putting together the finished product, sometimes drawing directly from log entries. Mohr (1984) suggests topics like the following for research logs: my research questions, what I already know about my subject, my data collection plan, my research progress so far, my biases and assumptions prior to doing the research, the most important thing I've found so far, my progress so far, in retrospect: what I learned.

- Real world application journal. Newspapers, magazines, and other media are often full of material that directly relates to what is being studied in class. For this journal, students are told to clip pertinent materials, paste them in the journal, and for each one write a journal entry discussing how it applies to or reflects the concepts being studied in the course. A successful format for showing students the relevance of what they are learning, this journal can be used in courses as diverse as government, history, math, science, art, music, and literature.

- Course log. This is a collaborative record of daily class activities and assignments with students taking turns being the class record-keeper. In one class we know of, two students are assigned each day; one records the facts—class work, homework—while the other is responsible for describing students' responses, questions, and concerns. The teacher can check the class log daily to get a sense of how the class is progressing. The log also frees the teacher from the constant hassle of bringing absentees up-to-date. But it is even more powerful as a record of the course, available for review by administrators, parents, and the students themselves, who enjoy reading the diverse voices of their classmates and rereading their own entries written weeks earlier.

Using Journal-Writes in the Classroom

If you want to use the journal writing to start a class discussion, it is best to ask for volunteers. Write with your students whenever possible, and share yours first if no one else is willing, or promise to read yours if two or three others will also read theirs. Sometimes, if the class is not too large, it can be highly effective to go around the room and give everyone who wishes to an opportunity to read theirs to the class. Asking students to pair up with a classmate to read and discuss each other's journal entries is another good way to use journals in class. Teachers can move on from this to having students share their work in small groups, with one person assigned to take notes on the journal ideas and ensuing discussion and report back to the whole group. If individual students are shy about volunteering to read their writing aloud to the class, have each group choose one person to read his or her piece aloud. Students are flattered to be chosen by the group and the group is more likely to exert just the right amount of coercion to get a reluctant student to read an exceptionally insightful entry to the class.

To model good journal writing, the instructor can put two or three of the best or most interesting responses on the overhead projector and discuss what makes them effective (Beall and Trimbur 1993). This also serves as a quick review of the material.

The informal sharing of journal work does not have to take much time. Students can write for five minutes, then another five to eight minutes can be devoted to having a few students read their pieces to the class to get things started or the same few minutes can be spent exchanging writings with a partner. On occasion, it may be enough to have students write in order to get them thinking about the topic and then just file the piece away in the journal notebook. On the other hand, the journal writing can become the focus for the lesson. Students can work in groups for ten or fifteen minutes, reading their pieces aloud, discussing and comparing their entries, coming to consensus or generating a collaborative statement. Each group can then report back to the class.

Responding to, Evaluating, and Grading the Learning Log

If you believe that students won't do these writings unless you collect them, then by all means do so and give students some daily credit for doing the writing. It has been our experience, however, that students soon understand the purpose for these writings and learn to value the sharing that follows since it gives them a chance to exchange ideas and make their own voices heard. It may be necessary to collect them the first few times, but eventually students are content with a periodic evaluation of the entire collection.

Even if you only take the entire journal when it is necessary to evaluate it, we suggest that you also collect and respond to an entry from each member of the class now and then, both to see how the class is doing in their entries and also to give students feedback on their ideas. When reading students' journal entries, look for positive things to comment upon. The learning log is not a place for negative response from the teacher or comments on matters not related to content, such as grammar and mechanics. The more positive the comments you make, the more students write in subsequent entries. Look for good ideas, personal reactions, clarity of meaning, interesting use of language, examples and details that illustrate what students are thinking. Respond honestly and positively to these, even if it is just with an asterisk in the margin, a "yes!" or "good idea."

When we are ready to evaluate a journal for grading, we ask students to prepare their journals for this by numbering pages or entries, adding a table of contents or introduction, and completing the journal with a reflection about its contribution to their learning in the course and some discussion of entries they feel are especially valuable (Fulwiler 1982). A sample of end-of-the-term directions for the class journal follows:

Reading Response Journal Final Directions

Your complete Reading Response Journal will be collected on the last day of class. My records show that you should have about 25 entries. Please include all the journal entries you have made throughout this semester, including any you may have done on your own. Please *don't* give me your class notes, too.

Directions for Preparing your Notebook:

1. Arrange all your entries in chronological order and number each separate entry consecutively from one to whatever the final number of entries is.
2. Title each entry with its topic or some other name indicating what it is about.
3. Make a Table of Contents for major entries.
4. Conclude with a final reflection one to two pages long evaluating the way this journal related to your learning in this class .

Some things to do and think about before you write your final reflection:

- Read through your entries as you organize them, evaluating the kind of reading and responding you did in this journal.

- Do you see any change over the term in your reading and writing for this course? If so, what do you see?
- Were any entries valuable to you when you worked in groups or we held discussions in class?
- Were any entries useful in writing the longer papers or studying for tests?
- Are there any special entries that represent insights you had while reading and thinking about the course material?
- Are there any entries that you feel are especially strong?
- Do any entries show your own growth as a learner or your own interest in this subject?
- Finally, try to assess the influence of this journal on your understanding of the material we studied and on the quality of your learning in this class. Was it worthwhile? If so, why? If not, why not?

We skim the individual entries but take a few minutes to read the student's reflection in its entirety and make a final comment on the quality of work, thought, and insight in the journal. The final reflection often gives us a good indication of how the student perceives his or her own work as well as how much thoughtful writing went into the journal itself. Extended entries, insights, speculations, personal reflections, and evidence of involvement with the material should be rewarded here.

"How do you grade journals?" is a common question from teachers. It has been our experience that it is more rewarding for the teacher than it looks. The pile of journals may seem intimidating, but a sane and reasonable grading system makes the process manageable. The reward is in seeing evidence of growth, of real learning, of involvement, plus the opportunity to hear the authentic voices of your students.

Some teachers like to grade on sheer quantity: so many pages for an A, so many pages for a B, so many pages for a C, etc. Or they count the number of entries assigned over the grading period and give students an A if every entry is there, with a sliding scale downward for missing entries. Others use a check-plus, check, check-minus system for the entire journal, which usually translates into a grade of A, B, or C. One teacher we know guarantees students at least a B if all entries are there; higher grades are based on the quality of the entries and the final reflection, which ensures that both quality and quantity count toward the grade. Another method is to use a credit/no-credit system, giving students credit for the journal as long as there is evidence they kept one. Still others believe that learning logs should not be graded at all, just responded to by the teacher when collected and used in class as much as possible.

No matter which method is used, grading should not become a deterrent from using these writing-to-learn techniques in the classroom. Keep in mind that the value of journal-writes lies in the actual act of writing combined with the use of journals as part of classroom teaching. Minimize grading as much as possible; maximize writing, sharing, and response. And be sure to make liberal use of the copy machine to save examples of students' work when their informal writings and final reflections exhibit learning in progress.

Writing to Communicate to Readers

In some classes, the consistent use of writing-to-learn activities may suffice for involving students in appropriate ways with the course material; teachers may not feel it is necessary for students to spend extended time producing longer, more formal pieces of writing. This may hold true, for example, in performance-based music and art classes, physical education, or math. However, for many teachers in all content areas there does come a time when they want students to explore a topic in more depth, producing a finished, polished product that synthesizes material, shows learning has taken place, and communicates clearly to readers. We are talking here about such "transactional" and "poetic" writing as essays, book and movie reviews, editorials, lab reports, research papers, essays of literary analysis, historical surveys, editorials, short stories, poetry, and other extended writings. Such assignments can foster complex thinking in a more sustained way than informal journal writing.

Historically, these longer, more formal writing assignments have been the dominant format for student writing throughout school. Usually they are dealt with as follows. The teacher gives the assignment and the due date, explains how it should be done, offers suggestions, and answers students' questions. Students do the assignment on their own, usually at home, and arrive in class on the due date with a final copy ready to be turned in for a grade. Alternatively, the writing topic is given at the beginning of the class period. Students write all period, are reminded to reread and correct errors for the last five minutes of class, and then turn in what is actually a rough first draft for grading. In either case, the teacher then takes the papers home to mark, going through each paper carefully with a red pen to circle mistakes, point out problems, make a final comment, and assign a grade. More often than not, the paper is tossed in the wastepaper basket once the student sees the grade. In this model, the teacher is the only audience for the paper, and the authentic purpose is to receive a grade. Each piece of writing is really a test of what the student already knows about writing rather than a chance to develop more fully as a writer in the process of exploring a topic.

Under these circumstances, many students fear and come to dislike writing assignments, often feeling isolated and insecure as they do their best to fulfill what they hope is expected of them, defeated if they receive a disappointing grade. Teachers, too, are frustrated when students' writing fails to exhibit the quality of thinking, writing, and mechanical/grammatical correctness they hoped to find.

The writing-to-learn strategies described earlier in this chapter take a very different approach to writing, one that tends to be less frustrating for both teachers and students as well as beneficial for students' learning. But writing to learn is only one way in which recent composition research has influenced writing in the classroom. This research has also led to new understanding of how writers write, and how teachers can make use of this information to provide a more supportive environment for writing and help students improve their final products. The following sections of this chapter will discuss what we now know about the writing process and present ways in which content area teachers can ensure more successful formal writing experiences for their students when they assign such writing.

The Process of Writing

The term "the writing process" seems to suggest that there is one monolithic process all writers go through in a lock-step fashion each time they compose. This is not so. The steps, stages, and strategies used by writers are as various as the writers themselves and may be different each time a writer works on a new piece. However, most writers can identify several stages they go through as they compose a piece and prepare it for a reader. Even the most successful professional writer does not produce a perfect final product in one fell swoop, the exact words just flowing from pen or computer, although students seem to believe that's what "good" writers do. Donald Murray (1982), a Pulitzer Prize –winning writer and also a writing teacher, divides the writing process into three stages: prewriting—"everything that takes place before the first draft"; writing—"the act of producing a first draft"; and rewriting—"reconsideration of subject, form, and audience . . . and finally, line-by-line editing" (15). Other discussions of the writing process divide writing into prewriting, drafting, revising, editing/proofreading, and postwriting phases. Figure 9–2, Stages of the Writing Process, outlines what the writer might be doing at any of these stages and the role a teacher might play to support the student's process.

All of these descriptions recognize the complexity of writing, the need for time to think and plan (which Murray claims is 85 percent of the entire time spent on a piece) and to write a rough first draft. After this, the emphasis is on "revision": reseeing the piece to develop its ideas and sharpen its form and focus. Finally, the writer pays attention to language at the sentence level and the more rigid constraints of correctness in grammar, punctuation, spelling, and usage. It is important to note here that writing is a more "recursive" process than the linear movement these stages suggest. Writers move back and forth among these stages, for example, revising as they compose drafts, jotting notes or freewriting about one part of the paper as ideas come to them while composing another part of the paper, rereading to position themselves before moving on (Perl 1980). Skilled writers have learned to manage their own writing processes. Developing writers are not as successful in understanding what might be helpful at any given time as they compose, which makes teacher intervention and support especially important.

School-based writing throughout much of this century did little to recognize the complexity of composing or to help students as they worked on their pieces. This led Janet Emig (1971) to characterize school-sponsored writing for American secondary students as "a limited, and limiting, experience" (97) in which teachers "truncate the process of composing" (98) by not offering prewriting activities and reducing revision to a narrow emphasis on error. The

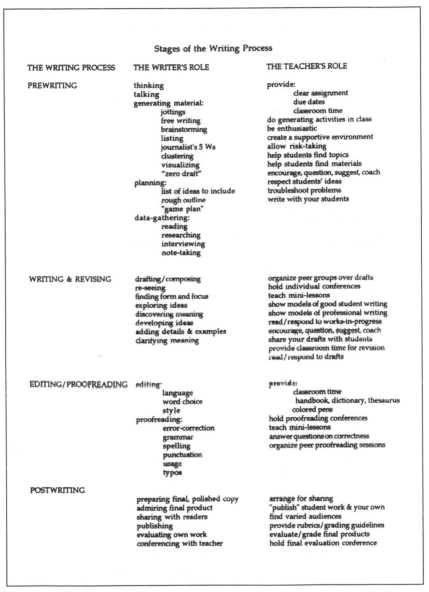

Stages of the Writing Process

THE WRITING PROCESS	THE WRITER'S ROLE	THE TEACHER'S ROLE

PREWRITING	thinking
	talking
	generating material:
	    jottings
	    free writing
	    brainstorming
	    listing
	    journalist's 5 Ws
	    clustering
	    visualizing
	    "zero draft"
	planning:
	    list of ideas to include
	    rough outline
	    "game plan"
	data-gathering:
	    reading
	    researching
	    interviewing
	    note-taking
		provide:
		    clear assignment
		    due dates
		    classroom time
		do generating activities in class
		be enthusiastic
		create a supportive environment
		allow risk-taking
		help students find topics
		help students find materials
		encourage, question, suggest, coach
		respect students' ideas
		troubleshoot problems
		write with your students

WRITING & REVISING	drafting/composing re-seeing finding form and focus exploring ideas discovering meaning developing ideas adding details & examples clarifying meaning	organize peer groups over drafts hold individual conferences teach mini-lessons show models of good student writing show models of professional writing read/respond to works-in-progress encourage, question, suggest, coach share your drafts with students provide classroom time for revision read/respond to drafts

EDITING/PROOFREADING	editing:
	    language
	    word choice
	    style
	proofreading:
	    error-correction
	    grammar
	    spelling
	    punctuation
	    usage
	    typos
		provide:
		    classroom time
		    handbook, dictionary, thesaurus
		    colored pens
		hold proofreading conferences
		teach mini-lessons
		answer questions on correctness
		organize peer proofreading sessions

POSTWRITING	preparing final, polished copy admiring final product sharing with readers publishing evaluating own work conferencing with teacher	arrange for sharing "publish" student work & your own find varied audiences provide rubrics/grading guidelines evaluate/grade final products hold final evaluation conference

FIGURE 9–2.

classroom focus has been on the form and correctness of the written product rather than on assisting the writer throughout the composing process.

Current writing theory and research support the view that if we want our students to become better writers and want the writing we collect to be worth our careful scrutiny, we should teach our students to do what successful writers do: "All teaching writing as a process tries to do is to bring writing in the classroom closer to what 'real' writers do when they write" (Kirby and Liner 1988,

18). Furthermore, Hull and Bartholomae (1986) claim that students can benefit from having this complex process "staged out for them so that they can learn not to try to do everything at once—so they can learn, that is, to manage the process of writing" (47).

This takes more classroom time than simply going over an assignment, then collecting it a week later. But the rewards are tangible to the observant teacher: increased student motivation and self-confidence, a final product that more closely meets both teacher and student expectations, and evidence that real learning has taken place as students explore a topic, revise, and polish to achieve a finished product. The classroom focus becomes the student writer and his writing process rather than teaching of forms and skills. This is especially relevant for the content area teacher who values writing as a way of learning in her class. The teacher is free to concentrate on helping students articulate and develop their ideas fully in order to communicate them to readers. Emphasis remains on the subject of the course rather than on making teachers feel they must play the role of the English teacher and teach "writing skills."

Guidelines for Content Area Writing Assignments

We have found the following guidelines useful in designing and carrying out more formal writing assignments in content area classes. They have been adapted from principles set out by Tchudi and Huerta (1983), Fulwiler (1986), and Ryder and Graves (1994), plus our own experiences with content area writing.

1. Keep content central to the writing assignment; students' ideas, information, and insights about a subject should be the focus. Be sure students write about subjects they know well or are interested in learning about. Encourage them to teach you and other readers something new instead of just regurgitating information to prove that they know it. Tchudi and Huerta (1983) suggest that "Content-area writing works best when it involves *discovery*, *synthesis*, and *inquiry* rather than recitation of factual material" (9).

2. Provide options and choices if possible. Allow students to formulate their own topics and approaches whenever it is feasible.

3. Create an atmosphere of trust, enthusiasm, interest in their topics, freedom to take risks, support rather than criticism, and encouragement for students to engage intellectually with the material they are writing about.

4. If you are asking for a specific type of writing—research paper, editorial, lab report—find out what students already know about that mode. Discuss the how-tos of composing such a piece. Using the overhead projector or duplicated handouts, show students the characteristics of that type of writing, drawing on both student and professional examples.

5. Create assignments that specify purpose for the writing (why are students doing this writing? what are they expected to learn or experience?), the

audience (who are possible readers for the finished piece?), your expectations and requirements, some suggestions for how to go about producing a finished piece, and any information they might need about resources to use, citation format, etc. Put this in writing on a handout so students can refer to it whenever necessary. Include due dates for drafts and finished copy.

6. Have students write for a variety of audiences: themselves, classmates, other students in the school or even in other schools, public figures, parents, the community beyond school.

7. Help students move through all phases of the writing process when it seems appropriate to your goals for the writing assignment. Doing some or all of the following activities in class will help students produce more well-developed and polished pieces of writing:

    a. Generating: do some in-class generating activities such as brainstorming, clustering, freewriting.

    b. Revising: have students work with each other over drafts in class using peer groups and critique sheets. Hold conferences with individual students who request your help. Cruise the room, leaning over shoulders to skim drafts, asking "How can I help you?" or "How's it going?" Offer suggestions; ask questions to help students clarify ideas; praise good work.

    c. Polishing: hold final editing and proofreading workshops in class, again using pairs or small groups.

8. Allow for talk to support writing. Go around the room and have each student tell what he or she is writing about. Let students share in pairs or small groups the jottings from the informal generating activities so they get a chance to discuss their ideas before they begin forming the paper. Let students work together revising drafts, polishing and proofreading their final copies. It is perfectly normal for a writing workshop session to have a low buzz of student-to-student and student-to-teacher conversation.

9. Allow time for thinking and planning, drafting, revising, and final proofreading and polishing. Most formal assignments may require two or three days of attention for at least a part of the daily class meeting. Some, such as a major research project, may require much more.

10. "Publish" student writing, don't just collect and grade it. Vary the publication technique from assignment to assignment: a class anthology from one assignment, a bulletin board display with another, presentations to the class with another.

11. Make grading standards explicit. Provide grading guides or checklists (discussed later in this chapter); include this with the assignment if possible so students are aware of expectations from the start. Or involve students in designing the grading criteria for the assignment.

12. Stay involved with your students throughout the writing process, focusing on their developing ideas and the content of their writing. Kirby and

Liner (1988) note that "extraordinarily successful teachers of writing have one thing in common: they spend very little time in isolation, reading and marking papers, and a great deal of time responding and discussing student writings with the writers themselves" (235).

Assignments and Assignment-Making

Topics and Forms

When we ask our college students what kinds of formal writing assignments they were given in secondary school content area courses, they mention predominantly three modes: the book review, the essay, and the research report. There's nothing inherently wrong with such traditional formats, and we aren't suggesting that teachers abandon them. However, these conventional forms often fail to excite students either intellectually or imaginatively, offering them fairly limited opportunities to explore topics in their own ways. The list of discourse forms in Figure 9–3 provides a rich source of ideas for possible writing assignments that can help students engage with course material in many different ways.

Most of the forms for writing in Figure 9–3 are adaptable to any subject area. For example, biology classes studying primitive life-forms such as amoeba and paramecium can write about these creatures in traditional lab report format, as "guess who" descriptions, imaginary interviews, "a day in the life of" stories or journal entries, poetry, or poster displays with written explanations. Math and history teachers can have students do research on famous men and women in the field, then write biopoems, incorporating the information they find into the following format:

First name _____

Title_____

Four words describing the person_____ , _____ ,

_____ , _____

Lover of _____ , _____ , _____

Who believes (believed) _____ , _____ ,_____

Who wants (wanted) _____ , _____ , _____

Who uses (used) _____ , _____ , _____

Who gives (gave) _____ , _____ , _____

Who says (said) _____

_____

Last name _____

Journals and diaries
  (real or imaginary)
Biographical sketches
Anecdotes and stories:
  from experience
  as told by others
Thumbnail sketches:
  of famous people
  of places
  of content ideas
  of historical events
Guess who/what descriptions
Letters:
  personal reactions
  observations
  public/informational
  persuasive:
    to the editor
    to public officials
  to imaginary people
  from imaginary places
Requests
Applications
Memos
Resume's and summaries
Poems
Plays
Stories
Fantasy
Adventure
Science fiction
Historical stories
Dialogues and conversations
Children's books
Telegrams
Editorials
Commentaries
Responses and rebuttals
Newspaper "fillers"
Fact books or fact sheets
School newspaper stories
Stories or essays for local papers
Proposals
Case studies:
  school problems
  local issues
  national concerns
  historical problems
  scientific issues
Songs and ballads
Demonstrations
Poster displays

Reviews:
  books (including textbooks)
  films
  outside reading
  television programs
  documentaries
Historical "you are there" scenes
Science notes:
  observations
  science notebook
  reading reports
  lab reports
Math:
  story problems
  solutions to problems
  record books
  notes and observations
Responses to literature
Utopian proposals
Practical proposals
Interviews:
  actual
  imaginary
Directions:
  how-to
  school or neighborhood guide
  survival manual
Dictionaries and lexicons
Technical reports
Future options, notes on:
  careers, employment
  school and training
  military/public service
Written debates
Taking a stand:
  school issues
  family problems
  state or national issues
  moral questions
Books and booklets
Informational monographs
Radio scripts
TV scenarios and scripts
Dramatic scripts
Notes for improvised drama
Cartoons and cartoon strips
Slide show scripts
Puzzles and word searches
Prophecy and predictions
Photos and captions
Collage, montage, mobile,
  sculpture

FIGURE 9–3. Some Discourse Forms for Content Writing

Literature teachers can ask students to write biopoems describing characters in literature or to write additional sections of a story or novel beyond the author's ending. Writing in imaginative discourse forms—poetry, song, drama, story—can have the same intellectual rigor as more conventional formats while also challenging students to approach the subject from a different angle.

When you plan the types of thinking and learning you want to happen in your classes through formal writing assignments, we suggest you review the list in Figure 9–3 and consider which discourse forms might best serve your purposes. Whenever possible, offer your students a range of possibilities both in the topics they might choose to write about and in the form this writing might take. Also give them the option of formulating their own assignment with your approval. Student involvement will be much higher if they have some control over what they write about and the structure it takes. This also avoids boredom for the teacher who has to read thirty-five essays on exactly the same topic.

Designing Assignments

In designing well-made assignments, it is helpful to consider all the aspects of writing that the writer must contend with in order to produce a successful piece: the rhetorical context or total writing situation. Writers must make decisions based on the following variables when they compose because all of these issues influence the shaping of the paper:

- Who is my *audience* for this piece? Whom do I expect to read it?
- What is my *purpose* in writing this piece? What am I trying to accomplish?
- What is my *message* to readers? What do I want them to learn, understand, or take away from this piece? What is the main point I want to convey?
- What is the *form* that best suits this purpose and audience?
- What *persona* or role will I take on in this piece? Formal or informal? Myself or another? How do I want readers to picture me?

Writing assignments that address these variables help writers produce better papers. In particular, if writers have a clear sense of what they are supposed to accomplish—e.g., explain a process, investigate a problem and suggest a solution, gather and organize evidence to support an argument—and can keep real readers in mind as they compose, they are more likely to produce pieces that meet the teacher's expectations.

One final word here about assignment-making. We like to give students a handout for each formal assignment that contains all the information we think they might need, as explained in item 5 of the guidelines presented earlier. We also include, whenever possible, a copy of the Reader Response Sheet if we are planning to use peer response groups, and the final grading guide we will use when marking the paper. These items suggest the processes the class will follow as the assignment is carried out and make final grading criteria explicit from the start. This does a lot to clear up misunderstandings and confusions about the assignment, making writing easier for the student.

The Research Paper

The formal research paper is so pervasive in the schools, starting as early as the middle elementary grades, that it deserves some special attention here. The assignment to do independent reading and research on a topic related to course material is an excellent way to extend students' knowledge beyond the text and stimulate personal involvement. Too often, however, the research paper assignment flounders in two ways: (1) It becomes a matter of copying material word for word from encyclopedias and books, then pasting these assorted bits of information together into a "report" of other people's ideas; and (2) kids and teachers get bogged down in the paraphernalia of research—notecards, citation format, bibliography—at the expense of the inquiry and discovery that should be the central focus. In *Coming to Know* (1990), Nancie Atwell contends that the problem stems from the way teachers handle these reports: "We need to put the emphasis where it belongs—on meaning—and show students how to investigate questions and communicate their findings, how to go beyond plagiarism to genuine expertise and a 'coming to know'" (xiv). Ken Macrorie (1988) describes an approach that he calls the "I-Search Paper" in his book by the same name: students must do research to fulfill a personal need, resulting in papers that "tell stories of quests that counted for the questers" (preface). He suggests dividing the written report into four parts: (1) What I knew (and didn't know) about my topic when I started out; (2) Why I'm writing this paper; (3) The search; and (4) What I learned (or didn't learn) (64). Teachers at any level who value original inquiry by their students will find many practical ideas in both these books.

We offer the following suggestions for engaging students in effective research processes:

1. Long, twenty-page formal research papers are unnecessary, even at the upper senior high level. Students can ask specific questions and report results in much shorter pieces of writing ranging from the three- to five-page paper to a fuller eight- to ten-page report.

2. A research paper should not just be a collection of information. It should ask a question or formulate a hypothesis and then report the findings and their meaning. An effective research paper takes a stance toward the topic and presents an argument, supporting it with evidence from the research. Teachers can encourage students to analyze their material instead of just collecting it by asking such questions as "What's most important?" "What did you learn?" "Did you find what you expected?" "What does your information seem to suggest about your topic?" "How do your findings apply to our world or to this course?"

3. Students should be guided toward formulating research questions about which they are genuinely curious, so the research process involves exploration, meaning-making, and the excitement of discovery.

4. Students should be encouraged to gather data from nontext sources: interviews, visits, field trips, videos, original documents. In other words, show them that inquiry is much more than copying material from books and pasting a report together.

5. It is important to get students to talk and write constantly about what they are learning as data collection is in progress: learning logs, freewriting, letters to the teacher, small-group discussions. Tell them to use *this* writing and talking, their own language, in the final report and only use a few quotes when the language is so fine they want that exact wording in the paper.

6. Students should be taught the difference between an acceptable paraphrase —restating someone else's ideas in your own language—and direct copying or echoing someone else's language without using quotation marks, which is considered a form of plagiarism. Plagiarism caused by lack of understanding about how to paraphrase is one of the biggest problems students must overcome in college research papers. Most research guides present models and hands-on exercises for paraphrasing information and avoiding plagiarism; every publishing company produces one or more of these and many are excellent. If you are asking students to write research papers based on written sources, it is worthwhile to spend class time teaching them how to use their sources properly.

7. If you want to teach documentation, we suggest the in-text citation format of the Modern Language Association (MLA). In Michigan, this is taught throughout the state in college freshman composition courses. Research guides exist that include other formats such as American Psychological Association, but if a student understands what citation is all about, it is easy enough to learn another format when necessary. Many of our colleagues in disciplines across the curriculum just tell students to be consistent in the citation format they use for a given paper.

8. While students are working on their papers, use the process approach described below so they get the support they need as they collect data, write, revise, polish, and publish their work.

The Teacher's Role as Students Write

Teachers can assist students in many ways as they work on formal writing assignments, setting up classroom activities to support students' writing processes and offering suggestions just as students need them most—when they are actively working on their pieces. A useful analogy here is to coaching: a good coach supports and praises what athletes do well yet also suggests ways they could achieve even more. In addition, the good coach designs practice sessions and specific workouts to improve athletes' performances. The teacher working with students during the composing process is, in effect, a writing coach, structuring the classroom so that students produce their very best work. The previous guidelines for content area writing assignments and Figure 9–2, the overview of the writing process, offer suggestions for working with student writers. Here are some specific methods that content area teachers can use with their students to ensure maximum success and learning when formal writing is assigned. You may not want to use all of these strategies for each assignment, but we assure you that the improved quality of students' final papers proves it is worth the time it takes.

Ideas for Generating Writing

Nothing is more intimidating to a writer than a blank sheet of paper that must be filled up and then followed by more pages of written language. Responding to this sometimes paralyzing experience (writer's block is not just a myth), one of us always tells students, "Never start writing with a blank sheet of paper. Start writing by collecting ideas with language on the page." Generating activities do just that: they help students find what they have to say and think through a topic in the process of shaping it with language. Also, the physical and mental act of writing often generates more writing as if a dripping faucet were turned on, releasing a flood, in this case, of writing.

The journal writings described earlier in this chapter all make good generating activities, especially *free writing*. As a first step in a writing assignment, ask students to write freely about their topic, to just spill onto the page whatever they think they might want to include in their paper. Students can also do *listing*, making the longest list they can of ideas, words, phrases, sentences, images, and information they might use in the paper. Asking students to respond to the *journalist's five Ws* is another generating technique that writers find useful: who? what? where? when? why? (sometimes "how?" is added). Or teachers may create their own set of generating questions designed for the specific writing assignment.

Students who are visual learners respond positively to *clustering* when collecting material on a subject. Gabriele Rico (1983) describes clustering as "a nonlinear brainstorming process akin to free association" (28). Put a nucleus word or the paper topic in the center of a clean sheet of paper, circle it, and then draw spiderweb arms from it, putting an idea, word, or association down at the end of each arm and circling it, filling up the page with a web of thoughts radiating from the central topic. Figure 9–4 is an example of clustering done by a student in an eighth-grade science class before writing a paper about sound. The clustering process is freeing for some students, producing many more ideas than the linear use of written language would. It also offers an opportunity to see connections among ideas and to organize them into subsections or paragraphs for a paper.

Talk also serves as a generating technique: students can discuss possible topics in small groups, share jottings or clusterings, or brainstorm together over one another's topics. In a whole-class format, each student can briefly describe his or her paper topic while others in the class offer suggestions or ask questions. It is enormously useful for students to hear what others are considering; this often gives them good ideas for their own papers.

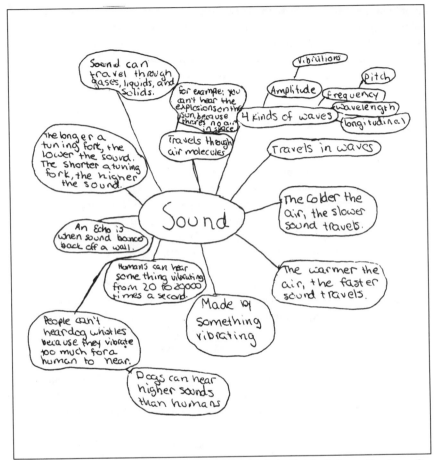

FIGURE 9–4. Clustering Done by Annie, an Eighth-Grade Science Student, for a Paper on Sound

All of these techniques lead to a "zero draft" (Kirby and Liner 1988), the exploratory first beginnings of a paper or report. One teacher we know always ends an in-class generating session by having students write in response to the question, "What else do you need to know before you can write your paper?"

Revision Workshops

For practicing writers, revision is the heart of the writing process, the time when a rough first draft is developed, focused, and crafted to convey the writer's best possible meaning. The inexperienced writer often treats the original draft as if it were engraved in cement; revision may amount to some tinkering with spelling or punctuation, but it rarely involves the "re-seeing" of content and structure that leads to a better piece of writing. Our task as teachers is to create classroom experiences that will help students understand the importance of revising their drafts and also offer them specific assistance in how to do this.

When we talk of revision, we mean crafting for focus and clarity, working on ideas and their organization. It is useful to separate this as much as possible from attention to mechanics, or revision sessions are likely to center on error correction instead of content. When you ask students to produce formal, finished, polished pieces, we suggest you include a revision workshop session as part of your writing assignment, specifying a due date for the complete first draft. Teachers usually give credit for this draft either by checking it in class or giving points for it when the completed assignment is collected. Revision sessions can include any or all of the following: peer response groups, conferences, mini-lessons, and planning and revising of drafts.

Writing Response Groups

Writing response groups give students an opportunity to get feedback and suggestions on their drafts, putting the responsibility for revision on the students, not the teacher. But there are other benefits to the content area teacher as well. In these small groups, students hear how other student writers have responded to the assignment, which gives them a sense of how well their own writing is coming along in comparison. The help they get from peers also lessens some of the paper burden for the teacher, who gets better papers than ones dashed off as a first draft. While students are in their groups, the teacher can sit in with each group briefly to assess their progress and answer questions. But this group work also frees the teacher to hold conferences with individual students who request them or with those who clearly need additional assistance.

With guidance, secondary school students can be very helpful responders to one another's work. For writing groups to work effectively, however, students need specific tasks and procedures to follow. Here are some suggestions:

1. Prepare students. Before students work together with drafts, explain the purpose of response groups, stressing the benefits of getting feedback from real readers. Students also need to be reminded to be sensitive to one another's feelings; to focus comments on the papers, not each other; and to make helpful suggestions, not negative comments. Disruptive or insensitive group members should be denied the privilege of working with groups—a penalty most students will take care to avoid because working together like this is enjoyable as well as helpful.

2. Structure group membership. We usually let students choose their own partners for any work done in pairs; the intimacy of a twosome seems to work better this way. We do suggest, however, that teachers structure larger response groups heterogeneously, putting three to five students together with as much diversity as the classroom population allows. If you know who the better and weaker writers in the class are, put one strong writer and one weak writer in each group to maximize the group's effectiveness.

3. Teach the PQP response format. Bill Lyons' (1978) Praise, Question, Polish (PQP) response technique is the best method we have found for

encouraging positive yet helpful response to any type of student writing. Students first tell the writer what they like about the paper (Praise). Second, they ask any questions they might have about the paper (Question). Finally, they offer specific suggestions for revision (Polish). Starting off any response session with praise for what the writer did well does much to alleviate negative feedback; the questions suggest places where the writer must clarify meaning or might develop ideas more fully, and the final suggestions offer concrete places to revise.

4. Structure peer response sessions. Group procedures and the Reader Response Sheets described below keep students on task. Successful response groups don't just happen; they are as carefully planned as a solid lecture. Students work well together when they have a specific process to follow as they share their papers in groups. We like to have the writer read his or her piece aloud to the group while the other group members follow along on their own copies of the draft. This is an important way for the writer to hear the piece; it often leads to on-the-spot revision as the writer recognizes problem areas while reading aloud. If it is impossible for each group member to have a copy of the paper, students should be instructed to listen "actively" while the writer reads, and to jot notes on a sheet of paper about things they want to comment on or question. After the piece is read aloud, the group should take a few minutes to write a response to the writer or fill out a Reader Response Sheet. Responders then spend another five to ten minutes discussing the paper, drawing on their written critiques, while the writer takes notes on suggestions and asks for help with trouble spots. Finally, the members of the group give the writer the written responses to use in revising. It is helpful to put these procedures in writing in a handout for students.

5. Use reader response sheets. For most secondary school students, directions to "write a response" are too general. They need a more concrete task to focus their comments in productive ways or they may never venture much beyond "That's good" in responding to one another's work. Response sheets with several questions for students to write about and then discuss facilitate effective group work over drafts. For example, if we want students to use the PQP format in their groups, we put the three questions on a handout, leaving space for a written comment under each question. But students can also be asked to focus their responses on certain aspects of the writing. The following sample Reader Response Sheet uses the PQP format but adds questions that focus on development of ideas through details and examples.

Reader Response Sheet

Writer's Name _____

Responder's Name _____

Title of the Paper _____

Directions: When you work in your writing response groups for this paper, I want you to focus your discussion on whether or not the writer has fully developed the main idea of the paper with good use of details and examples to support his or her points. Please write comments about the following questions after the writer reads the piece aloud and then discuss your responses in the group.

1. What do you like about this paper? What do you remember? What did the writer do particularly well?
2. What questions do you have for the writer about the paper?
3. What do you think is the central point the writer is making? What is his or her message to readers? Please state this in a sentence or two.
4. What details and examples has the writer used to illustrate and support the main point? Please list them here.
5. Are there any spots in the paper where the writer could add an example or give additional details to more fully explain something for readers?

Reader response questions can also focus on content (What parts of the paper did you find most interesting? Is the writer's position on the argument supported with enough evidence?); on clarity (Are there any areas where the meaning is unclear?); on organization (Are the main points arranged in the best order? Is the paper easy to follow? Does the paper have a "grabber" beginning and a solid conclusion?); on grammar, mechanics, and proofreading (Has the paper been carefully proofread to correct errors in punctuation, spelling, and usage?).

Mini-Lessons: Teaching at the Point of Need

While students are revising drafts, the teacher can sometimes see that many students misunderstand a point in the assignment or are making the same error. This is the time for a brief lesson perhaps five or ten minutes long, sometimes called a "mini-lesson" in writing texts. For example, one of us, in a class working on a paper comparing the work of two black women writers, discovered that students were not paying attention to the difference between "women" and "woman" in their writing. Other students were referring to the authors by their first names, comparing Toni to Alice instead of Morrison to Walker—small points, but ones that competent writers in all fields should use correctly. A mini-lesson, followed by direct application to the drafts students were working on, cleared up these problems immediately. In a history class working on papers about World War II, the teacher saw that most students started their papers with "My report is about. . . ". A brief mini-lesson in which she brainstormed with the class about possibilities for the opening led to much more interesting and creative introductions than she usually got for this kind of formal assignment.

Final Editing, Proofreading, and Polishing

Content area teachers will be much more pleased with the quality of the papers they read and grade if they allot a classroom session to copyediting after students have revised papers and are ready to make a final draft. This is the time to focus on correctness, setting students on an "error-hunt" in their own papers. They may not recognize every run-on sentence, misspelled word, or awkward phrasing, but they do find and correct many mechanical errors, especially if allowed to work together on this since it is usually easier to recognize errors on someone else's paper than on your own. We tell students to get as many readers as possible and to concentrate solely on punctuation, spelling, grammatical correctness, and appropriate usage. As students work on this, the teacher can circulate in the class, helping individual students. Handbooks, dictionaries, and a thesaurus or two piled on a table for reference can encourage students to find their own answers to matters of correctness. They also free the content area teacher from having to be an authority on grammar and mechanics. Students also profit from a proofreading checklist of what to look for in their papers: run-on sentences, fragments, spelling errors, typos, etc. The message to students is clear: correctness is important; it is also *your* responsibility as a writer.

Sharing and Publishing Student Writing

The single most effective way we know of to involve students more fully in their writing is to provide real readers. We do our best to make sure that every assignment that ends in a formal, polished piece has a wider readership than just the teacher. This encourages better writing and gives students an authentic reason for proofreading. Nothing is more discouraging than to have a piece the student has labored upon for a week or more disappear into the teacher's desk drawer on the day it is due and then reappear with a grade a few weeks later when the assignment has been completely forgotten.

A personal story bears telling here. One of our daughters was given an excellent writing assignment in an eleventh-grade history class studying the Depression: interview someone who had lived through the Depression and write it up. We arranged an interview with a seventy-eight-year-old family friend who had lived in Manhattan, working as a bank teller on Wall Street in the late 1920s. This assignment soon became a family project: we helped our daughter develop questions, transcribe her tape, analyze and write up the results (which were, by the way, astonishing because neither this woman nor her family had really felt the brunt of the Depression; no one lost jobs; no one went hungry though soup lines formed throughout the city). We could hardly wait to hear what had happened in class on the day everyone came in with their interviews. What had the other interviews been like? What had the class learned about the Depression from this assignment? The answer was *nothing*. The teacher collected the interviews at the start of the period, then went on to lecture about FDR and the New Deal, the next chapter in the textbook. A month later, our student got the paper back with a grade and "good job" written at the end of it. The assignment was just a grade in a teacher's roll book. What a missed opportunity for students to develop genuine understanding of how the Depression affected those who lived through it! What a turnoff for students as developing researchers and writers!

"Publication" can be construed very broadly, from exchanging papers in class to sending students' editorials to the local newspaper, where they might be published in a "Citizens' Voice" column. Students can make individual books for the class library, the school library, or lower grade levels. They can publish their information in class newspapers, or send pieces off to magazines that publish student writing such as *Merlyn's Pen* (P.O. Box 716, East Greenwich, Rhode Island 02818), which accepts all kinds of writing from students in grades seven through ten, or *Scholastic Voice* (50 West 44th St., N.Y., N.Y. 10036), for grades seven through twelve. The idea is to develop real readership for students' work. Post well-written pieces on bulletin boards or, if finances permit, publish a class anthology of everyone's paper on a given topic. (This would have been ideal for those Depression interviews.) Or simply pass the final papers around in class with a blank sheet attached for readers' comments. Science lab reports, even if about the same experiment, can be shared in small groups for students to see how others have dealt with the same material; so can narrative descriptions of problem-solving in math. For some writing assignments such as research reports, presentations in small groups, to the whole class, or beyond the classroom are the best way to publish students' findings.

Classroom *Strategies That Work* (Nathan, et al. 1989) has a list of forty-three different ways to publish student writing (58–59), and a full chapter in Kirby and Liner's *Inside Out* is devoted to publishing strategies (237–249). *In the Middle* by Atwell also has a set of publishing ideas plus a list of names and address of writing contests and publications that accept student work (265–268).

Evaluation and Response to Students' Finished Pieces

If students have spent class time working on drafts in small groups, revising and proofreading their work, a great deal of informal evaluation has already taken place by the time the teacher gets the finished copy. Brief teacher-student conferences, feedback from peers over drafts, responses from readers, and exposure to other papers in the class give students a reasonably good sense of the strengths and weaknesses of their own work by the time it is completed. When we ask students in our classes to evaluate their own writing, they are remarkably accurate in recognizing what they've done well on an assignment and where the weak spots remain. This kind of information gives the teacher valuable insights into how the student perceives his or her work, making it possible for evaluation to become a dialogue instead of a one-sided judgment on the teacher's part. A teacher's comments can often refer directly to the student's own self-evaluation, agreeing or disagreeing with the student and explaining why. For this reason, we recommend that the last step in any formal assignment be a brief self-evaluation based on two or three questions drawn from the following: What do you like best about your paper? Least? Are there any parts you think still need more work? How did you write this piece? What would you do to this piece if you could write one more draft? What problems did you have while you wrote this piece? How would you like readers to react to your piece? How do you think they *will* react to it?

We suggest three guidelines for making written comments on students' papers:

- Focus on content, not mechanics.
- Emphasize the main purpose of the assignment; don't try to comment on everything.
- Respond as an interested reader, not a "teacher-corrector."

Content area teachers sometimes feel they are shirking their duty if they don't point out every mechanical/grammatical error they see in a student's paper. We would like to suggest that this is not your role, nor is it necessary. If students have spent time proofreading their papers, your message about the importance of correctness has already been aired, and the students have taken appropriate responsibility for the copyediting of their work. In addition, a large body of research shows the futility of teachers' intensive marking of student papers for error. (See Braddock, Lloyd-Jones, and Schoer 1963; Haynes 1978; and Rosen 1987 for a discussion of the research in this area.) Unless mechanics are so poor that they interfere with meaning, your marking time is better spent on the content-related goals of the assignment. If a student has clearly not proofread carefully or really needs to do much more work polishing a paper, comment on this at the end of the paper and reduce the grade accordingly if that's part of your grading criteria. Fulwiler (1986) suggests that another way to handle this is to correct the errors on the first page or two of the paper and then write a comment at the bottom for the student to do the same for the rest of the paper, which again puts the responsibility with the student, where it belongs.

This same philosophy holds true for features of nonstandard dialect in students' writing. Developing writers are still learning the formal written structures of our language; therefore, you may get many features of a nonstandard-dialect speaker's oral language in a formal paper. Circling all the missing "-eds" and "s's" or changing every "him and me" to "he and I" will not eradicate these problems in future writing. We suggest, instead, that you discuss the importance of using written standard English in formal papers, use editing workshops, and be as helpful as possible in answering students' questions about correctness. To encourage nonstandard-dialect speakers to move toward standard English, create situations and assignments for students to communicate both orally and in writing to audiences for which they must shift to more formal language registers: the school newspaper, a parents' night research presentation, an editorial for the local newspaper, a science poster display for the school hallway. Correcting every nonstandard feature or taking points off a grade for dialect influence does little to move students toward control of the surface features of standard English and will most certainly make them less than eager to tackle future writing assignments in your course.

Content area teachers shouldn't try to respond to everything when marking papers—too many comments, even good ones, only overwhelm students. Instead, respond to evidence of genuine inquiry, discovery, and learning in your subject; note effective use of the vocabulary and terminology of your discipline; look for how well the student fulfilled the central purpose of the assignment. Especially with weak papers, it is more useful to center comments and suggestions on one problem in the paper than to tackle everything that needs to be worked on.

Finally, we suggest you try to set aside your "teacherly" stance when commenting on student writing. Read students' papers as genuine efforts to communicate a message to a reader and respond accordingly with questions, personal responses, and suggestions. Above all, look for the good things in a paper, giving honest praise whenever possible. Kirby and Liner (1988) quote Paul Diederich, senior research associate at the Educational Testing Service, on this issue:

> I believe very strongly that noticing and praising whatever a student does well improves writing more than any kind or amount of correction of what he does badly, and that it is especially important for the less able writers who need all the encouragement they can get. (236)

Grading

You have probably noticed that we separated evaluation and response from the issue of grading. This is a deliberate stance toward the subject. Students need lots of the *formative* evaluation and response described above as they are learning: feedback that will help them grow as writers, readers, and learners in your field. Grading is usually *summative,* final, the end of that particular learning process, and should, therefore, be kept to a minimum. In the case of writing, grades should be reserved for those pieces that students have taken through at least some writing process activities, so they have opportunities to improve the piece until it is an example of their best work. Grading should be the final step of postwriting. Under these circumstances, teachers will find grading easier, and the grades may be quite high. It is not unusual for most paper grades to be As and Bs when students have worked on their pieces using the methods described earlier in this chapter. We suggest, too, that grades include some credit for the writing process as well as the final written product.

Two things make grading papers easier, faster, and more consistent:

- a clear set of criteria so you know what you're looking for (and the students do, too)
- grading guides to make the actual grading process less labor-intensive.

Analytic Scales, Grading Guides, Grading Checklists

Analytic scales are grading guides that contain a list of qualities or features of writing with a numerical rating or ranking for each separate item. We highly recommend these for grading student writing, especially if lots of formative evaluation has been given during the writing process in teacher conferences and peer responses. These guides speed up the grading process while giving students some feedback on their writing. In addition, the qualities that are rated give students specific criteria to consider while writing. Students benefit from being involved in creating the criteria for assessment or identifying the characteristics of writing to be evaluated, but the teacher can also design these based on the qualities he or she would like to see in the paper. Figure 9–5 is a grading scale created by teachers in the Flint Area Writing Project.

Notice that the criteria to be evaluated include the student's use of prewriting and revision (The Writing Process) and the appearance of the finished piece (Form). The possible points for each feature, listed down the left column, are

Flint Area Writing Project
Grading Guide

Content/Meaning	Possible Points	Points Given
Main point		
Ideas		
Creativity	30	
Effective use of language		
Interesting to readers		
Organization/Structure		
Introduction		
Body: Development		
Examples		
Use of details	25	
Conclusion		
Mechanics		
Paragraphing		
Complete sentences		
Punctuation	15	
Grammar		
Spelling		
Capitalization		
The Writing Process		
Pre-writing		
Rough draft	15	
Second draft		
Form		
Cursive		
One side		
Margins	15	
Ink		
Neatness		

Total Points Received _____

Comments:

FIGURE 9–5.

weighted according to their relative value to these teachers, with content and structure given the most points.

Tim Holcomb, a high school science teacher, uses the grading guidesheet in Figure 9–6 for a long-term research project on fruit flies that students do in his genetics course. The format for this piece is a formally structured scientific research report; each section of the report is fully described for the students in a two-page handout accompanying the assignment. Note that both neatness and correctness are not ignored, but they are given the relatively small number of points appropriate for this assignment.

Drosophila Research Project Evaluation Sheet
Tim Holcomb, Linden High School, Linden, Michigan

SECTION	POINTS POSSIBLE	POINTS EARNED
I. II. Title Page and Introduction	10	_____
III. Hypothesis	10	_____
IV. Materials and Methods	50	_____
V. Observations	10	_____
VI. Conclusion	70	_____
VII. Recommendations	10	_____
VIII. Weekly Fly Reports	20	_____
IX. Neatness/Grammar/Spelling/Presentation	20	_____
Total	200	_____

FIGURE 9–6.

Cliff Totzke uses a totally different grading guidesheet in his high school social studies course, Contemporary World Problems. Students go through prewriting and editing processes for a formal position paper, which he evaluates as follows:

Prewriting	10 points
Peer editing	10 points
Introduction	5 points
Content	60 points

Conclusion	5 points
Mechanics	10 points

Total Points Possible   100 points

Kirby and Liner (1988) offer yet another type of scoring guide in Figure 9–7. In this case, each characteristic is rated on a scale of one to five with a brief description given of weak to excellent work in each area. These ratings are then multiplied to weight them according to their relative worth for the assignment.

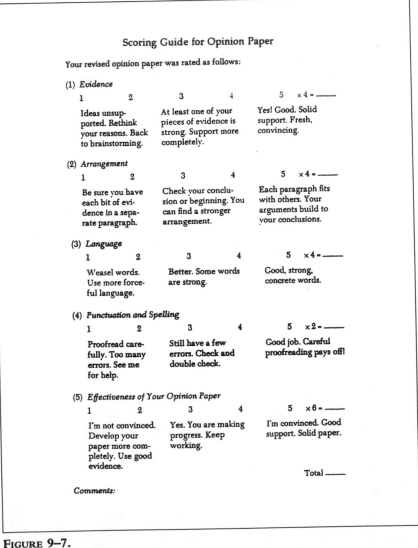

Scoring Guide for Opinion Paper

Your revised opinion paper was rated as follows:

(1) *Evidence*

1   2   3   4   5   x 4 = ____

Ideas unsup-   At least one of your   Yes! Good. Solid
ported. Rethink   pieces of evidence is   support. Fresh,
your reasons. Back   strong. Support more   convincing.
to brainstorming.   completely.

(2) *Arrangement*

1   2   3   4   5   x 4 = ____

Be sure you have   Check your conclu-   Each paragraph fits
each bit of evi-   sion or beginning. You   with others. Your
dence in a sepa-   can find a stronger   arguments build to
rate paragraph.   arrangement.   your conclusions.

(3) *Language*

1   2   3   4   5   x 4 = ____

Weasel words.   Better. Some words   Good, strong,
Use more force-   are strong.   concrete words.
ful language.

(4) *Punctuation and Spelling*

1   2   3   4   5   x 2 = ____

Proofread care-   Still have a few   Good job. Careful
fully. Too many   errors. Check and   proofreading pays off!
errors. See me   double check.
for help.

(5) *Effectiveness of Your Opinion Paper*

1   2   3   4   5   x 6 = ____

I'm not convinced.   Yes. You are making   I'm convinced. Good
Develop your   progress. Keep   support. Solid paper.
paper more com-   working.
pletely. Use good
evidence.

                                                   Total ____

Comments:

FIGURE 9–7.

These sample grading guides illustrate various ways teachers can go about designing their own based on their criteria for each assignment. To create a grading guide, ask yourself, "What traits are present in an effective piece of writing for this assignment?" List these characteristics down one column and either assign points for them according to your emphasis in the assignment or rate each feature one to five and use a multiplier that allows you to weight some traits more than others, as in the Kirby and Liner scoring guide.

Conclusion

This chapter has presented many different ways to use writing to support reading and learning in all courses across the curriculum. These range from informal writings used to stimulate more personal learning and discovery to more formal writing assignments that require students to collect, organize, and synthesize ideas to communicate them to readers. Writing can be used to support the readings, lectures, discussions, and other activities of a course or it can give students an opportunity to extend their learning beyond the boundaries of the course material. In all these writing activities, writing provides the means by which students explore and internalize new information to make it their own. Writing-centered classrooms become "educational settings with thinking-centered learning, where students learn by thinking through what they are learning about" (Perkins 1992, 7).

Suggested Further Reading

Brown, Jean E., Lela B. Phillips, and Elaine C. Stephens. 1993. *Toward Literacy: Theory and Applications for Teaching Writing in the Content Areas.* Belmont, CA.: Wadsworth Publishing Co.

Countryman, Joan. 1992. *Writing to Learn Mathematics: Strategies That Work, K–12.* Portsmouth, NH: Heinemann.

Farrell-Childers, Pamela, Anne Ruggles Gere, and Art Young. 1994. *Programs and Practices: Writing Across the Secondary School Curriculum.* Portsmouth, NH: Boynton/Cook.

Irvin, Judith, John Lunstrum, Carol Lynch-Brown, and Mary Shepard. 1995. *Enhancing Social Studies Through Literacy Strategies.* Washington, D.C.: National Council for the Social Studies.

Maxwell, Rhoda. 1996. *Writing Across the Curriculum in Middle and High Schools.* Boston: Allyn and Bacon.

WORKS CITED

Adams, Marilyn J. 1990. *Beginning to Read: Thinking and Learning about Print*. Cambridge: The MIT Press.

Alcott, Louisa May. 1869. *Little Women*. Boston: Roberts Brothers.

Allington, Richard L. 1983. "The Reading Instruction Provided Readers of Differing Reading Abilities." *Elementary School Journal* 83: 548–559.

Ambrose, Stephen. 1994. *D-Day: June 6, 1944*. New York: Simon and Schuster.

Angelou, Maya. 1969. *I Know Why the Caged Bird Sings*. New York: Random House.

Applebee, Arthur N. 1981. *Writing in the Secondary School: English and the Content Areas*. Urbana, IL: NCTE.

Applebee, Arthur N., Judith A. Langer, and Ina V. S. Mullis. 1986. *The Writing Report Card: Writing Achievement in American Schools*. Princeton, NJ: National Assessment of Educational Progress (NAEP), ETS Report #15-W-02.

Artley, A. Sterl. 1977. "Phonics Revisited." *Language Arts* 54 (February 1977): 121–126.

Asimov, Isaac. 1966. *Fantastic Voyage*. New York: Bantam Books.

Atwell, Nancie. 1987. *In the Middle: Writing, Reading, and Learning with Adolescents*. Portsmouth, NH: Boynton/Cook Publishers, Inc.

————, ed. 1990. *Coming to Know: Writing to Learn in the Intermediate Grades*. Portsmouth, NH: Heinemann.

Au, Kathryn H. 1993. *Literacy Instruction in Multicultural Settings*. New York: Harcourt Brace Jovanovich College Publishers.

Baldwin, R. S., and R. Kaufman. 1979. "A Concurrent Validity Study of the Raygor Readability Estimate." *Journal of Reading* 23: 148–153.

Barnes, Douglas, James Britton, Harold Rosen, and the London Association for the Teaching of English (LATE). 1969. *Language, the Learner and the School*. Harmondsworth, Middlesex, England: Penguin Education.

Baumann, James F. 1988. *Reading Assessment: An Instructional Decision-Making Perspective*. Columbus, OH: Merrill Publishing Co.

Beall, Herbert, and John Trimbur. 1993. "Writing in Chemistry: Keys to Student Underlife." *College Teaching* 41 (Fall): 50–54.

Becoming a Nation of Readers: The Report of the Commission on Reading. 1984. Washington, D.C.: The National Institute of Education.

Bishop, Rudine Sims, editor. 1994. *Kaleidoscope: A Multicultural Booklist for Grades K–8*, Urbana, IL: NCTE.

Bissex, Glenda L. 1980. *GNYS AT WRK: A Child Learns to Write and Read*. Cambridge: Harvard University Press.

Black, Laurel. 1992. "Portfolios for Placement: The Portfolio Writing Program at Miami University." *Composition Chronicle* 5 (February): 4–6.

Bloom, Benjamin S., ed. 1968. *Taxonomy of Educational Objectives: The Classification of Educational Goals.* Handbook 1. Cognitive Domain by a Committee of College and University Examiners. New York: David McKay Company, Inc.

Braddock, Richard, Richard Lloyd-Jones, and Lowell Schoer. 1963. *Research in Written Composition.* Urbana, IL: NCTE.

Brent, Doug. 1992. *Reading as Rhetorical Invention: Knowledge, Persuasion, and the Teaching of Research-Based Writing.* Urbana, IL: NCTE.

Britton, James. 1970. "Talking and Writing" and "Progress in Writing." In *Explorations in Children's Writing,* Eldonna Evertts, ed. Urbana, IL: NCTE.

Britton, James, Tony Burgess, Nancy Martin, Alex McLeod, and Harold Rosen. 1975. *The Development of Writing Abilities (11–18).* London: Macmillan Education.

Brontë, Charlotte. 1847. *Jane Eyre.* In the *Norton Anthology of Literature by Women,* 2nd edition, ed. Sandra M. Gilbert and Susan Gubar. New York: Norton, 1996.

Brozo, W. G. 1990. "Hiding Out in Secondary Content Classrooms: Coping Strategies of Unsuccessful Readers." *Journal of Reading* (November): 324–328.

Brozo, W. G., and M. L. Simpson. 1991. *Readers, Teachers, Learners: Expanding Literacy in the Secondary Schools.* New York: Merrill.

Bruner, Jerome S. 1971. *The Relevance of Education.* NY: W. W. Norton, pp. 7–8. Cited in 'Writing as a Mode of Learning.' Reprinted in *The Web of Meaning: Essays on Writing, Teaching, Learning, and Thinking.* Portsmouth, NH: Boynton/Cook, 1983.

Bryant, J. A. R. 1984. "Textbook Treasure Hunt." *Journal of Reading* 27: 547–548.

Burke, Carolyn. 1972. "Dialect and the Reading Process." In *Language Differences: Do They Interfere?* Newark, DE: International Reading Association.

Byers, P., and H. Byers, 1972. "Nonverbal Communication and the Education of Children." In *Functions of Language in the Classroom,* ed. Cazden et al. New York: Teachers College Press.

Cazden, Courtney B. 1988. *Classroom Discourse: The Language of Teaching and Learning.* Portsmouth, NH: Heinemann.

Chall, Jeanne. 1967. *Learning to Read: The Great Debate.* New York: McGraw-Hill.

———. 1992 and 1993. "Research Supports Direct Instruction Models." *Reading Today* International Reading Association (December and January): 8ff.

Collier, James Lincoln, and Christopher Collier. 1974. *My Brother Sam Is Dead.* New York: Four Winds.

Collins, Cathy. 1987. "Content Mastery Strategies and Class Discussion." *The Reading Teacher* 40: 816–818.

Cooke, David. 1941. *War Wings: Fighting Planes of the American and British Air Forces.* New York: R. M. McBride.

———. 1942. *War Planes of the Axis.* New York: R. M. McBride.

⸺an, Joan. 1992. *Writing to Learn Mathematics: Strategies That Work, K–12.* ⸺uth, NH: Heinemann.

⸺84. "A Message to Authors About Metadiscourse Use in Instructional ⸺nging Perspectives on Research in Reading/Language Processing and Instruc- ⸺Niles and L. A. Harris, 66–74. Thirty-third Yearbook of the ⸺g Conference. Rochester, NY: National Reading Conference.

Cuban, L. 1993. *How Teachers Taught: Constancy and Change in American Classrooms, 1890–1990.* New York: Longman.

Cunningham, Patricia. 1982. "Diagnosis by Observation." In *Approaches to the Informal Evaluation of Reading,* ed. by J. Pikulski and T. Shanahan, 12–22. Newark, DE: International Reading Association.

Cunningham, Dick, and Scott Shablak. 1975. "Selective Reading Guide–O–Rama: The Content Teacher's Best Friend." *Journal of Reading* 18: 380–382.

Dahl, Roald. 1950. *Someone Like You.* New York: Knopf.

Dale, E., and J. Chall. 1948. "A Formula for Predicting Readability." *Educational Research Bulletin* 27: 11–20, 37–54.

Davey, B. 1983. "Think-aloud—Modelling the Cognitive Processes of Reading Comprehension." *Journal of Reading* 27(1): 44–47.

Day, Frances Ann. 1994. *Multicultural Voices in Contemporary Literature: A Resource for Teachers.* Portsmouth, NH: Heinemann.

Day Lewis, C, quoted in "Internal Revision: A Process of Discovery." In *Learning by Teaching,* Donald Murray. Portsmouth, NH: Boynton/Cook, 1982.

DeGroat, Bernie. 1994. "New Students Required to Submit Writing Portfolios." *The University Record* 49 (February 28): 9.

Delpit, Lisa. 1995. *Other People's Children: Cultural Conflict in the Classroom.* New York: W. W. Norton.

Devine, Thomas G. 1986. *Teaching Reading Comprehension: From Theory to Practice.* Boston: Allyn and Bacon.

Dewey, John. 1938. *Experience and Education.* New York: Collier Books, 1963.

———. 1899. *The School and Society in John Dewey: The Middle Works, 1899-1924.* Carbondale: Southern Illinois University Press, 1976.

———. 1933. *How We Think: A Restatement of the Relation of Reflective Thinking to the Educative Process.* Boston: D. C. Heath.

Dillon, J. T. 1979. "Alternatives to Questioning." *High School Journal* 62: 217–222.

——— 1981. To Question and Not to Question During Discussion. I. Questioning and Discussion; II. Non-questioning Techniques. *Journal of Teacher Education* 32: no. 5: 51–55; and no. 6: 15–20.

Duvoisin, Roger. 1961. *Veronica.* New York: Knopf.

Edelsky, Carole. 1991. *Literacy and Justice for All: Rethinking the Social in Language and Education.* New York: Falmer Press.

Elbow, Peter. 1973. *Writing Without Teachers.* New York: Oxford University Press.

Emig, Janet. 1971. *The Composing Processes of Twelfth Graders.* Urbana, IL: NCTE.

———. 1977. "Writing as a Mode of Learning." Reprinted in *The Web of Meaning: Essays on Writing, Teaching, Learning, and Thinking.* Portsmouth, NH: Boynton/Cook, 1983.

Evertts, Eldonna L., and Myron H. Van Roekel. 1966. *Seven Seas.* Harper & Row Basic Reading Program. Evanston, IL: Harper & Row.

Farr, Marcia, and Harvey Daniels. 1986. *Language Diversity and Writing Instruction.* Urbana, IL: NCTE.

Farr, Roger, and Robert Carey. 1986. *Reading: What Can Be Measured?* 2d ed. Newark, DE: International Reading Association.

Fitzgerald, F. Scott. 1953. *The Great Gatsby*. New York: Charles Scribner's & Sons.

Flesch, R. 1951. *How to Test Readability*. New York: Harper & Row.

————. 1955. *Why Johnny Can't Read*. New York: Harper & Row.

Flower, Linda. 1979. "Writer–Based Prose: A Cognitive Basis for Problems in Writing." *College English* 41 (September): 19–37.

Forbes, Esther. 1943. *Johnny Tremain*. New York: Houghton.

Fordham, Signithia, and John Ogbu. 1986. "Black Students' School Success: Coping with the 'Burden of Acting White.'" *Urban Review* 18: 176–206.

Forman, James. 1969. *My Enemy, My Brother*. New York: Meredith Press.

Frank, Anne. 1952. *Anne Frank: The Diary of a Young Girl*. New York: Doubleday.

Fry, E. 1977. "Fry's Readability Graph: Clarifications, Validity, and Extension to Level 17." *Journal of Reading* 21: 242–252.

Fry, Roger. 1971. "The Orangoutang Score." *The Reading Teacher* 24 (January): 360–363.

Fulwiler, Toby. 1982. "The Personal Connection: Journal Writing." In *Language Connections: Writing and Reading Across the Curriculum*, ed. Toby Fulwiler and Art Young. Urbana, IL: NCTE.

————. 1986. "The Argument for Writing Across the Curriculum." In *Writing across the Disciplines: Research into Practice.*, ed. Art Young and Toby Fulwiler. Portsmouth, NH: Boynton/Cook.

————. ed. 1987. *The Journal Book*. Portsmouth, NH: Boynton/Cook.

Gambrell, L., R. Wilson, and W. Bantt. 1981. "Classroom Observations of Task Attending Behaviors of Good and Poor Readers." *Journal of Educational Research* 74: 400–404.

Gardner, Howard. 1983. *Frames of Mind: The Theory of Multiple Intelligences*. New York: Basic Books.

————. 1991. *The Unschooled Mind: How Children Think and How Schools Should Teach*. New York: Basic Books.

Gere, Anne Ruggles, ed. 1985. *Roots in the Sawdust: Writing to Learn Across the Disciplines*. Urbana, IL: NCTE.

Gibson, Margaret A. 1991. "Minorities and Schooling: Some Implications." In *Minority Status and Schooling: A Comparative Study of Immigrant and Involuntary Minorities*, ed. Margaret A. Gibson and John U. Ogbu. New York: Garland Publishing.

Goodman, Kenneth. S. 1965. "A Linguistic Study of Cues and Miscues in Reading." *Elementary English* 42: 639–643.

————. 1967. "Reading: A Psycholinguistic Guessing Game." *Journal of the Reading Specialist* 6: 127–135.

————. ed. 1973a. *Miscue Analysis: Applications to Reading Instruction*. Urbana, IL: NCTE.

————. 1973b. "Testing in Reading: A General Critique." In *Accountability and Reading Instruction*, edited by Robert Ruddell: 21–33. Urbana, Illinois: NCTE. ERIC Document 073448.

————. 1973c. "Psycholinguistic Universals in the Reading Process." In *Psycholinguistics and Reading*, ed. Frank Smith. New York: Holt, Rinehart, and Winston.

————. 1986. *What's Whole in Whole Language*. Portsmouth, NH: Heinemann.

————. 1992 and 1993. "Gurus, Professors, and the Politics of Phonics." *Reading Today* International Reading Association. (December/January): 8ff.

Goodman, Yetta. 1976. "A Study of the Development of Literacy in Preschool Children." Research grant proposal. Washington, D.C.: National Institute of Education.

————. 1978. "Kid Watching: An Alternative to Testing." *Journal of National Elementary Principals* 57: 41–45.

Goodman, Yetta, and Carolyn Burke. 1972. *Reading Miscue Inventory: Procedure for Diagnosis and Evaluation.* New York: Macmillan.

Goodman, Yetta, Dorothy Watson, and Carolyn Burke. 1996. *Reading Strategies: Focus on Comprehension.* New York: Holt, Rinehart, and Winston.

Gunderson, Lee, and Jon Shapiro. 1987. "Some Findings on Whole Language Instruction." *Reading-Canada-Lecture* 5(i): 22–26, Quoted in Constance Weaver, *Understanding Whole Language: From Principles to Practice.*

Guthrie, J. 1974. "The Maze Technique to Assess, Monitor Reading Comprehension." *Reading Teacher* 28: 161–168.

Harste, Jerome C., and Robert F. Carey. 1979. "Comprehension as Setting." In *New Perspectives on Comprehension: Monograph in Language and Reading Studies.* Monographs in Teaching and Learning. Bloomington, IN: Indiana University School of Education.

Harste, Jerome C., Virginia A. Woodward, and Carolyn L. Burke. 1984. *Language Stories and Literacy Lessons.* Portsmouth, NH: Heinemann.

Haynes, Elizabeth. 1978. "Using Research in Preparing to Teach Writing." *English Journal* 67 (January): 82–88.

Hayslip, Le Ly, with Jay Wurts. 1989. *When Heaven and Earth Changed Places: A Vietnamese Woman's Journey from War to Peace.* New York: Doubleday.

Heath, Shirley Brice. 1983. *Ways With Words: Language, Life, and Work in Communities and Classrooms.* Cambridge: Cambridge University Press.

Heath, Shirley Brice, and Leslie Mangiola. 1991. *Children of Promise: Literate Activity in Linguistically and Culturally Diverse Classrooms.* Washington, D.C.: National Education Association.

Heilman, Arthur W. 1981. *Principles and Practices of Teaching Reading.* Columbus, OH: Charles E. Merrill.

Hemingway, Ernest. 1936. "The Short Happy Life of Francis Macomber." In *Introduction to Literature,* 3d ed., eds. Louis G. Locke, William M. Gibson, and George Arms. New York: Rinehart and Company, Inc., 1957.

Herber, Harold. 1978. "Levels of Comprehension." *Teaching Reading in Content Areas.* Englewood Cliffs, NJ: Prentice-Hall.

Hofstetter, Fred T., with CD-ROM by Patricia Fox. 1995. *Multimedia Literacy.* New York: McGraw-Hill.

Huey, Edmund Burke. 1908. *The Psychology and Pedagogy of Reading.* Cambridge: The MIT Press.

Hull, Glynda, and David Bartholomae. 1986. "Teaching Writing as Learning and Process." *Educational Leadership* 43 (April): 44–53.

Hunt, Irene. 1964. *Across Five Aprils.* Chicago, IL: Follett.

Ingarden, Roman. 1973. *The Cognition of the Literary Work of Art*. Trans. Ruth Ann Crowley and Kenneth R. Olson. Evanston, IL: Northwestern University Press. 1973.

Irmscher, William. 1979. "Writing as a Way of Learning and Developing." *College Composition and Communication* 30 (October): 240–244.

Irwin, J., and C. Davis. 1980. "Assessing Readability: The Checklist Approach." *Journal of Reading* 24: 129–130.

Isaacson, Judith. 1990. *Seed of Sarah: Memoirs of a Survivor*. Urbana: IL: University of Illinois Press.

Jackson, Shirley. "The Lottery." In *Literature: The Human Experience*, 2d ed., eds. Richard Abcarian and Marvin Klotz. New York: St. Martin's Press, 1978.

Johnson, D., and P. D. Pearson. 1984. *Teaching Reading Vocabulary*. 2d ed. New York: Holt, Rinehart, & Winston.

Judy, Stephen N. 1974. *Explorations in the Teaching of English*. New York: Dodd, Mead.

Kirby, Dan, and Tom Liner with Ruth Vinz. 1988. *Inside Out: Developmental Strategies for Teaching Writing*, 2d ed. Portsmouth, NH: Boynton/Cook.

Knowles, John, 1960. *A Separate Peace*. New York: Bantam Books.

Kutz, Eleanor, and Hephzibah Roskelly. 1991. *An Unquiet Pedagogy: Transforming Practice in the English Classroom*. Portsmouth, NH: Boynton/Cook.

Labov, William, and C. Robins. 1969. "A Note on the Relation of Reading Failure to Peer-Group Status in Urban Ghettos." *Florida F[oreign] L[anguage] Reporter* 7: 54–57.

Lambert, Dorothy. 1967. "Keeping a Journal." *English Journal* 56 (February): 286–288.

Lee, Harper. 1960. *To Kill a Mockingbird*. Philadelphia: Lippincott.

Leo, John. 1994. "Affirmative Action History." *U.S. News & World Report* (March 28): 24.

Long, Maxine. 1995. "Composition in the Newspapers." *Composition Chronicle* 8 (September): 11.

Lyons, Bill. 1978. "Well, What Do You Like About My Paper?" *Iowa English Newsletter* (September).

Macrorie, Ken. 1988. *The I-Search Paper*. Portsmouth, NH: Boynton/Cook.

McDermott, R. P., and Kenneth Gospodinoff. 1981. "Social Contexts for Ethnic Borders and School Failure." In *Culture and the Bilingual Classroom: Studies in Classroom Ethnography*, ed. Henry Trueba, Grace Guthrie, and Kathryn Au. Rowley, MA: Newbury House Publishers.

McLaughlin, H. 1969. "SMOG Grading—A New Readability Formula." *Journal of Reading* 12: 639–646.

Meinbach, Anita Meyer, Liz Rothlein, and Anthony D. Fredericks. 1995. *The Complete Guide to Thematic Units: Creating the Integrated Curriculum*. Norwood, MA: Christopher Gordon Publishers.

Meltzer, Milton. 1976. *Never to Forget: The Jews of the Holocaust*. New York: Harper & Row.

———. 1989. *Voices from the Civil War: A Documentary History of the Great American Conflict*. New York: Thomas Y. Crowell.

Mohr, Marian M. 1984. *Revision: The Rhythm of Meaning.* Portmouth, NH: Boynton/Cook.

Moore, D. 1986. "A Case for Naturalistic Assessment of Reading Comprehension." In *Reading in the Content Areas: Improving Classroom Instruction*, Second Edition, ed. by E. Dishner, T. Bean, J. Readance, and D. Moore: 159–170. Dubuque, IA: Kendall/Hunt.

Moore, D., S. Moore, P. Cunningham, and J. Cunningham. 1994. *Developing Readers & Writers in the Content Areas K–12*, 2d ed. New York: Longman.

Moore, D. W. and Cunningham, J. W. 1986. "The Confused World of Main Idea." In J. F. Baumann, ed. *Teaching Main Idea Comprehension.* Newark, DE: International Reading Association.

Murray, Donald. 1982. *Learning by Teaching: Selected Articles on Writing and Teaching.* Portsmouth, NH: Boynton/Cook.

Myers, Miles. 1996. *Changing Our Minds: Negotiating English and Literacy.* Urbana, IL: NCTE.

Myers, Walter Dean. 1988. *Fallen Angels.* New York: Scholastic.

Nathan, Ruth, Frances Temple, Kathleen Juntunen, and Charles Temple. 1989. *Classroom Strategies That Work: An Elementary Teacher's Guide to Process Writing.* Portsmouth, NH: Heinemann.

Neeld, Elizabeth Cowan. 1990. *Writing*, 3d ed. Glenview, IL: Scott, Foresman/Little, Brown Higher Education.

Nieto, Sonia. 1992. *Affirming Diversity: The Sociopolitical Context of Multicultural Education.* New York: Longman.

Ogle, Donna. 1986. "K–W–L: A Teaching Model That Develops Active Reading of Expository Text." *The Reading Teacher* 39: 564–570.

Oliver, Eileen. 1994. *Crossing the Mainstream: Multicultural Perspectives in Teaching Literature.* Urbana, IL: NCTE.

Olsen, M., D. Kirby, and G. Hulme. 1982. *The Writing Process: Composition and Applied Grammar, Grade 7.* Boston: Allyn and Bacon.

Parsons, Michael. 1987. *How We Understand Art: A Cognitive Developmental Account of Aesthetic Experience.* Cambridge: Cambridge University Press.

Paulson, F., P. Paulson, and C. Meyer. 1991. "What Makes a Portfolio a Portfolio?" *Educational Leadership* 48 (7): 60–63.

Pearson, P. David. 1993. "Teaching and Learning Reading: A Research Perspective." *Language Arts* 70 (6): 502–511.

Pearson, P. David and Dale D. Johnson. 1978. *Teaching Reading Comprehension.* New York: Holt, Rinehart, & Winston.

Perkins, David. 1992. *Smart Schools: From Training Memories to Educating Minds.* New York: Macmillan.

Perl, Sondra. 1980. "Understanding Composing." *College Composition and Communication* 31 (December): 363–371.

Pesick, Stan. 1996. "Writing History: Before and After Portfolios." *The Quarterly of the National Writing Project and the Center for the Study of Writing and Literacy* 18 (1): 20–29.

Philips, Susan U. 1972. "Participant Structures and Communicative Competence: Warm Springs Children in Community and Classroom." In *Functions of Language in the Classroom*, ed. C. B. Cazden et al. New York: Teachers College Press.

Poe, Edgar Allan. 1843. "The Pit and the Pendulum." In *The Complete Tales and Poems of Edgar Allan Poe*. New York: Vintage Books, 1975.

Postman, Neil, and C. Weingarten. 1969. *Teaching as a Subversive Activity*. A Delta Book. New York: Dell.

Rakes, Thomas A., and Lana Smith. 1986. "Assessing Reading Skills in the Content Areas." In *Reading in the Content Areas: Improving Classroom Instruction*, 2d ed., ed. by E. Dishner, T. Bean, J. Readence, and D. Moore: 145–159. Dubuque, IA: Kendall/Hunt.

Raygor, A. L. 1977. "The Raygor Readability Estimate: A Quick and Easy Way to Determine Difficulty." In *Reading: Theory, Research, and Practice*, ed. by P. D. Pearson. Twenty-sixth Yearbook of the National Reading Conference: 259–263. Clemson, SC: National Reading Conference.

Read, Charles. 1975. *Children's Categorization of Speech Sounds in English*. Research Report no. 17. Urbana, IL: NCTE.

Readence, John E., Thomas W. Bean, and R. Scott Baldwin. 1981 and 1989. *Content Area Reading: An Integrated Approach*, 2d and 3d eds. Dubuque, IA: Kendall/Hunt.

Revard, Carter, ed. 1993. *Native Heritage: American Indian Literature*. Urbana, IL: NCTE.

Reyes, Maria de la Luz. 1991. "Bilingual Student Writers: A Question of Fair Evaluation. *English Journal* 80 (December): 16–23.

Rhodes, Lynn, and Curt Dudley-Marling. 1988. *Readers and Writers with a Difference: A Holistic Approach to Teaching Learning Disabled and Remedial Students*. Portsmouth, NH: Heinemann.

Ribowsky, Helene. 1985. *The Effects of a Code Emphasis Approach and a Whole Language Approach upon Emergent Literacy of Kindergarten Children*. Alexandria, VA: Educational Document Reproduction Service, ED 269 720.

Richardson, S. 1991. *Magazines for Children*. Chicago: American Library Association.

Richter, Hans Peter. 1970. *Friedrich*, trans. Edite Kroll. New York: Holt.

Rico, Gabriele. 1983. *Writing the Natural Way*. Los Angeles: J. P. Tarcher.

Rose, Mike. 1989. *Lives on the Boundary*. New York: Penguin.

Rosen, Lois Matz. 1987. "Developing Correctness in Student Writing: Alternatives to the Error-Hunt." *English Journal* 76 (March): 62–69.

Rosenblatt, Louise. 1978. *The Reader, the Text, the Poem: The Transactional Theory of the Literary Work*. Carbondale: Southern Illinois University Press.

Rosow, La Vergne. 1988. "Adult Illiterates Offer Unexpected Cues into the Reading Process." *Journal of Reading* (November): 120–124.

Rumelhart, David E. 1984. "Understanding Understanding." In *Understanding Reading Comprehension: Cognition, Language and Structure of Prose*. ed. James Flood. Newark, DE: International Reading Association: 3.

Ryder, Randall J., and Michael F. Graves. 1994. *Reading and Learning in Content Areas*. New York: Macmillan College Publishing Company.

Russell, Ron. 1986. "Romulus: A Lesson on Testing." *The Detroit News*, Sunday, January 12.

Schell, Leo M., ed. 1981. *Diagnostic and Criterion-Referenced Reading Tests: Review and Evaluation.* Newark, DE: International Reading Association.

Scholes, Robert. 1985. *Textual Power: Literary Theory and the Teaching of English.* New Haven, CT: Yale University Press.

Shannon, Patrick. 1989. *Broken Promises: Reading Instruction in Twentieth Century America.* New York: Bergin & Garvey.

———. 1990. *The Struggle to Continue: Progressive Reading Instruction in the United States.* Portsmouth, NH: Heinemann.

———. 1992. "Reading Instruction and Social Class." In *Becoming Political: Readings and Writings in the Politics of Literacy Education,* ed. Patrick Shannon. Portsmouth, NH: Heinemann.

Shelley, Mary. 1818, revised 1831. *Frankenstein.* New York: The New American Library, A Signet Classic, 1983.

Singer, Harry. 1986. "Friendly Texts: Description and Criteria." In *Reading in the Content Areas: Improving Classroom Instruction,* 2d ed., ed. by E. Dishner, T. Bean, J. Readence, and D. Moore: 112–128. Dubuque, IA: Kendall/Hunt.

Smith, Frank. 1973. *Psycholinguistics and Reading.* New York: Holt, Rinehart, & Winston.

———. 1975. *Comprehension and Learning: A Conceptual Framework for Teachers.* New York: Holt, Rinehart, & Winston.

———. 1978. *Understanding Reading,* 2d ed. New York: Holt, Rinehart, & Winston

———. 1994. *Understanding Reading,* 5th ed. Hillsdale, NJ: Lawrence Erlbaum Associates, Publishers.

Smith, Nila Banton. 1986 ed. *American Reading Instruction.* Newark, DE: International Reading Association.

Stauffer, Russell. 1969. *Directing Reading Maturity as a Cognitive Process.* New York: Harper and Row.

Stenmark, Jean Kerr. 1989. *Assessment Alternatives in Mathematics: An Overview of Assessment Techniques That Promote Learning.* Berkeley, CA.: Lawrence Hall of Science.

Stice, Carole, and Nancy Bertrand. 1989. *The Texts and Textures of Literacy Learning in Whole Language Versus Traditional/Skills Classrooms.* Unpublished manuscript, Tennessee State University.

Stoll, D. R. 1990. *Magazines for Children.* Newark, DE: International Reading Association.

Sullivan, Anne McCrary. 1988. "The Personal Anthology: A Stimulus for Exploratory Reading." *English Journal* 77: 27–30.

Taba, Hilda. 1967. *Teacher's Handbook for Elementary Social Studies.* Reading, MA: Addison-Wesley.

Taylor, Mildred. 1976. *Roll of Thunder, Hear My Cry.* New York: Dial.

Taylor, W. S. 1953. "Cloze Procedure: A New Test for Measuring Readability." *Journalism Quarterly* 30: 415–433.

Tchudi, Stephen N., and Margie C. Huerta. 1983. *Teaching Writing in the Content Areas: Middle School/Junior High.* Washington, D.C.: National Education Association.

Thomas, Sharon, and Marilyn Wilson. 1993. "Idiosyncratic Interpretations: Negotiating Meaning in Expository Prose." *English Journal* 82: 58–64.

Thorndike, Edward L. 1915. *The Principles of Teaching Based on Psychology*. New York: A. G. Seiler.

————. 1917. "Reading as Reasoning: A Study of Mistakes in Paragraph Reading." *The Journal of Educational Psychology* 8: 323–326.

Tierney, Robert J., Mark A. Carter, and Laura E. Desai. 1991. *Portfolio Assessment in the Reading-Writing Classroom*. Norwood, MA: Christopher Gordon.

Tierney, Robert J., J. Readence, and E. Dishner. 1990. *Reading Strategies and Practices: A Compendium*, 3d ed. Boston: Allyn and Bacon.

Vacca, Richard T. 1981. *Content Area Reading*. Boston: Little, Brown & Company.

————. 1975. "Development of a Functional Reading Strategy: Implications for Content Area Instruction." *Journal of Eduational Research* 69: 108–112.

Vacca, R. T. and J. L. Vacca. 1989 and 1993. *Content Area Reading*, 3d and 4th eds. Glenview, IL: Scott, Foresman and Company.

Van Allen, Roach. 1982. *Language Experience Activities*, 2d ed. New York: Houghton Mifflin.

Vaughn, S., Sharon Crawley, and L. Mountain. 1979. "A Multiple-modality Approach to Word Study: Vocabulary Scavenger Hunts." *The Reading Teacher* 32: 434–437.

Vygotsky, Lev S. 1978. *Mind in Society: The Development of Higher Psychological Processes*, ed. Michael Cole, Vera John-Steiner, Sylvia Scribner, and Ellen Souberman. Cambridge: Harvard University Press.

Wade, Suzanne E., and Ralph E. Reynolds. 1989. "Developing Metacognitive Awareness." *Journal of Reading*: 6–14.

Walshe, R. D. 1987. "The Learning Power of Writing." *English Journal* 76 (October): 22–27.

Watson, James D. 1968. *The Double Helix: A Personal Account of the Structure of DNA*. New York: Atheneum.

Weaver, Constance. 1988. *Reading Process and Practice: From Socio-Psycholinguistics to Whole Language*. Portsmouth, NH: Heinemann.

————. 1990. *Understanding Whole Language: From Principles to Practice*. Portsmouth, NH: Heinemann.

Whaley, Liz, and Liz Dodge. 1993. *Weaving in the Women: Transforming the High School English Curriculum*. Portsmouth, NH: Boynton/Cook.

Wiesel, Elie. 1960. *Night*. New York: Bantam.

Willinsky, John. 1990. *The New Literacy: Redefining Reading and Writing in the Schools*. New York: Routledge.

Wilson, Marilyn and Sharon Thomas. 1995. "'Holy Smoke! Did I Miss Something Here?': Cultural Experience and the Construction of Meaning." *English Education* 27: 53–64.

Winsor P., and P. David Pearson. 1992. *Children At Risk: Their Phonemic Awareness Development in Holistic Instruction* (Tech. Rep. No. 556). Urbana, IL: Center for the Study of Reading, University of Illinois.

Zemelman, Steven, and Harvey Daniels. 1988. *A Community of Writers: Teaching Writing in the Junior and Senior High School*. Portsmouth, NH: Heinemann.

Zemelman, Steven, Harvey Daniels, and A. Hyde. 1993. *Best Practice: New Standards for Teaching and Learning in America's Schools*. Portsmouth, NH: Heinemann.

Zorn, Jeff. 1994. "The NAEP 1992 Reading Report Card: Useless-and-Worse Psychometry." *English Journal* 83 (April): 38–39.

INDEX